Council Tax Handbook

••

Martin Ward

8th edition updated by Alan Murdie

Child Poverty Action Group

CPAG promotes action for the prevention and relief of poverty among children and families with children. To achieve this, CPAG aims to raise awareness of the causes, extent, nature and impact of poverty, and strategies for its eradication and prevention; bring about positive policy changes for families with children in poverty; and enable those eligible for income maintenance to have access to their full entitlement. If you are not already supporting us, please consider making a donation, or ask for details of our membership schemes, training courses and publications.

Published by Child Poverty Action Group
94 White Lion Street, London N1 9PF
Tel: 020 7837 7979
staff@cpag.org.uk
www.cpag.org.uk

A CIP record for this book is available from the British Library

ISBN: 978 1 906076 33 7

Child Poverty Action Group is a charity registered in England and Wales (registration number 294841) and in Scotland (registration number SC039339), and is a company limited by guarantee, registered in England (registration number 1993854). VAT number: 690 808117

Cover design by Devious Designs
Typeset by David Lewis XML Associates Ltd
Printed in the UK by CPI William Clowes Beccles NR34 7TL
Cover photo by Christopher Thomond/Reportdigital

The author

Alan Murdie (LLB) is a barrister, specialising in local taxation law. He is Director of the McKenzie Friends of the Zaccheus 2000 Trust. He was co-founder of the Poll Tax Legal Group in 1990 and is co-author of *Enforcement of Local Taxation*, published by the Legal Action Group. He writes and lectures extensively on local government finance issues and is involved in many legal test cases.

Acknowledgements

Many people have provided valuable information and suggestions with respect to the eighth edition of this book and a number deserve a special mention.

I would like to express my gratitude to Martin Ward who wrote the first two editions of the *Council Tax Handbook*, upon which this new edition is broadly based.

Thanks are due to Paul Russell's scrutiny of legal issues, and to Carolyn George and Sarah Clarke for re-writing and checking the council tax benefit chapter. I am also particularly grateful to Robert Telfer for his knowledge of and contribution on the situation in Scotland.

I would also like to thank Alison Key, Paula McDiarmid and Paul Levay for editing, proofreading and indexing the book.

Thanks are due to staff at Nucleus Legal Advice and to Nadine Clarkson of Ole Hanson and Partners, London.

Finally, I would like to thank Andy Love MP, Karen Buck MP and Andrew Dismore MP, the Reverend Paul Nicolson and Ian Wise, barrister, of the Zacchaeus 2000 Trust, Philip Evans and members of the Enforcement Law Working Group and Councillor Ben Grower of Bournemouth, all of whom provided information and insights on different aspects of the tax and appeals system, and its impact on vulnerable people. The library staff of the Honourable Society of Lincoln's Inn once again gave invaluable help with obtaining key references throughout.

Alan Murdie

The law covered in this book was correct on 1 October 2009 and includes regulations up to this date.

Contents

Abbreviations

AA	attendance allowance
ABI	Association of British Insurers
CA	carer's allowance
CTB	council tax benefit
CTC	child tax credit
DLA	disability living allowance
DHP	discretionary housing payment
DWP	Department for Work and Pensions
ESA	employment and support allowance
HB	housing benefit
IB	incapacity benefit
IS	income support
JSA	jobseeker's allowance
LSC	Learning and Skills Council
MP	Member of Parliament
NI	national insurance
PC	pension credit
SDA	severe disablement allowance
The Revenue	HM Revenue and Customs
VOA	Valuation Office Agency
WTC	working tax credit

Introduction

This is the eighth edition of the *Council Tax Handbook* since 1993. It will be the last during the current Parliament and charts the changes in the law since the previous edition was published in autumn 2007.

The trend for fine tuning the council tax by regulation identified in previous editions has continued over the last two years, with a number of significant changes across the system which are covered here. There are growing differences between the way in which the tax operates in England, Wales and Scotland. Many of these variations are addressed in this latest edition, together with the extensive reform of the valuation tribunal system in England, which became part of the Valuation Tribunal for England on 1 October 2009, with an integrated structure and approach to council tax appeals.

As will be apparent, the council tax system remains complex and, in the view of the author and many others, is ripe for consolidation and reform. Values for property bandings in England and Scotland remain based on presumed values made in April 1991. These are lapsing into historical memory and are increasingly difficult to use as a benchmark as time goes on. The collection of council tax by local authorities in England, Wales and Scotland occurs against the backdrop of a global economic downturn and recession that began in autumn 2008. Many people in the UK are facing financial hardship as a consequence, with council tax being a debt that is increasingly difficult to pay. Signs of growing numbers of people experiencing difficulty in paying council tax began to emerge in rising default levels three years ago. Statistics indicate that in 2006/07 some 2,181,031 liability orders were issued for non-payment of council tax. This represents a 37 per cent increase from the figures for 2000/01 and default levels look set to increase with rising unemployment.

It is worth recalling that originally one of the key functions of local taxation in Great Britain was to help support the poorest and most vulnerable in society. From Elizabethan times, and the Poor Law Act 1601, the rating system was known as the 'poor rates', supporting those with no means of support. Rating was based on the value of properties, the assumption being that those with larger and more expensive homes could afford to pay more. However, as local authorities expanded the range of services provided to inhabitants, local taxation became understood in the twentieth century primarily as a way of raising revenue for local authority services needed by the wider population, not simply those in poverty. The attempt to transform local taxation on ideological grounds began in the mid-1980s. Reform was based on introducing ideological notions of a market model of society, based on the idea that ratepayers were mobile consumers who exercised choices in a free market. This led to the ill-fated experiment with the poll tax attempted between 1989 and 1993, and for which the council tax was introduced as an emergency bale-out measure. While council tax was an improvement on the poll tax, its hasty introduction re-enacted a number of the worst features of community charge virtually unchanged. These have meant a legacy of legal and administrative problems. As recently as August 2009, the Department of Communities and Local Government has had to address remaining community charge legislation in the process of reforming valuation tribunals in England. Fortunately, it is reassuring to learn from the *Explanatory Memorandum* to the most recent regulations that 'The Government has no plans to re-introduce the community charge.'

Currently there is no doubt that the complexities of the council tax system are posing real problems for the poorest and most vulnerable members of the community who are least able to deal with them. This concern is also shared by many in local authorities and in the court system. Lord Justice Wall in the Court of Appeal remarked in December 2008:

> In my view it remains an apparently non-eradicable blemish on our operation of the rule of law that the poorest and most disadvantaged in our society remain subject to regulations which are complex, obscure and, to many, simply incomprehensible.

Certainly, there is a growing awareness of the difficulties experienced in dealing with council tax matters by vulnerable sectors of the community and one of the aims of this *Handbook* is to make key aspects of the law clear and accessible. Among points deserving particular notice are the following:

The power under section 13A of the Local Government Finance Act 1992 (as inserted by the Local Government Act 2003) to reduce amounts of council tax. This power allows a local authority to reduce or remit a sum in council tax for a taxpayer. Although this power has existed for five years, anecdotal evidence suggests that it is rare for advisers to apply for it to be exercised in favour of a person facing financial hardship. For example, it emerged in 2008 that Westminster City Council had received only two such applications in the previous four years. Clearly, this power could be used more often in appropriate cases.

The right of appeal regarding erroneous calculations on the amount of tax payable on a dwelling to a valuation tribunal or appeal committee. Appeals may be brought in disputes over liability, discounts, exemptions and any calculation on an amount of tax (with the exception of council tax benefit). Despite valuation tribunals and valuation appeal committees having been integral parts of the council tax system since its inception, and free procedures, it is surprising how few advisers are aware of them and the role they can perform.

It is important to note that valuation tribunals and appeal committees are not just limited to determining disputes over property bands. In a dispute with a local authority over how much money should be paid, the valuation tribunal body provides a route of appeal to determine the matter conclusively. In theory, tribunals are meant to be a relatively simple way of resolving a dispute. However, as this *Handbook* outlines, their procedures have now been streamlined in England by the introduction of the Valuation Tribunal for England. This will make tribunal procedures more formal, but still sufficiently flexible that no one should be deterred from using them.

Page 9 of the National Standards for Enforcement Agents issued in April 2002. This provides guidance for enforcement agents and creditors regarding vulnerable people. The guidance emerged partly over concern about local authorities using bailiffs to enforce community charge and council tax debts in the period 1991 to 2001. Page 9 is reproduced in Appendix 2. In essence, local authorities must take particular care when enforcing debts by way of distress against anyone falling into a vulnerable category.

The status of this guidance is yet to be tested in the court, but failure to observe these standards may result in maladministration where prejudice occurs. It deserves to be better known, particularly in light of the most welcome announcement by the Government in March 2009 that it was postponing the introduction of new powers for bailiffs, introduced under the Tribunals Courts and Enforcement Act 2007. If enacted, regulations under this Act threaten to allow forced entry to private dwellings and the use of force against occupiers. Fortunately, the Government has reconsidered taking this dangerous and irrational step, which would have taken human rights back more than 400 years.

The role of the Local Government Ombudsman in rectifying mistakes. The average citizen often feels powerless in seeking redress against officialdom and legal action is likely to prove expensive. This is particularly so in the field of council tax administration where there is potential for error throughout the system. Fortunately for the citizen, the role of Ombudsman may be of assistance where complaints made to a local authority have failed to resolve a problem or correct a mistake. The Commissioner for Local Administration in England, the Scottish Public Services Ombudsman and the Public Services Ombudsman for Wales may provide a way of redress to victims of council tax maladministration. This latest edition lists a number of rulings relevant to council tax, which establish principles that may be of assistance to those who have suffered injustice.

The reform of local taxation seems to follow a 20 to 25-year cycle: 1925, 1948, 1967 and 1988. On this basis, the timetables of history would suggest that reform of our local taxation is due and that council tax will be consolidated and changed. In the meantime, it is hoped that this edition of the *Council Tax Handbook* will provide all those seeking information to deal with the system we have with the law stated as believed correct as at 1 October 2009.

Alan Murdie

Chapter 1

Overview

This chapter covers:
1. Administration (below)
2. Chapter summary (p2)
3. Legal background and references (p8)

This *Handbook* describes the council tax as it operates throughout Great Britain and the Scottish Water charges for the supply of household water and the collection of waste water in Scotland. It should be of value to taxpayers, advisers and administrators.

The council tax is best understood as a cross between a land tax and a personal tax. It is levied on domestic dwellings, but the number of people and the type of people who are living in a dwelling will affect the amount of tax to be paid and who should pay it. This *Handbook* provides a guide to the relevant rules.

There are a number of differences in the way the scheme operates in England, Wales and Scotland. In some chapters these are indicated as they arise; in others there are separate sections on the different arrangements. Domestic rates are still payable in Northern Ireland. This *Handbook*, therefore, does not apply to Northern Ireland.

1. Administration

In England and Wales, district councils, metropolitan districts and London boroughs, unitary authorities, the Common Council of the City of London and the Council of the Isles of Scilly are responsible for setting the council tax, as well as billing and collection in their area. They are known as 'billing authorities'.[1] In 2009 the number of district councils in some regions was reduced and further reductions are likely between 2010 and 2011.

In Scotland, new single-tier, all-purpose councils were introduced in April 1996, replacing district, island and regional councils. Both billing and levying is performed by these local authorities. Scottish local authorities remain legally obliged to collect Scottish Water charges (for household water and waste water). These charges are included in the annual council tax bill.

2. **Chapter summary**

The following paragraphs provide an overview of the scheme and the related chapter in the *Handbook* which describes a particular aspect of the scheme in greater detail.

Chargeable dwellings (Chapter 2)

The council tax is a tax on a domestic property known as a 'dwelling'. Not all properties in a local authority's area count as dwellings. A property that is not a dwelling is usually subject to non-domestic rates. In England and Wales, the valuation officer at the local valuation office of HM Revenue and Customs and, in Scotland, the assessor appointed by the regional or islands council, decides whether or not a property is a dwelling. An appeal may be made against a decision that a property is, or is not, a dwelling.

Valuation (Chapter 3)

Since 1993 governments have attempted to relate the amount people pay in council tax to their ability to pay by basing it, in the first instance, on the assumed value of their dwelling. In England and Scotland, dwellings are allocated to one of eight valuation bands by the local valuation officer or assessor on a list which first came into operation on 1 April 1993. In Wales, they are allocated into one of nine bands on a list effective from 1 April 2005. Information about the dwelling and its valuation band appears on valuation lists maintained by the listing officer at the local valuation office, or the assessor in Scotland. The public has the right to inspect and obtain copies of the valuation list. A proposal may be made to change, and an appeal can be made against, a dwelling's valuation band.

The amount of tax (Chapter 4)

The amount of council tax payable varies between and, in certain instances, within local authorities. Prior to the start of each financial year (April to March), each local authority must set an amount of council tax that enables it to meet its budgeted expenditure and the budgeted expenditure of certain related bodies. For example, in England and Wales the county council raises money via the district council's council tax. In certain instances the amount of money that may be raised through the tax can be restricted by central government.

The council tax payable on each dwelling in the local authority depends, in the first instance, on the valuation band to which it has been allocated. Different valuation bands apply in England, Wales and Scotland. These reflect the different range of property prices in the three countries. There are a number of ways in which the council tax payable on a particular property may be reduced and these are examined in the next chapters.

From 1 April 2004, local authorities have a discretionary power to reduce council tax bills. They can do so in individual cases – eg, to prevent financial hardship, and in groups of cases – eg, if several properties have been affected by flooding.

Transitional relief

Transitional relief reduction schemes operated in a number of local authority areas prior to 2000/01. In England, no new schemes have been introduced and, with the postponement of a revaluation of homes for council tax purposes, none are anticipated to come into operation during the lifetime of the current Parliament.

In Wales, transitional relief remained available until 1 April 2008. Transitional relief was available on dwellings which, on 31 March 2005, moved by two or more valuation bands from their previous banding. The relief takes effect as a reduction in banding – ie, a dwelling is treated as falling into a lower band than that actually shown on the valuation list, for up to three years, depending on the size of the shift in banding.

Exempt dwellings (Chapter 5)

Certain categories of dwelling are exempt from the tax. New exempt categories have been added and the definition of others amended since the tax was first introduced. There are now 23 classes of exempt dwellings. The exemption may be either indefinite or for a fixed period. No council tax is payable while the dwelling is exempt. In Scotland, no Scottish Water charges are payable during the period of exemption. An appeal may be made if a local authority refuses to grant an exemption. There is no time limit for obtaining exemptions. A list of exempt dwellings is given in Appendix 1.

Liability (Chapter 6)

The council tax is usually payable by someone aged 18 or over who is solely or mainly resident in the dwelling. Where there is more than one such person, the liable person is the one with the greatest legal interest in the dwelling. Normally it is the owner or the tenant who must pay the council tax. However, in some circumstances a non-resident owner may be liable instead of a resident.

If the liable person is married, or has an unmarried partner of the opposite sex, the partner is normally jointly liable for the council tax even if s/he has no legal interest in the dwelling. Also, where two or more people, other than partners, have the same legal interest in the dwelling, they may all be jointly liable for the council tax.

From 1 April 2006, council tax law was amended to apply the rules on joint liability to couples of the same sex who have entered into civil partnerships under the Civil Partnership Act 2006 or those who are living as if they were civil partners. Special rules apply if a liable person or partner is 'severely mentally impaired' or a full-time student.

The local authority has the right to obtain information from a variety of sources to identify liable individuals. An appeal may be made against the local authority's decision on liability.

Disability reduction (Chapter 7)

The council tax payable on a dwelling can be reduced if the dwelling has certain features to meet the particular needs of someone (either an adult or a child) with a disability. The fact that a dwelling occupied by a person with a disability is not sufficient in itself; what is necessary is that there is an additional room, or a room which is adapted, to meet the needs of a disabled resident of the dwelling. Annual applications must be made for these reductions, but there is no time limit for applying. An appeal may be made if the local authority refuses to award a disability reduction.

Discounts (Chapter 8)

A council tax bill is based on the assumption that there are two or more residents aged 18 or over in the dwelling. If there are more than two the bill does not increase, but it may be reduced by:
- a variable percentage, typically 50 per cent if the dwelling is no one's sole or main residence; *or*
- 25 per cent if it is only one person's sole or main residence.
- 25 per cent if all but one person fails to be a 'disregarded person'.

In deciding how many people are solely or mainly resident in the dwelling, certain categories of people are disregarded – effectively the dwelling is treated as if these people were not actually living in it. The local authority must consider whether a discount applies in any particular case. There is no time limit for applications. Appeals may be made against the local authority's decision not to apply a discount.

A local authority may reduce the amount awarded in a discount if the dwelling fits into one of the classes of dwellings prescribed by the Secretary of State for England and/or the Welsh Assembly Government. A number of local authorities are also operating a scheme which provides for rebates on council tax bills to householders undertaking certain energy efficiency measures. In addition, individual local authorities may also grant special discretionary discounts in certain situations.

Council tax benefit (Chapter 9)

Additional assistance is available to meet the council tax in the form of council tax benefit (CTB).

CTB is one benefit, but it takes two forms:
- main CTB; *and*
- alternative maximum CTB – more commonly referred to as 'second adult rebate'.

Main CTB may be awarded in addition to the other forms of assistance already identified. If the claimant, together with any partner of the opposite or same sex, has more than a certain amount of capital, s/he is not entitled to CTB. The benefit calculation is based on the claimant's council tax liability less any disability reduction or discount. It is also based on the claimant's (and any family's) assumed needs and resources. Main CTB provides up to 100 per cent help with the council tax if the liable person is on income support (IS), income-based jobseeker's allowance (JSA), income-related employment and support allowance (ESA), the guarantee credit of pension credit (PC), or has an income at or below these levels. The amount may be reduced, however, if:
- the claimant is jointly liable for the council tax with someone other than a partner of the opposite sex or same sex if under a civil partnership; *or*
- a non-dependant, such as an adult son or daughter, lives with the claimant; *or*
- the claimant's (and any partner's) income is above IS/income-based JSA levels.

Second adult rebate must be claimed by the liable person, but her/his own income and capital are ignored. It is awarded on the basis of the income of other adults who live with the claimant, except her/his partner or someone who is jointly liable for the council tax. Rebates of up to 25 per cent of the claimant's council tax are usually available. If the liable person is a student, the rebate may be for 100 per cent of the council tax liability.

An application for main CTB is also an application for second adult rebate. If the claimant is entitled to both main CTB and second adult rebate, the local authority should award whichever is the greater. An appeal may be made to the First-tier Tribunal about the amount of CTB awarded and the local authority's refusal to award CTB.

The council tax benefit regulations have been revised and consolidated in the Council Tax Benefit Regulations 2006.

A person may also be eligible for a **discretionary housing payment (DHP)** from her/his local authority if s/he is in financial need. The local authority has a very broad discretion on the amount of the DHP and the form it may take. There is no restriction on the amount of a DHP. One-off and weekly payments may be made, although a weekly payment must not exceed the weekly council tax liability. Since a Court of Appeal ruling in December 2008, a DHP is potentially available to cover arrears of rent and council tax.[2]

Bills and payments (Chapter 10)

The council tax is not payable until a demand notice (bill) has been issued and served on the taxpayer. Liability for the council tax arises on a daily basis, but bills are raised on the assumption that the circumstances on which they are based will remain the same throughout the year. Where this is not the case they may be adjusted and, in certain circumstances, the taxpayer has the right to receive a refund of any overpayment.

People have a right to pay their council tax in instalments. There will usually be ten each year, but if a first demand notice is issued part-way through the year the number of instalments is reduced. Local authorities may also offer council tenants up to 52 instalments so that they can pay their council tax with their rental payments. Local authorities also have the power to enter into special payment arrangements with individual taxpayers, to offer discounts for lump-sum payments and adopt non-cash payment methods. Provisions allowing for electronic service of council tax bills have been brought into operation.

Enforcement (Chapter 11)

The local authority may use a variety of measures to ensure that a liable person pays the tax and any related costs and penalties. These methods range from issuing reminders to taking legal action. If someone fails to pay council tax, a local authority may apply to a magistrates' court for a liability order (or, in Scotland, to the sheriff court for a summary warrant).

A liability order (or summary warrant) enables the local authority to:
- make deductions from the debtor's earnings;
- seize and sell the debtor's goods;
- obtain a charging order against the debtor's home;
- request the local Department for Work and Pensions office to make deductions from the debtor's IS/JSA/PC and, from October 2008, ESA;
- use bankruptcy proceedings to make the taxpayer bankrupt;
- if the taxpayer is a councillor, obtain deductions from her/his councillor's allowances.

In addition, English and Welsh local authorities may apply to the magistrates' court for a warrant committing the debtor to prison, but only in certain limited circumstances.

Both the magistrates' court and the sheriff court have the power to remit the debt (in whole or in part) if the debtor is unable to pay.

There are various ways of appealing against a liability order or against improper enforcement action.

Appeals (Chapter 12)

Many decisions concerning the council tax can be appealed. Appeals may be made against:

- valuation;
- liability;
- completion notices;
- calculation of the amount of tax;
- penalties.

Appeals on matters to do with property valuation should go first to the listing officer or the assessor. From 1 July 2007, if the proposed change is not agreed, the person making the proposal will be required to take an appeal directly to a valuation tribunal if s/he wants to challenge the decision of the listing officer. So, the case should automatically go to a valuation tribunal in England and Wales. In England, this system is called 'Appeals Direct' by the Government and replaces the previous system whereby the listing officer automatically transferred the matter to the tribunal as an appeal. The structure of valuation tribunals has been changed and centralised, and, in future, will be subject to direction from a President appointed by the Lord Chancellor. In Wales, the appeals system remains as it was in England before the introduction of 'Appeals Direct'. In Scotland, an appeal goes to a valuation appeal committee.

Appeals on matters to do with liability, including the amount of tax payable on a dwelling, should first be addressed to the local authority. This includes matters such as whether or not the aggrieved person is liable to pay the tax, or whether or not a disability reduction, exemption or discount should be awarded. If the local authority fails to respond within two months, or the aggrieved person is still dissatisfied, a further appeal may be made to a valuation tribunal in England and Wales, and via the local authority to a valuation appeal committee in Scotland.

In England and Wales, the local authority and, in Scotland, the assessor may issue a completion notice that states the date on which a newly erected or structurally altered property is considered to be a dwelling. In England and Wales, an appeal against the completion date must normally be made directly to a valuation tribunal within four weeks of the notice being sent. In Scotland, an appeal to the valuation appeal committee must be made via the local assessor within 21 days of receiving the completion notice.

There are various circumstances in which people may have to pay a penalty if they fail to provide information. Appeals against the imposition of penalties may be made directly to a valuation tribunal in England and Wales or via the local authority to a valuation appeal committee in Scotland.

Complaints to the Ombudsman (Chapter 13)

In some cases, local authorities make mistakes in the administration of council tax, which cannot be rectified by either appealing to a valuation tribunal or to the courts.

Such errors may fall within the remit of the Local Government Ombudsman. The Ombudsman seeks to obtain redress for people who have suffered injustice as a result of maladministration. The Ombudsman may mount an independent investigation with a view to obtaining a remedy. Complaints may be resolved by a local settlement or proceed to a full investigation. If a complaint is upheld, the Ombudsman may recommend compensation for the person bringing the complaint.

Details of the work of the Ombudsman, an outline of the complaints procedure, and details of reports and examples of compensation are included in this chapter.

3. Legal background and references

The legal framework for the council tax is contained in the Local Government Finance Act 1992, as amended by the Local Government Act 2003. The Act includes sections and Schedules that apply throughout England and Wales and Scotland, as well as sections and Schedules that apply exclusively to one or other of the two jurisdictions. The functions of the Secretary of State were transferred to the Scottish Ministers by section 53 of the Scotland Act 1998.

The Acts enable the Secretary of State, the Welsh Assembly Government or the Scottish Parliament to formulate legislation (statutory instruments) in the form of regulations which contain and amend the details of the scheme. In practice, it is these regulations that govern the operation of the council tax. Different sets of statutory instruments apply to England and Wales and to Scotland. Additionally, certain statutory instruments only apply to England or to Wales or Scotland. Most of the regulations have been amended since they were first made. The text of many of these regulations is available from the internet.

Relevant caselaw is also identified in the appropriate paragraphs of this *Handbook*.

Electronic communication

Under powers derived from the Electronic Communications Act 2000, local authorities in England, Wales and Scotland may serve certain notices and information required for council tax by electronic means. These provisions require the agreement of the taxpayer to be effective. Information and notices may also be served electronically on local authorities by taxpayers, although to be effective in law the communication must be recorded on a local authority computer. Electronic communications can also be used for the alteration of lists and appeals before a valuation tribunal or regional appeal committees.

Human rights

Human rights principles are incorporated into English law under the Human Rights Act 1998 and therefore also apply to local taxation matters. Section 3(1) provides that, 'So far as it is possible to do so, primary legislation and subordinate legislation must be read and given effect in a way which is compatible with the Convention rights.' Under section 4(2) and (5) the courts may make a declaration of incompatibility.

Among issues likely to arise are questions as to whether certain enforcement remedies are disproportionate in the private lives of citizens. Human rights principles also extend to the actions and defaults of private bodies, which will be classed as 'public authorities' if they conduct work on behalf of state bodies. This may mean that private firms employed as enforcement agents for the collection of council tax debts may be subject to human rights principles.

Freedom of information

The Freedom of Information Act 2000 enables anyone to seek and obtain information held by state bodies, subject to certain exceptions. The Act may be used to discover information about aspects of the council tax, both national and local, in addition to information which is already available to the public (such as the valuation list). If a request to supply information is unreasonably refused, an appeal can be made to the Information Commissioner. Not all information is available – eg, personal records.

Future changes

This *Handbook* is up to date as the law stood on 1 October 2009 and the benefit rates used in Chapter 9 are those that apply from 1 April 2009.

Legislative change for council tax continues to be on the Government's agenda and more regulations are possible during the lifetime of the current Parliament.

The process of revaluing all domestic dwellings in England was abandoned in October 2005 and there will be no attempt to revalue dwellings until after the next general election. Valuations for domestic dwellings in Wales have been effective since 1 April 2005.

Council tax bills are calculated in accordance with existing law; bills for earlier years are calculated with respect to earlier legislation.

Practice Notes and Implementation Letters

In addition to the legislation, the Department of Communities and Local Government (in England), the Welsh Assembly Government and the local authority associations have together produced, and periodically revise, a series of Practice Notes. These are listed in Appendix 4. They advise on the interpretation of the legislation, on administrative arrangements and highlight a number of good practice points. There is no Scottish equivalent. The Department of Communities and Local Government also produces council tax Implementation Letters that have been formalised in the CTIMPL series. These advise local authorities about the latest changes in legislation or decisions of the courts. Points from the Implementation Letters are periodically included in revisions of the Practice Notes. While the legislation is binding on local authorities, neither the Practice Notes nor the Implementation Letters have the force of law and local authorities are not bound by them. Particularly useful comments from the Practice Notes are identified in this *Handbook*. The Valuation Tribunal Service also issues newsletters, which may be consulted online.

Notes in the *Handbook*

References to the law are given in notes at the end of each chapter. The notes usually begin with the letters E, W or S or a combination of these, indicating references to English, Welsh and/or Scottish law. The abbreviations used in the notes can be found in Appendix 4. The full details of the regulations contained in Appendix 4 include the years and statutory instrument (SI) numbers of amending legislation.

References to chapters and pages in the main text of the *Handbook* are to other chapters and pages where a term or concept is defined or further discussed. References to Practice Notes followed by a number and a paragraph are references to the revised council tax Practice Notes mentioned above.

Legal and other references

Butterworth's loose-leaf work, *Ryde on Rating and the Council Tax*, reproduces all the relevant English and Welsh legislation and the council tax Practice Notes. Most main public reference libraries should have this two-volume work.

CPAG's Housing Benefit & Council Tax Benefit Legislation contains the legislation on council tax benefit.

Rating and Valuation Reporter covers changes to council tax and reports decisions of the courts in valuation and local taxation matters. Other unreported decisions may be available on LEXIS, a database of court decisions and law reports; some judgments will also be available on the internet at www.hmcourts-service.gov.uk.

The most detailed guide to enforcement in England and Wales remains the Legal Action Group's *The Enforcement of Local Taxation: an adviser's guide to non-payment of the council and poll tax* (2000).

Detailed information on proceedings in the civil and criminal courts, which may involve council tax matters, can be found in specialist works of law and procedure, published annually. Details of procedures in the magistrates' court can be found in *Stones' Justices' Manual*. Details of procedures in the county court can be found in the *County Court Practice*, and details of High Court procedures can be found in the *Supreme Court Practice*.

The Department of Communities and Local Government publishes council tax Information Letters detailing legislative changes. Policy changes and council tax research can be found on its website at www.odpm.gov.uk.

Information on valuation matters and appeals can be found at the Valuation Office Agency website at www.voa.gov.uk and the Valuation Tribunal website at www.valuation-tribunals.gov.uk. The Valuation Tribunal website is regularly updated with summaries given in recent valuation tribunal decisions.

Outlines of future changes to council tax in England can be found at www.local.dtlr.gov.uk/finance/ctax/consult/02.htm. Details of future developments and updates can also be found at the website for Communities and Local Government at www.communities.gov.uk.

Individual local authority websites may also provide useful information on the payment and collection of council tax in local areas. It seems likely that the provision of information in this area will increase in the next few years and some local authorities are developing schemes to share information with advice agencies such as Citizens Advice Bureaux at a local level.

Reports of the Local Government Ombudsman decisions in England can be obtained from the Ombudsman at: The Commission, 10th Floor, Millbank Tower, Millbank, London SW1P 4QP or www.lgo.org.uk

Notes

1. **Administration**
   1 **EW** s1 LGFA 1992
   2 *R (Gargett) v London Borough of Lambeth*
     [2008] EWCA Civ 1450, 18 December
     2008

2

Chapter 2

Chargeable dwellings

This chapter covers:
1. What counts as a dwelling in England and Wales (below)
2. Dwellings in two or more local authorities or different parts of the same authority in England and Wales (p17)
3. What counts as a dwelling in Scotland (p17)
4. When a new or altered building counts as a new dwelling (p19)

Council tax is payable on any dwelling which is not an exempt dwelling (see Chapter 5). Properties on which the tax must be paid are referred to as 'chargeable dwellings'.[1] The definition of a 'dwelling' is therefore a fundamental one for council tax purposes.

In most cases, whether or not a property constitutes a dwelling is not in question. Houses, flats, bungalows, cottages and maisonettes used for domestic purposes all normally count as dwellings. However, sometimes it may not be clear whether or not a property constitutes a dwelling. This might occur, for example, where one property consists of a number of dwellings or where a number of properties constitute one dwelling. Whether or not a specific property constitutes a dwelling is one of the grounds for making a proposal to alter the valuation list (see Chapter 3) and could be the subject of an appeal (see Chapter 12).

The definition of a dwelling which applies in England and Wales differs from that which applies in Scotland. In the majority of cases, however, the effect is the same.

---

1. What counts as a dwelling in England and Wales

The legal definition of a dwelling for council tax purposes in England and Wales is far from straightforward. The Local Government Finance Act 1992 defines a '**dwelling**' as any property which:[2]
- would have been a 'hereditament' (a rateable unit – see p13) for the purposes of section 115(1) of the General Rate Act 1967 if that Act remained in force; *and*

- is not shown, or required to be shown, on a local or a central non-domestic rating list; *and*
- is not exempt from local non-domestic rating; *or*
- is a 'composite hereditament' (see p16).

The Act goes on specifically to exclude certain properties from being dwellings in their own right, unless they constitute part of a larger property which is itself a dwelling. These are:[3]
- a yard, garden, outhouse or other land or building belonging to, or enjoyed with, property used wholly for the purposes of living accommodation; *or*
- a private garage which either has a floor area of not more than 25 square metres or is used wholly or mainly to accommodate a private motor vehicle; *or*
- private storage premises used wholly or mainly to store articles of domestic use.

These exclusions mean, for example, that a garage used to keep a private car that is not part of a larger property does not constitute a dwelling and should not be included in the valuation of any other dwelling.

Hereditaments

The General Rates Act 1967 charged general rates on domestic and non-domestic property. Section 115(1) of that Act defined a **'hereditament'** as a 'property which is or may become liable to a rate, being a unit of such property which is, or would fall to be, shown as a separate rate item in the valuation list'. The exact identity of the hereditament has been the subject of numerous legal cases. In the leading case on the issue Denning LJ said:[4]

> Where two or more properties are within the same curtilage or contiguous to one another, and are in the same occupation, they are as a general rule to be treated for rating purposes as if they formed part of a single hereditament. There are exceptional cases, however, where for some special reason they may be treated as two or more hereditaments. That may happen for instance, because they were valued at different times, or because they were at one time in different occupations, or because one part is used for an entirely different purpose. Where the two properties are in the same occupation but are not within the same curtilage nor contiguous to one another each of them must as a general rule be treated as a separate hereditament for rating purposes: and this is the case even though they are used by the occupier for the purposes of his one whole business.

In the same case, Parker LJ said that the following should be considered when determining what was a hereditament:
- whether two or more parts of the premises are capable of being separately let;
- whether the premises form a single geographical unit;

- whether, though forming a single geographical unit, the premises' structure and layout consist of two or more separate parts;
- whether the occupier uses the whole of the premises for one purpose or whether s/he uses different parts for different purposes.

Dwellings in a state of disrepair

In some cases, a property may be in such a state of disrepair that it cannot be classed as a dwelling at all. It could be so derelict that even with a reasonable amount of repairs, no one could be expected to live in it. In such cases, such a property ceases to be a hereditament under the definition of section 115(1) of the General Rate Act 1967 and may be removed from the valuation list altogether.

In deciding whether a dwelling should be removed, a key test is whether a reasonable amount of repair work would make it habitable. If the answer is 'no', the dwelling can be taken off the list entirely. Past valuation tribunal decisions on this question show that the state of dereliction must be severe and it must be uneconomical to undertake repairs. A tribunal may establish that if it were unreasonable to undertake repairs and no reasonable owner would attempt them, then the dwelling should be removed from the list.

It should be noted that the actual intentions of the landlord or owner are not relevant to this test – the tribunal looks at the actions of a hypothetical reasonable owner. Thus, an owner or landlord who is willing to spend more than what a reasonable person would to repair a property may still have the dwelling removed from the list for the period it is uninhabitable. For example, in *Z Munter Farms Ltd v Pettitt*, the Suffolk Valuation Tribunal held that a dwelling with dangerous electrical wiring and lacking a gable wall should not appear in a valuation list whilst undergoing rebuilding. The building was uninhabitable during rebuilding and failed to meet the definitions of a rateable hereditament.[5] In other cases where a dwelling can be repaired, it should remain on the valuation list but may be entitled to an empty dwelling exemption for 12 months whilst repairs are taking place. For more information on exemptions, see Chapter 5.

Self-contained accommodation and 'granny flats'

If a dwelling is considered a single dwelling under the above definition of a hereditament, but consists of more than one 'self-contained unit' of living accommodation, the local authority will treat each self-contained unit of accommodation as a separate dwelling.[6]

A '**self-contained unit**' is a building, or part of a building, which has been constructed or adapted for use as separate living accommodation. A caravan or boat which has been constructed or adapted for use as separate living accommodation is also considered to be a 'self-contained unit'. Local authority listing officers are advised to look for living and sleeping accommodation, and at least minimal separate cooking and washing facilities before they decide that the property constitutes 'self-contained' living accommodation. For example, properties that contain more than one self-contained unit – eg, a large house that has been adapted to provide a separate 'granny' annex, should be treated as two or more dwellings. The 'granny' annex may then be an exempt dwelling if unoccupied (see Chapter 5). Key factors which will be examined include whether a self-contained unit or annex has all the features necessary for independent living.

There not being an independent outside access to a living unit does not make the annex part of a single dwelling.[7] The subjective view of the occupier – for example a claim that the accommodation is in fact used as a games room rather than living accommodation – will not prevent a listing officer from deciding a separate dwelling exists.

If you are an 'interested person' (see p30), you can make a proposal to the listing officer not to show your home as a separate unit of accommodation on the valuation list. The process of making a proposal is described in Chapter 3.

The listing officer also has discretion to treat a property which would otherwise be considered to be two or more separate dwellings as single if it:[8]

- consists of a single self-contained unit, or such a unit together with or containing premises constructed or adapted for non-domestic purposes; *and*
- is occupied as more than one unit of separate living accommodation.

This could apply, for example, to a property occupied by more than one household, but where the residents share facilities such as kitchens or bathrooms – eg, a group of bedsits or a hostel. The listing officer must exercise her/his discretion reasonably and should take into account all the circumstances of the case, including the extent to which the parts of the property separately occupied have been structurally altered.

The listing officer's decision that a property with a number of different households consists of only one dwelling rather than several may have an impact not only on the single dwelling's valuation band but also on liability and entitlement to discounts or benefits. In one case concerning general rates, *James v Williams*, it was held that at least four factors should be considered by a valuation officer when exercising her/his discretion.[9] These are:

- the degree to which facilities, such as kitchens and bathrooms, are shared;
- the degree of internal adaptations, such as entrance doors;
- the degree of identifiability of separate parts;
- the degree of transience in the occupiers' residence.

The Court of Appeal has confirmed that the principles in *James v Williams* continue to apply.[10] On the other hand, where two flats are converted to a single property, a new dwelling is created for council tax purposes.[11]

Property on the non-domestic rating list

Property is 'domestic' if it is used wholly for the purpose of living accommodation. If it is not in use it is still considered to be domestic property if its next use will be domestic. Most non-domestic property, such as business or industrial property, is shown on either the local or central non-domestic rating list. By definition, such properties are not dwellings for council tax purposes but are subject to non-domestic rates.

Caravans and houseboats

A pitch for a caravan and a mooring for a houseboat are hereditaments (see p13) and are, therefore, considered dwellings for council tax purposes if they are occupied by a caravan or houseboat (including a boat which is no longer navigable[12]) which is someone's sole or main residence (see p71). If not in use, even if the pitch or mooring is empty, it is still considered a dwelling if it appears that its next use will be domestic, but it may be an exempt dwelling (see Chapter 5).

Holiday caravans and other caravans used for non-domestic purposes are subject to non-domestic rates. If you keep a caravan at home for use on holidays you are not liable to pay non-domestic rates or council tax on it. If, however, the listing officer considers it to be a self-contained unit constituting separate living accommodation (see p14), it would be a dwelling for council tax purposes.

Timeshare property

Timeshare accommodation does not count as domestic property and is subject to non-domestic rates.

Composite hereditaments

A property is a 'composite hereditament' if only part of it is used solely for the purpose of living accommodation. For example, some rooms in a property may be used only for business purposes and others used only for domestic purposes. Council tax is payable on the domestic portion and non-domestic rates are payable on the business portion. It is possible to appeal against a decision that a property is a composite hereditament, or against a decision on the proportion of a property that is used for domestic or non-domestic purposes. The key question is whether the character of a dwelling house has been lost.[13] For example, a dwelling in which a room or garage is predominantly used for business purposes is a composite hereditament.

2. Dwellings in two or more local authorities or different parts of the same authority in England and Wales

The location of a dwelling is a major determining factor in how much council tax is payable. Different local authorities may have different levels of council tax for dwellings in the same valuation band (see Chapter 4). Additionally, where there are parish or community councils, different parts of the same local authority may have different levels of council tax for dwellings in the same valuation band.

If a dwelling (including a dwelling that is part of a larger single property) falls within the area of two or more local authorities, or two or more parts of an authority's area, it should be treated as being in the area in which the greatest part of the dwelling is situated.[14]

3. What counts as a dwelling in Scotland

In Scotland, a **'dwelling'** means any lands and heritages (rights that exist with the land, such as farming and fishing):

- which consist of one or more dwelling houses with any garden, yard, garage, outhouse or pertinent other area belonging to and occupied with such dwelling house(s); *and*
- which would, but for the fact that it is a dwelling, be entered separately in the valuation roll.[15]

The valuation roll is now limited to recording the details of non-domestic and part-residential properties. Details of domestic dwellings are now contained in the valuation lists.

A Scottish dwelling includes:

- the residential part of part-residential property (see p18); *and*
- that part of any premises which has been apportioned, as at 1 April 1989, as a dwelling house.

It includes caravans, but only if they are someone's sole or main residence (see Chapter 6).

Property that counts as a dwelling

Certain types of property are explicitly included or excluded from the Scottish definition of a dwelling. The following properties are specifically included in the definition of a dwelling if, but for the fact that they were dwellings, they would be entered separately on the valuation roll:[16]

- a garage, carport or car parking space wholly or mainly used, or last used, for private motor vehicles;[17]
- certain private storage premises used, or last used, wholly or mainly to store domestic articles (including cycles and other similar vehicles);[18]
- bed and breakfast accommodation operated on a commercial basis by a person living there for letting to not more than six people a night;
- student halls of residence which include shared facilities;
- accommodation owned by the Ministry of Defence which are, or are likely to be, the sole or main residence of at least one member of the armed forces;
- school boarding accommodation;
- any part of communal residential establishments with shared facilities for residents, including those parts of a hostel or care home as defined for the purpose of a discount (see Chapter 8), which are used wholly or mainly as the sole or main residence of a person employed there (the other parts of this type of accommodation in which the ordinary residents live are not dwellings but are subject to non-domestic rates).

While the above count as dwellings, some of them are exempt from the tax (see Chapter 5).[19]

Excluded property

Certain properties are specifically excluded from the Scottish definition of a dwelling, but may be subject to non-domestic rates. These are:
- certain huts, sheds and bothies which are no one's sole or main residence;
- certain self-catering holiday accommodation which is no one's sole or main residence;
- women's refuges (except any part which is the sole or main residence of an employee of the voluntary organisation managing the refuge);[20]
- timeshare accommodation.[21]

Part-residential property in Scotland

Certain properties with a mixed domestic and non-domestic use, such as private nursing homes and hospitals (see above), are divided into their relevant parts. The non-domestic element is entered on the valuation roll and the domestic element is entered on the valuation list and treated as a dwelling for council tax purposes. With what are termed **'part-residential subjects'** (ie, premises that are used for commercial or sporting reasons), however, a different approach is taken. In these cases, the property is shown on the valuation roll, but an apportionment note on the roll indicates the net annual value and the rateable value based on the residential and non-residential use made of the property.[22] The residential part of a part-residential subject counts as a dwelling for council tax purposes. Those parts of a women's refuge, hostel or care home (see Chapter 8) used as accommodation for residents rather than employees are specifically excluded from the definition of part-residential subject.[23]

4. **When a new or altered building counts as a new dwelling**

A new dwelling may be created either by new building or by the structural alteration of an existing property. A new dwelling is considered to come into existence for council tax purposes from the day a completion notice is served, or from the completion date contained on the notice if later.[24] In the latter case, this will be if a dwelling is not completed but is believed by the local authority to be substantially completed and can be completed within three months from the date the notice is served.

A new or altered dwelling does not require a completion notice once someone starts to live there.

If a new or altered dwelling is unoccupied, it may be exempt from paying tax for a period (see Chapter 5). If a new dwelling is created by the structural alteration to a building, the former dwelling(s) is considered to have ceased to exist on the completion date.

Completion notices

The local authority (England and Wales) or assessor (Scotland), may serve completion notices on owners of buildings which have been completed or which can reasonably be expected to be completed within three months.[25] These notices propose a completion day for the building.

The proposed completion day becomes the actual completion day unless the aggrieved owner appeals. Prior to the outcome of the appeal, the proposed completion day is treated as the actual completion day.

Appeals against completion notices

Any disagreement over the date on a completion notice can be raised in the first instance with the local authority in England and Wales, or the assessor in Scotland, but appeals must be made within particularly short time periods (see Chapter 12).

In England and Wales, appeals should be made directly to the Valuation Tribunal for England (see p206) or valuation tribunal within four weeks of the notice being sent.[26] The President of the tribunal may, however, allow an out-of-time appeal if you have failed to meet this time limit for reasons beyond your control.[27]

In Scotland, an appeal must be lodged with the valuation appeal committee within 21 days of receiving the completion notice.[28] This is done by writing to the assessor stating the grounds of the appeal and enclosing a copy of the completion notice.

Notes

1 **EW** s4(1) and (2) LGFA 1992
S s72(6) LGFA 1992

1. What counts as a dwelling in England and Wales
2 s3(1) LGFA 1992
3 s3(4) LGFA 1992
4 *Gilbert (Valuation Officer) v Hickinbottom & Sons Ltd* [1956] 2 All ER 101 (CA)
5 *Z Munter Farms Ltd v Pettitt* [2006] RVR 332
6 CT(CD)O
7 *Vaziri v Listing Officer* [2006] RVR 329
8 CT(CD)O
9 *James v Williams* [1973] RA 305
10 *R v London South Eastern Valuation Tribunal and Neale ex parte Moore* [2001] RVR 94 (CA)
11 *R v East Sussex Valuation Tribunal ex parte Silverstone* [1996] RVR 203
12 *Nicholls v Wimbledon Valuation Officer* [1995] RVR 171
13 *Guthrie v Highland Region and Western Isles Assessor* [1995] RA 292

2. Dwellings in two or more local authorities or different parts of the same authority in England and Wales
14 CT(SVD) Regs; see also Practice Note No. 10

3. What counts as a dwelling in Scotland
15 s72 LGFA 1992
16 CT(D)(S) Regs
17 CT(Dw)(S) Regs
18 CT(Dw)(S) Regs
19 CT(ED)(S)O
20 CT(D)(S) Regs
21 CT(Dw)(S) Regs
22 s72(8) and Sch 5 LGFA 1992
23 CT(D)(S) Regs

4. When a new or altered building counts as a new dwelling
24 **EW** s17 LGFA 1992; Sch 4A LGFA 1988
S s83(1) and Sch 6 LGFA 1992
25 **EW** s17 LGFA 1992; Sch 4A LGFA 1988
S s83(1) and Sch 6 LGFA 1992
26 **EW** Reg 36(4) VCCT(Amdt) Regs
27 **EW** Reg 36(5) VCCT(Amdt) Regs
28 **S** Sch 6 LGFA 1992

Chapter 3

Valuation

This chapter covers:
1. Who is responsible for valuations (below)
2. The valuation officer's and assessor's powers (p22)
3. How dwellings are valued (p24)
4. Compiling and maintaining valuation lists (p27)
5. What the valuation list shows (p28)
6. Inspecting the valuation list (p28)
7. Altering a valuation list (p28)

1. Who is responsible for valuations

England and Wales

In England and Wales the valuation of dwellings for council tax purposes is carried out by the Valuation Office Agency (VOA), which is part of HM Revenue and Customs (the Revenue). There is a listing officer at the VOA for each local authority. The listing officer has various duties in relation to compiling and maintaining the valuation list, and is independent of the local authority.[1] The term **'valuation officer'** refers to any listing officer and any other officer appointed by the commissioners to carry out any of their functions.[2]

You can check the council tax banding of an individual property online by providing the address, postcode and billing authority area on the VOA website at www.voa.gov.uk.

Note: the procedure for challenging a property valuation in England changed on 1 October 2009. See p28 and Chapter 12 for more information.

Scotland

In Scotland the assessor, and any deputy assessor, for each regional and islands council decides which valuation band should apply to each dwelling in the area.[3] The assessor is a professional valuer who must comply with any directions on valuations given by the Revenue's commissioners.[4] The assessor is appointed and employed by the council.[5] Details of assessors can be found at www.saa.gov.uk

and council tax bandings in Scotland can be checked online by providing your postcode.

Appointees

In England and Wales the commissioners, and in Scotland the assessor, have the power to appoint other people, such as private surveyors, to carry out valuations.[6] The commissioners and the assessor are able to supply these appointees with relevant information obtained under their various powers – eg, any survey report obtained for rating purposes.[7] If the person assisting with the valuation discloses that information for reasons other than valuation purposes or pursuant to the provisions of the Freedom of Information Act 2000, s/he may be imprisoned for up to two years and/or fined.[8]

Complaints

If you wish to complain about the poor performance (as opposed to the decisions) of any local valuation office, you should write initially to the office concerned. If the response is unsatisfactory, a complaint can be made to the relevant regional director of the VOA, a Member of Parliament (MP), or to the Ombudsman (see Chapter 13).

If you are not satisfied with the regional director's response you can put your case to the Revenue Adjudicator. The Revenue Adjudicator should review all the facts and aim to reach a decision as speedily as possible. The VOA will normally accept the Revenue Adjudicator's decision unless there are exceptional circumstances. You can refer a complaint to the Revenue Adjudicator's Office by writing or by telephone. The contact details are: Revenue Adjudicator's Office, 3rd Floor, Haymarket House, 28 Haymarket, London SW1Y 4SP; Tel: 020 7930 2292; Fax: 020 7930 2298; email: adjudicators@gtnet.gov.uk; website: www.adjudicatorsoffice.gov.uk.

If you are unhappy with a decision of a local valuation office, see p28 and Chapter 12.

2. The valuation officer's and assessor's powers

The valuation officer and assessor have powers:
- to enter dwellings; *and*
- to obtain information from a past or present owner, occupier, the local authority and certain other people.

Powers of entry

A valuation officer and any assistant with written authorisation from the valuation officer (in Scotland, the local assessor or deputy assessor) may enter, survey and value a dwelling.[9] At least three clear days' written notice must be given. The three-day period excludes weekends and public holidays. Normally, the official concerned should try to arrange a suitable time for access and give you at least seven days' notice.

The Valuation Office Agency website also states that valuation officers will carry identity cards and ask permission to take photographs.

Someone who intentionally delays or obstructs the official may be liable on summary conviction to a fine not exceeding level 2 on the standard scale.[10]

The owner's and occupier's duty to provide information

The valuation officer (in Scotland, the local assessor) may require the present or past owner or occupier of a dwelling to supply information to assist her/him in carrying out the valuation.[11] If the information is in the owner's or occupier's possession or control it should be supplied within 21 days of a written notice being served. Failure to comply with this requirement, without reasonable excuse, may result in a fine up to level 2 on the standard scale.[12]

A current or past owner or occupier could be liable to be imprisoned for up to three months and/or for a fine up to level 3 on the standard scale if s/he makes a false statement, either deliberately or carelessly.[13]

The local authority's duty to provide information

The valuation officer (in Scotland, the local assessor) may require the local authority to supply information concerning a property to assist her/him in carrying out the valuation. In addition, if any information comes to the notice of a local authority, which it considers would assist the valuation officer or assessor in her/his duties, it should provide that information.[14] In practice, it is the local authority's task to identify new dwellings and refer existing ones that have been altered.

Right to use other sources of information

Certain other individuals and organisations, such as the former community charge registration officer and, in Scotland, the district council, must also supply information if the valuation officer or local assessor requests it.[15] A valuation officer or assessor may also take into account any other information available from other sources.

3. **How dwellings are valued**

In England and Scotland, each dwelling is valued on the basis of what it might reasonably have been expected to realise on the open market, subject to certain valuation assumptions, if sold on 1 April 1991 by a willing seller.[16]

The original use of 1 April 1991 for all valuations has meant that adjustments for changes in prices over time have not had to be made. However, with changes in property prices since 1991, the construction of many new dwellings and the alteration of others, an assumed valuation date of 1 April 1991 has become harder to justify or maintain. As a result, the Local Government Act 2003 introduced a new ten-year cycle of revaluations, but the process has so far only been completed for Wales.

Although a general revaluation was intended for England by 1 April 2007, these plans were abandoned in the autumn of 2005 when the Government introduced the Council Tax (New Valuations for England) Act 2005. This removed the requirement for a revaluation of domestic properties in England by 1 April 2007. The Act provides for future revaluation dates to be set by statutory instrument. The Government does not envisage that there will be a revaluation until after the end of the present Parliament. As a result, council tax valuations of dwellings in England will continue to be made based upon a theoretical sale price as at 1 April 1991.

In Wales, a revaluation of dwellings was completed by 1 April 2005 using the relevant date of 1 April 2003. The closing date for most appeals by taxpayers against the new valuation was 31 December 2005, with only limited rights of appeal thereafter (see Chapter 12).

When valuing a property in England for council tax purposes, the question asked is: 'What was this dwelling worth on 1 April 1991, assuming there was a buyer available and the valuation assumptions applied?' (see p25).

In Wales, until 1 April 2015, when valuing a property for council tax purposes the question asked will be: 'What was this dwelling worth on 1 April 2003, assuming there was a buyer available and the valuation assumptions applied?' (see p25).

Theoretical and actual value

The valuation for council tax purposes represents a *theoretical* value of what the property was worth on the relevant date (see above), *not* its actual value. Thus, a dwelling which, in reality, may have been in a bad state of repair will be treated as though it had been in a reasonable state of repair, as this is one of the valuation assumptions applied to all dwellings regardless of the circumstances. Similarly, fixtures inside a dwelling are ignored. For example, it makes no difference whether there is a modern kitchen range installed or no modern kitchen fittings at all. The consequences of this are that the *actual price* that a property achieved when put on the market in 1991, or since, will not be its value for council tax purposes unless the two figures happen to coincide. An actual sale price would simply count as evidence towards what a property was worth for the purposes of a council tax banding valuation, applying the valuation assumptions.

Banding details of domestic properties can be found on the Valuation Office Agency (VOA) website: www.voa.gov.uk. The Government is also proposing to allow the VOA to share information it holds on the sale prices of dwellings dating before 2000 which has hitherto been confidential unless used in a valuation appeal (see Chapter 12).

The valuation assumptions

To make all valuations on a common basis, properties are not only assessed on the basis of their market value on 1 April 1991 (or, in Wales, 1 April 2003), but certain valuation assumptions are also made. The factors that affect the market value of a property include the number of rooms, its age, the construction materials used, the presence of a garden and the nature of the neighbouring environment. The valuation assumptions are then applied.

Valuation assumptions
- The sale was with vacant possession.
- In England and Wales, a house was sold freehold and a flat (ie, part of a building divided horizontally to provide living units) was sold on a lease for 99 years at a nominal rent.
- In England and Wales, the dwelling was sold free from any rent charge (ie, rare rental payments on freehold land usually associated with covenants) or other incumbence.
- In Scotland, the dwelling was sold free from any 'heritable security' – ie, any mortgage is paid off.
- The size, layout and character of the dwelling, and the physical state of its locality, were the same as on the day the valuation was made.
- The dwelling was in reasonable repair.
- If there were common parts (eg, a hallway shared with another dwelling), these were in a reasonable state of repair considering the age and character of the dwelling and its locality, and the purchaser would be liable to contribute to the cost of keeping them in such a state.
- Fixtures designed for a person with a physical disability (see below), which increase the value of the dwelling, were ignored.
- The dwelling's use was permanently restricted to use as a private dwelling (see below).
- The dwelling had no development value other than that attributable to any development for which no planning permission is required.

Fixtures for a person with a disability

'Fixtures' are items in a dwelling which are permanently attached to it, such as a sink, lavatory or lift. The value of fixtures should be ignored in the valuation if: [17]

- they are designed to make the dwelling suitable for use by a person with a physical disability; *and*
- they add to the dwelling's value.

In other words, the dwelling is valued on the basis that those fixtures are not present. There is no requirement for someone with a disability actually to live in the dwelling. Such fixtures may have been taken into account during the valuation process. If this is the case, the valuation officer or local assessor should be advised of this possible oversight.

In addition to the above, there is a separate disability reduction scheme for people with disabilities. This is described in Chapter 7.

Dwellings with mixed domestic and business use

In England and Wales, properties which include both a domestic and non-domestic component (known as 'composite hereditaments' – see p16) are valued on the proportion of the market value which might reasonably be attributed to the domestic use of the property. The valuation is based on the same rules and assumptions outlined above, except that the assumption that the property is permanently restricted to use as a private dwelling is ignored.

Scottish farmhouses, crofts and fish farms

In Scotland, dwellings such as farmhouses or cottages and croft houses connected with agriculture or fish farms are valued on the assumption that their availability is restricted to being used in that way. This lowers the value of the property and may lead to it being placed in a lower valuation band. In valuing a dwelling for council tax, the effect of a planning condition restricting occupation to a person mainly employed on a farm must not be ignored.[18]

Proposals and appeals on valuations

The use of valuation assumptions (see p25) means that a dwelling's valuation band may not reflect its actual sale price in 1991 (or in Wales, 2003). Consequently, the actual selling price of a dwelling would not necessarily be useful evidence to support a proposal to alter its value on the valuation list (see p28) or at a valuation tribunal or valuation appeal committee hearing, unless the actual sale price happened to match the council tax valuation using the statutory valuation assumptions.

The valuation assumptions are applied whatever the condition of the dwelling (but see below if energy efficiency measures have been added). Thus, a valuation for council tax purposes may differ from a valuation for any other purpose. The VOA does not depart from these assumptions; they are applied in every case regardless of the actual circumstances on the relevant day (ie, 1 April 1991 for England and 1 April 2003 for Wales) and used by valuation tribunals and the High Court when considering appeals against banding decisions.

To be successful, a proposal to alter a dwelling's banding or an appeal must apply the assumptions described on p25.

Energy efficiency measures

The addition of energy efficiency or renewable energy measures such as ground source heat pumps, insulation or solar panels do affect the value of a dwelling for council tax purposes. If the property is sold and the measures have increased the value of the dwelling into the next council tax band level, it is possible to change the dwelling's valuation. However, in practice, only substantial improvements would be likely to move a property up a band upon sale, and energy efficiency measures in isolation are unlikely to do so.[19]

4. **Compiling and maintaining valuation lists**

The listing officer or assessor is responsible for compiling and maintaining each local authority's valuation list.[20]

Compiling the list

In England, the valuation list in operation was compiled on 1 April 1993 and came into force on that day. In Wales, the new list came into force on 1 April 2005. Prior to its compilation, the listing officer or assessor should have taken such steps as were reasonably practicable in the time available to ensure that the list was accurate.[21] Any new lists must – as far as is reasonably practicable – be accurate on the date on which they are compiled, therefore obliging the listing officer to revalue properties prior to the publication of each list. As soon as reasonably practicable after its compilation, a copy should be sent to the local authority. The local authority should deposit this at its principal office.[22] The public has the right of access to the valuation list (see p28), but the local authority does not have to advertise its availability.

Maintaining the list

The listing officer or assessor must maintain the list for as long as is necessary for the purposes of the council tax.[23] The listing officer or assessor notifies the local authority on a regular basis of any alterations to the compiled list to take account of new dwellings, demolitions, successful appeals and other changes. For the purpose of determining which valuation band (see p40) is applicable to a dwelling for any day, the state of affairs at the end of the day is assumed to have existed throughout that day.[24]

5. **What the valuation list shows**

A valuation list must show the items identified below.[25] The list does not contain any personal information. The omission from a list of any matter which should be included does not make it invalid.[26]

The contents of a valuation list
- Each dwelling in the local authority's area.
- Each dwelling's valuation band.
- A reference number for each dwelling.
- A marker indicating properties with mixed domestic and non-domestic use (England and Wales only).
- The effective date on which there has been an alteration.
- An indicator showing that an alteration has been made following an order of a valuation tribunal or the High Court or, in Scotland, a valuation appeal committee or the Court of Session.
- Notes indicating that a dwelling is a private garage or domestic storage premises (Scotland only).

6. **Inspecting the valuation list**

Everyone has the right to inspect the valuation list. Access to this information must be provided free of charge and at a reasonable time and place.[27]

The valuation lists for England and Wales can be viewed at www.voa.gov.uk/ and those for Scottish local authorities at www.saa.gov.uk/.

Members of the public may make copies or transcripts of the list, or parts of the list. Alternatively, the local authority, listing officer or assessor is required to supply a copy if requested to do so, but a reasonable charge may be made for this service. If someone is intentionally obstructed from exercising her/his rights in relation to the valuation list, the person responsible for the obstruction may be liable on summary conviction to a fine not exceeding level 2 on the standard scale.[28]

7. **Altering a valuation list**

A current valuation list can be altered by the listing officer:
- following the receipt of a proposal from an interested party or the local authority; *or*
- following a successful appeal to a valuation tribunal or the High Court.

The list below outlines the circumstances in which a dwelling's valuation band may be altered.[29]

Circumstances in which a valuation band may be altered

- The listing officer or assessor is satisfied that the valuation band is incorrect – eg, because of a clerical error.
- The listing officer or assessor is satisfied that the dwelling would have been allocated to a different valuation band had the valuation been carried out correctly.
- There has been a 'material increase' (see below) in the value of the dwelling since it was placed on the list and all, or part, of it has been sold or, additionally in England, let on a lease for a term of seven years or more.
- There has been a 'material reduction' (see p30) in the value of the dwelling.
- Part of the property has started to be used, or is no longer used, for business purposes, or the balance between business and domestic use has changed.
- There has been a successful appeal against the valuation band shown on the list.

The Valuation Office Agency should normally tell you within two months if it has decided to alter the list.

A 'material increase' in the dwelling's value

A **'material increase'** in the value of a dwelling means any increase which is caused (in whole or in part) by any:
- building; *or*
- engineering; *or*
- other operation

carried out in relation to the dwelling.[30]

This would apply to building or other works which either increase the size of the property or add to its market value. But the material increase only has an impact on the dwelling's valuation once the dwelling (or any part of it) has been sold. In England, this also applies where the dwelling is let on a lease for a term of seven years or more. Since 1 April 2008 in England, the material increase has effect from the date the transaction took place. In the case of a dwelling ceasing to be a composite hereditament, or if there is a reduction in the domestic use of a dwelling or if a new dwelling comes into existence, the relevant date is the date of the alteration. If a number of changes have taken place, the change in the valuation list is taken from the date of the last change.[31]

However, even when a dwelling has not been sold or let on a lease for a term of seven years or more, when a revaluation takes place in England in the future, all material increases will be taken into account in setting the banding for the dwelling concerned.

A 'material reduction' in the dwelling's value

A 'material reduction' in the value of a dwelling should lead to an immediate revaluation. This, if sufficiently significant, will also lead to an immediate re-banding of the dwelling. This only applies, however, if the material reduction is caused (in whole or in part) by:[32]
- the demolition (but not partial demolition during other building or engineering work) of any part of the dwelling; *or*
- any change in the physical state of the dwelling's locality; *or*
- any adaptation of the dwelling to make it suitable for a person with a physical disability.

Changes in the physical state of a dwelling's locality give the greatest scope for proposals to change a dwelling's valuation band (so-called 'blighting'). Such changes include, for example, a change in the character of the immediate environment brought about because of a road widening scheme, the deterioration of surrounding property or a change in the use of nearby business premises.

The reduction in value should post-date the entry of the dwelling in the valuation list. In one case it was pointed out: [33]

> [in]... some cases the reduction may follow very swiftly upon the change, in other cases it may not do so. It may take time after the change is known about before the impact of it is realised and it begins to affect the prices which people are prepared to pay for the affected dwellings.

How dwellings are revalued

When one of the conditions for the potential alteration of a dwelling's valuation band exists, there should be a revaluation. The valuation should be made on the basis of the rules and assumptions (see p25). In England, this means that its value, taking into account its current state, is still based on what it would have sold for on the open market by a willing vendor on 1 April 1991.[34] If the change in value is only small it might not be sufficient to move a dwelling from one valuation band to another.

Obtaining an alteration

Where a list is inaccurate, a proposal may be made to the listing officer or assessor for an alteration to the list. In many instances, there are time limits for this (see p31). Making a proposal is also a first and obligatory stage in the appeal process (see Chapter 12).

Who can make a proposal

Any 'interested person' can make a proposal for alteration to the list. An **'interested person'** on any particular day is:[35]

- the owner of the dwelling;
- anyone who is liable (either solely or jointly) to pay the tax on the dwelling;
- in the case of an exempt dwelling (see Chapter 5), or a dwelling on which the council tax has been set at nil, the person who would otherwise be liable to pay the tax.

Local authorities in England can also make proposals to the listing officer.[36]

Time limits

A proposal may be made at any time if:
- a property should be excluded from, or included in, the valuation list;[37]
- there has been a material increase (see p29) in the value of the dwelling and a relevant transaction;
- there has been a material reduction (see p30) in the value of a dwelling;
- part of a property starts to be used, or is no longer used, for business purposes, or the balance between business and domestic use has changed.[38]

In the following circumstances, however, there is a time limit in which to make a proposal.
- Proposals regarding a valuation band on the original list. Except in limited circumstances, the time limit to make a proposal has now expired.
- Banding proposals made by a new resident/owner or regarding a new property. A proposal can be made within a six-month period if:
  - someone first becomes liable for the council tax on a particular dwelling; *or*
  - the dwelling (eg, a new home) is first shown on the valuation list after 1 April 1993 or 1 April 2005 in Wales.[39]

  Such a proposal cannot be made, however, if:
  - it is based on the same facts that have already been considered and determined by a valuation tribunal or the High Court; *or*
  - the new taxpayer is a company which is a subsidiary of the preceding taxpayer; *or*
  - the preceding taxpayer is a company which is a subsidiary of the new taxpayer; *or*
  - the change of taxpayer has occurred solely because of a formation of a new partnership and any of the partners was a partner in the previous partnership.[40]
- Appeal decisions relating to a comparable dwelling. A proposal may be made within six months of an appeal decision on another comparable dwelling if this gives reasonable grounds for arguing that the valuation band of the dwelling in question should be changed.[41]
- Proposals regarding an alteration to the list. If the listing officer or assessor has altered the list in respect of a dwelling, a proposal can be made within six months from when the notice of the alteration was served.[42]

Making a proposal

You must make the proposal by writing to the listing officer at the local office of the Valuation Office Agency (the address should be on the council tax bill) or the local assessor.[43] Standard forms and explanatory notes are available from these offices to assist with the proposal. The completed form, or alternatively a letter, should contain all relevant information including:[44]

- your name and address;
- the capacity in which the proposal is being made – ie, whether as the liable person or the owner of the dwelling;
- the dwelling to which it relates;
- the date;
- the way in which it is proposed the list should be altered;
- the reasons for believing the list to be inaccurate, the relevant facts, any evidence supporting those facts and any relevant dates, such as the date you first became the liable person or the date when a material reduction in the dwelling occurred.

Normally a proposal can only deal with one dwelling. In England, however, a proposal can be made for more than one dwelling if:[45]

- you make the proposal in the same capacity (ie, as the owner) and each of the dwellings is within the same building or 'curtilage' as the other(s); *or*
- it arises because a property is shown as a dwelling when it should not be or should be shown as a number of dwellings.

The proposal should be addressed to the listing officer or assessor for the relevant area and delivered or posted to the appropriate address. To be on the safe side, it is sensible to keep a copy and obtain some proof of postage (eg, registered mail) or, if delivered by hand, a receipt.

In England, the listing officer should write within 28 days acknowledging receipt of the proposal, unless the proposal is considered to be invalid (see p33). In Scotland, the assessor should write acknowledging receipt of the proposal within 14 days. Again, the acknowledgement letter should include details of the procedures that will be followed.[46]

Joint proposals in Scotland

In Scotland, other interested people (see p30) may write to the assessor indicating that they wish to support the proposal.[47] As long as the proposal has not been withdrawn or referred to the local valuation appeal committee, the original proposal should then be treated as a joint proposal.

Invalid proposals

There are different procedures concerning invalid proposals that apply in England, Wales and Scotland. If the listing officer or assessor fails to identify an invalid proposal at this stage the point can still be raised at an appeal hearing.[48]

England

In England, if the listing officer considers that the proposal is invalid you will be sent an 'invalidity notice'. This should be done within four weeks of receiving the proposal. This notice gives:[49]

- the reasons why the proposal is considered invalid; *and*
- you a right either to make a further proposal in relation to the same dwelling or to appeal against the invalidity notice to the Valuation Tribunal for England (see p206).

The listing officer may at any time withdraw an invalidity notice by informing you in writing.

Unless an invalidity notice has been withdrawn, you can:

- make a further proposal, but only once and only if the original proposal was made within the appropriate time limit; *or*
- appeal to the Valuation Tribunal for England (see p206).

If a further proposal is made, the earlier proposal which resulted in the issue of the invalidity notice is treated as withdrawn.

From 1 April 2008 the 'Appeals Direct' system has operated in England. This requires you to appeal to the Valuation Tribunal for England (see p206) yourself, without further steps being taken by the listing officer. You must send a copy of the invalidity notice, together with a written statement. This should include the address of the dwelling and the reasons why the proposal is considered invalid.

Valuation tribunal hearings are described in Chapter 12. Action on the original proposal is suspended until either the listing officer withdraws the invalidity notice, or the tribunal or High Court reaches a decision on the validity of the proposal. If the listing officer withdraws an invalidity notice after an appeal has been started, s/he must inform the tribunal.

Scotland

In Scotland, a distinction is drawn between proposals that are considered invalid:[50]

- because you are not an appropriate person to make a proposal or because it is out of time; *and*
- because you do not include the required information.

In both instances, the assessor must write to you within six weeks of receiving the proposal. The letter must give reasons for the decision and describe your right to appeal in writing to the assessor within four weeks. If no such appeal is made, the matter will end. In the second instance, the letter must again give reasons for the decision, but should also identify the information that needs to be supplied. You may either:

- supply the information (this should be done within four weeks); *or*
- appeal in writing to the assessor within four weeks.

If the information is not supplied or an appeal is not made within the four-week period, the assessor treats the proposal as invalidly made and that is the end of the matter.

If an appeal is made in either case but the assessor still considers the appeal invalid, s/he should inform the secretary of the local valuation appeal committee in writing within four weeks that an appeal has been made. Details of the proposal and the assessor's reasons for considering the proposal invalid should also be given.[51]

Wales

In Wales, if the listing officer believes that a proposal has not been validly made, s/he may serve an invalidity notice on the proposer. This must be done within four weeks. The notice must explain the reasons for her/his opinion and that either a further proposal may be made or an appeal taken to a valuation tribunal. If a fresh proposal is made, the original is treated as withdrawn. The fresh proposal must be made within four weeks of the invalidity notice being served.

What happens after a valid proposal has been made

England

Within six weeks of receiving a valid proposal, the listing officer should send a copy of it to anyone else who appears to be liable for the tax on the dwelling. Copies should also be sent to the local authority if it has informed the listing officer in writing that it wishes to receive a copy of a class or classes of proposal, and the proposal falls within such a class. Each copy should be accompanied by a statement of the procedures to be followed.[52]

Following the receipt of a valid proposal:

- the listing officer may agree to the proposal (see below);
- all interested parties may agree to an alternative alteration to the list (see p35);
- an appeal may be made to the Valuation Tribunal for England (see p35);
- the proposal may be withdrawn (see p35).

The listing officer agrees to the proposal

If the listing officer agrees to the proposal, you and the liable person (if different) should be notified that the valuation list will be altered accordingly. The valuation list should be altered within six weeks of the date of the letter.[53]

Agreeing to a different alteration

Before an appeal, it is possible for the listing officer to agree an alteration to the list that is different from that proposed, but with which you agree. This requires the agreement of all interested parties. If such an agreement is reached, the listing officer should alter the valuation list within six weeks of the date of the agreement. The original proposal is treated as having been withdrawn.[54]

Appealing to the Valuation Tribunal for England

If the listing officer has made a decision and served a notice on the proposer, the taxpayer and any other competent person, appeal can be made to the Valuation Tribunal for England (see p206).

An appeal must be made within three months. If an appeal has not been made within this time, the President of the Valuation Tribunal for England may authorise the appeal if the delay has arisen because of circumstances beyond your control.

The appeal is started by serving the Tribunal with a copy of the decision notice containing the following information if this is not contained in the decision notice:

- the address of the dwelling;
- the reasons for the appeal;
- the name and address of:
  - the appellant;
  - the proposer (if different from the appellant);
  - the listing officer;
  - any other person who appears to be a taxpayer;
- any other interested person

Appeals are described in Chapter 12.

Withdrawing the proposal

You may withdraw the proposal at any time before an appeal by writing to the Valuation Tribunal for England, or orally at the hearing. If a proposal is withdrawn at the hearing, it will not take effect unless the panel consents. Each party must be notified in writing of a withdrawal and the date on which the proposal is withdrawn should be confirmed. Each party has the opportunity to commence a new appeal about the decision by serving a written notice. This must state that the new appellant wishes to proceed with an appeal and the reason for the appeal.

In the past, it was not unknown for the valuation office or for local authority staff to attempt to encourage people to withdraw their proposals and appeals. Such 'persuasion' may include claims that a tribunal has previously rejected a similar appeal so that an appellant has no prospect of success. A valuation tribunal decision on any point is merely persuasive, but not binding, on subsequent tribunals (see Chapter 12).

Scotland

In Scotland, once a valid proposal has been received:

- the assessor may agree to the proposal (see below);
- an appeal may be made to the local valuation appeal committee (see below);
- the proposal may be withdrawn (see below).

The assessor agrees to the proposal

If the assessor thinks the proposal is well founded, you (and any joint proposer) should be advised of this in writing. The list should be altered within six weeks of the date of that letter.[55]

Appealing to the local valuation appeal committee

If the assessor thinks that the proposal is not well founded, and it is not withdrawn, s/he should refer the disagreement to the local valuation appeal committe. This should be done within six months of the day the assessor received the proposal.[56]

If the assessor has previously issued an invalidity notice on the grounds that:

- you are not an appropriate person to make the proposal or the proposal is out of time, the six-month period starts from the day the assessor withdrew the notice or you won the appeal against the notice;
- the proposal does not include the required information, the six-month period starts from the day that all the relevant information was supplied or the day you won the appeal against the notice.[57]

A proposal may be adopted by another interested person (see p30) if the original proposer seeks to withdraw it. In such cases, the six-month period starts from the date the other person informed the assessor of her/his wish to adopt the proposal.[58]

The appeal is initiated by the assessor writing to the secretary of the valuation committee advising of the appeal. The following information should also be included:[59]

- the proposed alteration of the list;
- the date on which the proposal was received;
- the name and address of the proposer;
- the grounds on which the proposal was made.

Appeals are described in Chapter 12.

Withdrawing the proposal

The proposal may be withdrawn at any time if the proposer(s) writes to the assessor.[60] If none of the proposers are currently liable for the tax on the dwelling, the assessor must write to at least one currently liable person telling her/him about the proposed withdrawal. An interested person (see p30) has six weeks from the date of the letter to advise the assessor that s/he wishes to adopt the proposal. From that date it is then treated as having been made by that person.

Notification of an alteration

Within six weeks of altering the list, the listing officer or assessor should write to the local authority stating the effect of the alteration. The local authority should alter its copy of the valuation list as soon as is reasonably practicable.[61]

England

In England, the listing officer should also write to the person who is currently liable for the tax on the dwelling within six weeks of altering the list, advising her/him of the effect of the alteration and the process by which a proposal and appeal may be made.[62] This obligation to notify does not, however, apply if the alteration was made solely to correct a clerical error, or to reflect:

- a decision of the listing officer that a proposal is well founded; *or*
- an agreed alternative alteration; *or*
- a change in the address of the dwelling concerned; *or*
- a change in the area of the billing authority; *or*
- the decision of a valuation tribunal or the High Court in relation to the dwelling concerned.

The listing officer should take such steps as are reasonably practicable to ensure that the letter to the liable person is sent no later than the letter to the local authority.[63]

Scotland

In Scotland, the assessor must notify a liable person within six weeks of the alteration being made. Where the alteration involves the addition of the dwelling to the list, the owner must also be notified within six weeks of the alteration.

Additionally, the assessor must notify a liable person within six weeks of the alteration being made if:

- an alteration has been agreed, but the proposer is not a liable person at the time of the alteration; *or*
- an appeal decision has led to the alteration of the list but none of the parties to the appeal is a liable person on the date of the alteration.[64]

The above notification should include a statement about the process by which a proposal may be made. The assessor should take such steps as are reasonably practicable to ensure that the above letters are sent no later than the letter to the local authority.[65]

Notes

1. Who is responsible for valuations
1 **EW** s20 LGFA 1992
2 **EW** s26 LGFA 1992
3 **S** s84(1) LGFA 1992
4 **S** s86(5) LGFA 1992
5 **S** s86(10) LGFA 1992
6 **EW** s21 LGFA 1992
6 **S** s86(7) LGFA 1992
7 **EW** s21 LGFA 1992
  S s86(8) LGFA 1992
8 **EW** s21 LGFA 1992
  S s86(9) LGFA 1992

2. The valuation officer's and assessor's powers
9 **EW** s26 LGFA 1992
  S s89 LGFA 1992
10 **EW** s26 LGFA 1992
   S s89 LGFA 1992
11 **EW** s27 LGFA 1992
   S s90 LGFA 1992
12 **EW** s27 LGFA 1992
   S s90 LGFA 1992
13 **EW** s27 LGFA 1992
   S s90 LGFA 1992
14 **EW** s27(6) LGFA 1992
   S s90 LGFA 1992
15 **EW** s27 LGFA 1992
   S s90 LGFA 1992

3. How dwellings are valued
16 **E** s21 LGFA 1992 and CT(SVD) Regs
   W s21 LGFA 1992 and CT(SVD) Regs, as amended by CT(SVD)(W)(A) Regs
   S s86(2) LGFA 1992 and CT(VD)(S) Regs
17 **E** s21 LGFA 1992 and CT(SVD) Regs
   W s21 LGFA 1992 and CT(SVD) Regs, as amended by CT(SVD)(W)(A) Regs
   S s86(2) LGFA 1992 and CT(VD)(S) Regs
18 **S** Reg 3 CT(VD)(S) Regs; *The Appeal of Grampian Valuation Joint Board* [2003] RA 167 Sc
19 Parliamentary Answer by John Healy, Minister for Local Government, 13 December 2007

4. Compiling and maintaining valuation lists
20 **EW** ss22 and 22B LGFA 1992
   S s84 LGFA 1992
21 **EW** ss22 and 22B LGFA 1992
   S s84 LGFA 1992

22 **EW** ss22 and 22B LGFA 1992
   S s85 LGFA 1992
23 **EW** s22 LGFA 1992
   S s84 LGFA 1992
24 **EW** s2(2)(b) LGFA 1992
   S s71(2)(b) LGFA 1992

5. What the valuation list shows
25 **EW** s23 LGFA 1992 and CT(CVL) Regs
   S s84 LGFA 1992 and CT(CVL) Regs
26 **EW** s23 LGFA 1992
   S s84 LGFA 1992

6. Inspecting the valuation list
27 **EW** s28 LGFA 1992
   S s91 LGFA 1992
28 **EW** s28 LGFA 1992
   S s91 LGFA 1992

7. Altering a valuation list
29 **E** CT(ALA)(E) Regs; VTE(CTRA)(E) Regs
   W CT(ALA) Regs
   S CT(ALA)(S) Regs
30 **E** s24 LGFA 1992
   S s87 LGFA 1992
31 Reg 6 CT(SVD) Regs, as amended by CT(VALA)(E) Regs
32 **E** s24 LGFA 1992
   S s87 LGFA 1992
33 *Tilly v Listing Officer for Tower Hamlets* [2001] RVR 250
34 **E** CT(SVD) Regs
   W CT(SVD)(W)(A) Regs
   S CT(VD)(S) Regs
35 **E** Reg 2 CT(ALA)(E) Regs
   S Reg 3 CT(ALA)(S) Regs
36 **E** Reg 4 CT(ALA)(E) Regs
37 **E** Reg 4 CT(ALA)(E) Regs
   S Reg 5 CT(ALA)(S) Regs
38 **E** Reg 4 CT(ALA)(E) Regs
   S Reg 5 CT(ALA)(S) Regs
39 **E** Reg 4 CT(ALA)(E) Regs
   S Reg 5 CT(ALA)(S) Regs
40 **E** Reg 4(5) CT(ALA)(E) Regs
   S Reg 5 CT(ALA)(S) Regs
41 **E** Reg 4 CT(ALA)(E) Regs
   S Reg 5 CT(ALA)(S) Regs
42 **E** Reg 4 CT(ALA)(E) Regs
   S Reg 5 CT(ALA)(S) Regs
43 **E** Reg 5 CT(ALA)(E) Regs
   S Reg 6 CT(ALA)(S) Regs

44 **E** Reg 5 CT(ALA)(E) Regs
   S Reg 6 CT(ALA)(S) Regs
45 **E** Reg 5 CT(ALA)(E) Regs
46 **S** Reg 7 CT(ALA)(S) Regs
47 **S** Reg 12 CT(ALA)(S) Regs
48 **E** CT(ALA)(E) Regs
   W CT(ALA) Regs
   S CT(ALA)(S) Regs
49 **E** Reg 7 CT(ALA)(E) Regs
50 **S** Regs 8 and 9 CT(ALA)(S) Regs
51 **S** Reg 10 CT(ALA)(S) Regs
52 **E** Reg 8 CT(ALA) Regs
53 **E** Reg 9(3) CT(ALA) Regs
54 **E** Reg 9 CT(ALA) Regs
55 **S** Reg 14 CT(ALA)(S) Regs
56 **S** Reg 15 CT(ALA)(S) Regs
57 **S** Reg 15 CT(ALA)(S) Regs
58 **S** Reg 15 CT(ALA)(S) Regs
59 **S** Reg 15 CT(ALA)(S) Regs
60 **S** Reg 11 CT(ALA)(S) Regs
61 **E** Reg 12(1) CT(ALA) Regs
   S Reg 16 CT(ALA)(S) Regs
62 **E** Reg 12 CT(ALA)(E) Regs
63 **E** Reg 12(4) CT(ALA)(E) Regs
64 **S** Reg 16 CT(ALA)(S) Regs
65 **S** Reg 16 CT(ALA)(S) Regs

4

Chapter 4

The amount of tax

This chapter explains:
1. The valuation bands (below)
2. Reducing the amount of tax payable (p42)
3. Transitional relief in Wales (p43)
4. Discretionary reduction (p46)

1. The valuation bands

Each year local authorities must set a council tax to help pay for their expenditure and that of related bodies. They must publish the amounts of their council tax within 21 days of setting them, in at least one local newspaper. Failure to do so, however, does not invalidate the amounts set.[1] The set amount of council tax and Scottish Water charges for each dwelling depends on the valuation band to which it is allocated. Different valuation bands apply in England,[2] Scotland[3] and Wales.[4]

England and Scotland

The original bands from the 1993 valuation list continue to apply in England and Scotland until the next general revaluation date.

Valuation bands in England

Valuation band	Range of values
A	Up to £40,000
B	£40,001 to £52,000
C	£52,001 to £68,000
D	£68,001 to £88,000
E	£88,001 to £120,000
F	£120,001 to £160,000
G	£160,001 to £320,000
H	£320,001 and over

Valuation bands in Scotland

Valuation band	Range of values
A	Up to £27,000
B	£27,001 to £35,000
C	£35,001 to £45,000
D	£45,001 to £58,000
E	£58,001 to £80,000
F	£80,001 to £106,000
G	£106,001 to £212,000
H	£212,001 and over

Wales

Valuation bands before 1 April 2005

Before 1 April 2005 the effective valuation bands for Wales were as listed in the table below. These values apply to any calculation of council tax for a dwelling in Wales before 1 April 2005.

Valuation bands in Wales before 1 April 2005

Valuation band	Range of values
A	Up to £30,000
B	£30,001 to £39,000
C	£39,001 to £51,000
D	£51,001 to £66,000
E	£66,001 to £90,000
F	£90,001 to £120,000
G	£120,001 to £240,000
H	£240,001 and over

Valuation bands from 1 April 2005

From 1 April 2005 dwellings in Wales fall into one of the following band valuations, based upon a theoretical valuation date of 1 April 2003.[5]

Valuation bands in Wales from 1 April 2005

Valuation band	Range of values
A	Up to £36,000
B	£36,001 to £52,000
C	£52,001 to £73,000
D	£73,001 to £100,000
E	£100,001 to £135,000
F	£135,001 to £191,000

G	£191,001 to £286,000
H	£286,001 to £400,000
I	£400,001 and over

These bands apply to all domestic dwellings from 1 April 2005. A transitional relief scheme to reduce bills for people who are affected by certain banding changes will operate for three years (see p43).

How the amount of tax payable varies between bands

The council tax payable in any local authority depends on the valuation band in which the dwelling has been placed. The lower the value of the band is, the lower the bill will be. The amount of tax payable in respect of dwellings situated in the same area varies between valuation bands in England and Scotland in the following proportions:[6]

6(A):7(B):8(C):9(D):11(E):13(F):15(G):18(H)

This means, for example, that the tax payable on a Band H dwelling is three times more than that payable on a Band A dwelling and double that of a Band D dwelling. The local authority has no discretion to vary bands or the relative proportion of tax paid within each band.

In Wales from 1 April 2005, the amount of tax payable in respect of dwellings situated in the same area varies between valuation bands in the following proportions:[7]

6(A):7(B):8(C):9(D):11(E):13(F):15(G):18(H):21(I)

This means that those in the top Band I in Wales will pay three-and-a-half times more than those in the lowest Band A.

Daily liability

Liability to pay the tax arises on a daily basis. The situation at the end of the day is assumed to have existed throughout the day.[8] The amount payable for the day is the annual amount set by the local authority for that year for dwellings in the relevant valuation band, divided by the number of days in the financial year (365 or 366).

2. Reducing the amount of tax payable

Individual dwellings

The amount payable in respect of a specific dwelling may be reduced by:
- an alteration to the dwelling's valuation band (see Chapter 3);

- a fixed period, or indefinite, exemption (see Chapter 5);
- a disability reduction (see Chapter 7);
- a discount (see Chapter 8);
- council tax benefit (see Chapter 9);
- adopting certain payment arrangements, which may offer a discount (see Chapter 10);
- a discretionary reduction (see p46).

Tax capping

Under the Local Government Finance Act 1992, the Secretary of State can limit the amount of council tax set by individual local authorities (so-called 'capping'). The Government could use this power to tell councils to set a lower budget if it considers the budget requirement and the council tax to have increased by an excessive amount. In 2008 the power was exercised in relation to councils in Lincolnshire, resulting in re-billing for taxpayers at a lower amount.

---

3. **Transitional relief in Wales**

Properties in Wales have been revalued once since the introduction of council tax in 1992. From 1 April 2005, a transitional relief scheme existed for three years to smooth the transition to the new bandings. The scheme aimed to reduce the impact of banding changes on existing owners and occupiers of dwellings which moved by two or more bands in the three years between 1 April 2005 and 31 March 2008. Transitional relief may still be relevant if a bill has been served late for some reason, in respect of a past financial year.

Although the banding of a property may have increased, the dwelling was still treated for billing purposes as falling into a lower band than that actually shown on the valuation list in those years. This stopped taxpayers whose homes moved by two or more bands from being hit by steep rises in council tax during the first few years of the new list.

The scheme did not apply to homes in all bands, but only to those which previously fell into Bands C to G prior to 1 April 2005. Dwellings which fell into Bands A and B were not eligible for transitional relief. Dwellings which previously fell into Band H were not entitled to transitional relief since these could not, by definition, have moved more than two bands.

A dwelling was eligible for relief if:[9]
- it was on the valuation list on 31 March 2005; *and*
- it moved by two or more valuation bands on 1 April 2005; *and*
- the liable person on 1 April 2005 was the same as on 31 March 2005.

Transitional relief was applied automatically to a bill; taxpayers did not need to apply.

Dwellings that underwent the largest change in valuation attracted the most transitional relief spread over three years; those that underwent a smaller change in banding were entitled to transitional relief for only the first or second year. The number of years for which transitional relief was available, therefore, depended on the size of the shift in banding applicable to your home.

For example, a property that moved two bands only received a reduction equivalent to one band in the first year – ie, the property was charged an amount of tax as though it had moved one band instead of two – but nothing thereafter for 2006/07 and 2007/08. This means that the taxpayer was charged for the full amount of council tax after one year. Similarly, properties that moved by three bands were entitled to a reduction of two bands for the first year and one band in the second, but did not qualify for transitional relief in the third year or after. Other changes in the valuation bands can be calculated using the following table.

Number of valuation band increases above original	Number of bands by which column 1 increases are reduced in 2005/06	Number of bands by which column 1 increases are reduced in 2006/07	Number of bands by which column 1 increases are reduced in 2007/08
8	7	6	5
7	6	5	4
6	5	4	3
5	4	3	2
4	3	2	1
3	2	1	0
2	1	0	0

Example

A dwelling that fell into Band C before 31 March 2005 now falls into Band H on the new valuation list. This is a change in five valuation bands (column 1). Transitional relief reduces the amount of tax payable by four valuation bands in the first year (2005/06). This means the taxpayer pays the amount normally payable on a property in Band D instead of H (column 2).

In the second year (2006/07) transitional relief reduces the tax increase to the equivalent of three valuation bands, so the taxpayer pays the amount applicable to Band E (column 3).

In the third year (2007/08) transitional relief reduces the increase to two valuation bands from Band H, so the taxpayer pays the amount applicable to Band F (column 4). This is the last year transitional relief is awarded. Thereafter, the taxpayer will pay the full amount on Band H.

Details of the transitional relief, including the transitional valuation band and the amount of the reduction, was required to be shown on council tax bills.[10] The local authority should also have supplied additional information with the bill explaining how a transitional valuation band and reduction were arrived at.[11] If you do not agree with the amount of the reduction, you can appeal (see Chapter 12).

Note: if a local authority is late in serving a bill, transitional relief should still be applied.

Changes of valuation band between 2005 and 2008

In some cases, homes in Wales were not placed in a new band on 1 April 2005, but later – eg, following an appeal. If an alteration occurred between 2005 and 2008 which involved a change of two or more valuation bands, the liable person was entitled to transitional relief on her/his home.[12] A dwelling may have become entitled to transitional relief for the first, second or third years of the scheme, or part of each year, depending on the date of the banding change and between how many bands the dwelling moved.

Thus, a property may have attracted or lost its transitional relief if it moved band during the transitional period. For example, if after 1 April 2005 a dwelling moved by two or more bands from Band A or B it would have attracted transitional relief from the date of the change, provided the taxpayer was the same as on 31 March 2005. Similarly, transitional relief may have been available if the valuation officer changed a band after 1 April 2005. Thus, a dwelling may have attracted transitional relief not in the first year, but in the second.

Dividing a dwelling

If a change was made to the composition of a dwelling, for instance, by dividing it into two separate dwellings, after 1 April 2005, transitional relief was lost. Thus, if a single house was divided into two flats, the property would no longer have qualified for transitional relief as it would not have been the same dwelling it was on 1 April 2005, even if the taxpayer remained the same.[13]

Change in liable taxpayer

If a person was the liable taxpayer on both 31 March 2005 and 1 April 2005, transitional relief was applied on each day s/he was liable to pay thereafter during the transitional period. If a person moved out or let an empty property to tenants, the dwelling lost its transitional relief. It could have been applied for again, however, if the liable taxpayer on 31 March 2005 became liable again – ie, by moving back. Thus, a non-resident landlord of a property may have lost transitional relief during the period in which a dwelling was occupied by tenants, but may have been entitled during a later period or subsequent financial year when the dwelling was unoccupied.

Exempt dwellings

Exempt dwellings which were empty and unfurnished for up to six months were eligible for transitional relief. When the dwelling ceased to be exempt, it then attracted council tax a transitional reduction (see Chapter 5).[14]

---

4. Discretionary reduction

A local authority in England or Wales can reduce the amount of council tax payable on any dwelling or any class of dwelling by any amount it sees fit under s13A Local Government Finance Act 1992, as inserted by the Local Government Act 2003. Under the rates system local authorities had the power to reduce the amount payable in a case of poverty, but in council tax the power goes beyond reduction on ground of poverty.

From 1 April 2004, local authorities enjoy a discretionary power to reduce council tax bills. Local authorities can reduce sums payable in individual cases – eg, to prevent financial hardship, and in groups of cases – eg, if several properties have been affected by flooding.[15]

A local authority has the discretion to reduce the amount of council tax to nil.

A reduction can be made in respect of sums of council tax that have accrued in previous financial years, including arrears.

Explaining the scope of the power to reduce a council tax bill in Parliament in 2003, Lord Rooker stated: 'The billing authority would, of course, have to act reasonably and would have to justify to [their] auditors what [they] had done.'[16]

A reduction is applied in the same way as a discount (see Chapter 8) or disability reduction (see Chapter 7) – ie, it is deducted before council tax benefit is calculated.

Applications for discretionary reduction

Applications for discretionary reductions are best made in writing with supporting evidence. An application for a reduction should be made to the Chief Executive of the local authority, as decisions often have to be taken at a senior level.

So far, there has been no caselaw on how the discretion should be exercised, but the matter has been considered by the Local Government Ombudsman.[17] In December 2004 Redcar and Cleveland Borough Council decided that all empty homes in its area should pay the maximum 90 per cent council tax. Mr and Mrs Weaver (pseudonyms) bought a bungalow in the local authority district and renovated it, but then faced hostility from people in the area and decided not to move in. When they received a bill, Mrs Weaver wrote to explain their circumstances. The Council refused the reduction, stating that it had set the maximum discount and that the scheme '. . . does not allow for any individual discretion'.

The Ombudsman ruled that the blanket policy adopted by the Council was wrong in law, and the local authority had no basis for claiming it had no discretion on whether to grant a discount or not in individual cases. The Council could not fetter its discretion. Parliament had given it a discretion and the Ombudsman considered that a local authority should give consideration to cases on an individual basis. The failure to do so amounted to maladministration, and the Ombudsman directed the authority to give proper consideration to Mrs Weaver's request and invite her to state her reasons for seeking the reduction. Having considered her reasons, the Council was directed to give its reasons for either accepting or rejecting the application, as well as establishing proper arrangements for the consideration of such cases in future.

In theory, a local authority's refusal to consider an application might be challenged by judicial review in the High Court. Whilst the discretion given to a local authority is wide and cannot be expected as a right, there might also be situations in which the discretion to award or refuse might be considered unreasonable and open to challenge (eg, in a case of discrimination), and a local authority would be expected to give reasons explaining any decision.

Discretionary reduction in Scotland[18]

From 1 April 2005, Scottish local authorities may apply discretionary reductions to empty dwellings and dwellings that are second homes in different parts of their areas. The minimum reduction is 10 per cent and the maximum reduction is 50 per cent. However, certain classes of dwelling that are identified as second homes are protected from this power. This statutory protection is given to second homes where the liable person is the owner or a tenant and is required to reside elsewhere as a specific condition of her/his employment.

A dwelling is job-related if you or your spouse or civil partner are required under a contract to live there – eg, a manager of a public house who is required to reside within or near the premises, domestic staff, and service personnel who need special security arrangements, which require them to reside in other dwellings.

A dwelling is also job-related if you (or your spouse or civil partner) are a minister of religion and you live there in order to perform your ministerial duties.

Notes

1. The valuation bands
1 **EW** s38 LGFA 1992
  S s96 LGFA 1992
2 **E** s5(2) LGFA 1992
3 **S** s74(2) LGFA 1992
4 **W** s5(3) LGFA 1992
5 **W** s5(3) LGFA 1992
6 **E** s5 LGFA 1992
7 **W** s5 LGFA 1992
8 **EW** s2 LGFA 1992
  S s71 LGFA 1992

3. Transitional relief in Wales
9 Reg 3(2) CT(TA)(W) Regs
10 Sch 1 para 15 CT(DN)(W) Regs
11 Sch 2 CT(DN)(W) Regs
12 Reg 3(4) and (5) CT(TA)(W) Regs
13 s13B LGFA 1992
14 s13B LGFA 1992

4. Discretionary reduction
15 s13A(2) LGFA 1992
16 *Hansard,* Grand Committee, 16 June 2003, col 217
17 Complaint against Redcar and Cleveland Borough Council (05/C/03367)
18 CT(DUD)(S) Regs

Chapter 5

Exempt dwellings

This chapter covers:
1. Exempt dwellings in England and Wales (below)
2. Exempt dwellings in Scotland (p58)
3. How exempt dwellings are identified (p64)
4. Obtaining an exemption (p64)
5. Notification of exemption (p64)
6. Penalties (p65)
7. Appeals (p66)

The council tax and, in Scotland, Scottish Water charges are only payable for chargeable dwellings. Certain classes of dwelling are exempt from council tax.[1] No council tax is payable on a dwelling on any day when it falls into an exempt category. The local authority must take steps each year to establish which dwellings in its area are exempt. When determining whether the dwelling is exempt, the state of affairs at the end of the day is assumed to have existed throughout that day.[2]

1. Exempt dwellings in England and Wales

Vacant and unoccupied dwellings

Dwellings that are vacant or unoccupied may be exempt from council tax. Some occupied dwellings are also exempt (see p56). A list of all categories of exempt dwellings is set out in Appendix 1.

The term **'vacant'** refers to a dwelling which is both:[3]
- unoccupied; *and*
- substantially unfurnished.

The legislation contains no definition of 'substantially unfurnished'. In practice many local authorities regard a dwelling as **'substantially unfurnished'** if there are insufficient furnishings to enable someone to live in the dwelling. However, the quantity of furniture present in the dwelling, in relation to its size, should be the determining factor, ignoring anything other than 'furniture' – ie, appliances, fitted wardrobes, TV, DVD player and carpets. Thus, a studio flat with a table, two chairs, a sofa and a bed (plus a cooker, washer/drier, TV and hi-fi) would be substantially furnished, but the same goods would not make a four-bedroom house substantially furnished.

The legislation defines an **'unoccupied dwelling'** as one in which no one lives and an **'occupied dwelling'** as one in which at least one person lives.[4] There is, however, a significant distinction between occupying a home and being solely or mainly resident in it (see p71). While the same person may occupy two or more dwellings at any one time, s/he can only be mainly resident in one of them. The local authority must consider each case on its merits.

An unoccupied dwelling is exempt from council tax if:[5]

- it is substantially unfurnished and requires, or is undergoing, major repairs to make it habitable or is undergoing structural alterations (see below);
- it is substantially unfurnished and has recently received major repairs to make it habitable or structural alterations (see p51);
- it belongs to a charity and was last used for that charity's purposes (see p51);
- it is substantially unfurnished (see p51);
- it was previously the sole or main residence of someone in prison (see p52);
- someone has died in it (see p52);
- it is a property in which occupation is prohibited by law (see p53);
- it is being kept for occupation by a minister of religion (see p53);
- it was previously the sole or main residence of someone in a hospital, care home or certain hostels (see p53);
- it was previously the sole or main residence of someone who is receiving care in a place other than a hospital or a home (see p53);
- it is owned by and was previously the sole or main residence of someone who is resident elsewhere providing personal care (see p54);
- it was previously the sole or main residence of a student who is resident elsewhere or a person who will become a student within six weeks of vacating the dwelling (see p54);
- it is in the possession of a mortgage lender (see p55);
- it is held by bankruptcy trustees (see p55);
- it is an annexe and may not be let separately (see p55).

Vacant dwelling requiring or undergoing major repairs or alterations

In England and Wales a dwelling may be exempt for a maximum of 12 months if it:[6]

- is vacant (ie, unoccupied and substantially unfurnished) and requires, or is undergoing, major repair works to make it habitable; *or*
- is undergoing structural alteration which has not been substantially completed; *or*

- has undergone major repair work to render it habitable, but has remained continuously vacant since completion for less than six months; *or*
- has undergone structural alteration, but has remained continuously vacant for less than six months since the alteration was completed.

The vacant dwelling remains exempt for as long as it requires the major repair work or for as long as the works or alteration takes, subject to the 12-month limit.

Major repair works are not defined in the legislation apart from the fact that they include structural repair works. The phrase 'substantially completed' is not defined either.

In deciding whether a dwelling has been vacant, any period of not more than six weeks when it was not vacant is disregarded.[7]

Vacant dwelling recently repaired or altered

A vacant dwelling remains exempt from the council tax for an additional period of up to six months from the day on which the repair works were, or the structural alteration was, substantially completed. In deciding whether a dwelling has been vacant, any one period of not more than six weeks during which it was not vacant is disregarded.

Unoccupied dwelling owned by a charitable body

An unoccupied dwelling owned by a body established solely for charitable purposes is exempt for up to six months from the last day it was occupied. For this exemption to apply, the charity must be the freeholder or hold the most inferior (ie, shortest) leasehold interest for a term of six months or more. The dwelling may be furnished or unfurnished. The exemption only applies, however, if it was last occupied in connection with furthering the objectives of the charity. For the purpose of deciding the day on which the dwelling was last occupied, any period of occupation of not more than six weeks is disregarded.[8]

This disregard is a device to avoid abuse of the exemption. Without the disregard, the owner could ensure that the building is occupied for a few days near the end of the six-month period and thus trigger the exemption again for a further six months. This exemption can be repeated each time the dwelling is unoccupied following a period of occupation of six weeks or more, as long as the above conditions are met.

Almshouses and refuges are typical examples of properties that would be exempt.

Vacant dwelling

A vacant dwelling (one that is unoccupied and substantially unfurnished, or a caravan or houseboat which is unoccupied) is exempt for up to six months.[9] This exemption applies both to new and previously occupied dwellings. Any one period of not more than six weeks during which the dwelling is occupied is disregarded when deciding if the dwelling has been vacant.

Dwelling unoccupied because the former resident is in prison

An unoccupied dwelling is exempt indefinitely if the former resident is in prison or certain other forms of detention (see Chapter 8) and the dwelling was previously her/his sole or main residence (see p71).[10] For the purpose of this exemption, a person is considered detained if s/he would be regarded as such for the purpose of a council tax discount (see Chapter 8).[11] The definition includes people detained under immigration or mental health powers, but not those in prison for non-payment of council tax.

This exemption includes not only former residents who were owners (ie, the freeholder or the leaseholder with the shortest lease of six months or more) but also a former tenant or licensee, whether or not s/he is the person who is liable to pay council tax on the property.[12]

The dwelling is also exempt if the owner or tenant was previously the sole or main resident and since the end of her/his imprisonment has been in a hospital, care home, hostel or other accommodation where care is provided, or if s/he has been providing personal care to someone else.

Example
On leaving prison, Geoff moves in with his elderly mother to look after her. In such circumstances, Geoff's former home remains exempt.

Unoccupied dwelling in which someone has died

A dwelling is exempt if it has been unoccupied since the former resident's death and the only person liable for the tax on the dwelling would be the deceased's personal representative, and no grant of probate or letters of administration has been made.[13] The exemption ends six months after a grant of probate or letters of administration has been made.

Before 1 April 1994 for this exemption to apply, the dwelling only had to be unoccupied; it was not necessary for it to have been unoccupied since the death of the owner. From 1 April 1994, unoccupied dwellings are also exempt if the deceased was a tenant or licensee and an executor or administrator is now liable for the rent. The exemption lasts up to six months after the grant of probate or letters of administration. This is designed to discourage landlords, who would become liable for the council tax following a tenant's death, from pressing for the property to be cleared immediately in order to benefit from the six-month exemption for vacant dwellings or, alternatively from seeking to pass on to the deceased's relatives or estate the council tax payable on the dwelling which is now unoccupied, but not vacant (see p51).

In all cases, any one short occupation of less than six weeks following the death is disregarded. Thus, the exemption is not ended inadvertently if, for instance, a relative stays at the dwelling briefly in order to arrange the deceased's affairs.

This exemption does not apply if the deceased left the dwelling to a beneficiary in her/his will. In this case, the beneficiary becomes the taxpayer at the date of death, as s/he is deemed to become the owner (for council tax purposes) on that date.

Dwelling in which occupation is prohibited by law

In England, a dwelling is exempt indefinitely if its occupation is prohibited by law, including a condition imposed by planning control under the Town and Country Planning Act 1990.[14] It is also exempt if it is being kept unoccupied because legal action is underway to prohibit its occupation or to acquire it under a compulsory purchase order. For instance, a local authority serving a repair notice does not qualify even if the occupants have to move out temporarily.[15] If the dwelling is actually occupied – eg, by squatters, the dwelling is not exempt from the charge. The squatters would normally be liable to pay the tax (see Chapter 6).

Unoccupied dwelling held for a minister of religion

An unoccupied dwelling, such as a vicarage, is exempt indefinitely if it is held to be available for occupation by a minister of any religious denomination and from where s/he will perform the duties of her/his office.[16]

Dwelling unoccupied because the former resident is in hospital or a care home

An unoccupied dwelling is exempt indefinitely if it was previously the sole or main residence (see p71) of an owner, tenant or licensee:[17]
- who would be disregarded for the purpose of a council tax discount because s/he is a patient in hospital, or is in a care home or certain hostels; *and*
- who, since s/he last occupied the dwelling, has either been in that type of accommodation, in detention, or receiving or providing care elsewhere.[18] The care must be required for one of the reasons listed on p54.

During temporary stays in hospital people remain liable for council tax at their normal address. However, if someone's main residence is a hospital, their previous home is exempt from council tax provided it is unoccupied.[19]

Dwelling unoccupied because the former resident is receiving care elsewhere

An unoccupied dwelling is exempt indefinitely if it was the sole or main residence (see p71) of an owner, tenant or licensee who now has her/his sole or main residence elsewhere and where s/he is receiving personal care (but not a hospital, care home or certain hostels).[20] The personal care must be required because of her/his:

- old age; *or*
- disablement; *or*
- illness; *or*
- past or present alcohol or drug dependence; *or*
- past or present mental illness or disorder.

To qualify, the former resident must have been resident in such accommodation, or in prison or detention centre, or in a hospital, care home or hostel (as described on p53) since the dwelling last ceased to be her/his residence.

This exemption applies if the former resident was an owner and, in England, if s/he was a tenant or licensee, irrespective of whether s/he was liable for council tax on the dwelling. In Wales, this exemption extends to former tenants only if the person has been absent for the whole period since the dwelling last ceased to be his residence.

Dwelling unoccupied because the former resident is providing care elsewhere

An unoccupied dwelling is exempt indefinitely if it was previously the sole or main residence (see p71) of an owner, tenant or licensee who is now solely or mainly resident elsewhere because s/he is providing personal care to someone.[21]

This exemption applies to former residents who were owners, as well as tenants or licensees, irrespective of whether they were liable for council tax on the dwelling.

The carer does not have to be disregarded for the purpose of a council tax discount. However, the person being cared for must require the care because of her/his:

- old age; *or*
- disablement; *or*
- illness; *or*
- past or present alcohol or drug dependence; *or*
- past or present mental illness or disorder.

The carer must have been absent from her/his own dwelling since it was last occupied because s/he has been providing such care.

Dwelling left unoccupied by a student owner

An unoccupied dwelling is exempt indefinitely if it was last occupied as the sole or main residence (see p71) of its owner who is now a student and s/he:[22]

- has been a student since s/he last occupied the dwelling; *or*
- has become a student within six weeks of leaving the dwelling.

'Student' has the same meaning as for council tax discount purposes (see p95). If there are joint owners of the unoccupied property, all of them must be students and at least one of them must have been solely or mainly resident there on the last day it was occupied, and the last one must have become a student within six weeks of the day it was last occupied as a sole or main residence.

Example

Josie is a single student studying in London. She left her former home in Plymouth and came to London three weeks before her course was due to start. Josie owns a flat in Plymouth, which remains unoccupied apart from when she returns for short periods during college vacations.

The flat in Plymouth is exempt because it is unoccupied and Josie became a student within six weeks of having been solely resident there. It remains exempt when Josie returns in the vacations because, during these times, although it is occupied, the sole resident is a student. If Josie decided to let the flat in Plymouth to a tenant it would cease to be exempt because it would no longer be unoccupied. However, it would continue to be exempt if the new tenant were also a student.

Unoccupied dwelling in the possession of a mortgage lender

An unoccupied dwelling is exempt indefinitely if a mortgagee – ie, a bank, building society or finance company, is in possession under the mortgage.[23] This would arise, for example, if the lender has repossessed the property because of the borrower's failure to keep up her/his mortgage payments.

Unoccupied dwelling held by a trustee in bankruptcy

An unoccupied dwelling is exempt indefinitely if the liable owner is a trustee in bankruptcy under the Bankruptcy Act 1914 or the Insolvency Act 1986.[24] A trustee in bankruptcy is the person appointed by a general meeting of a bankrupt person's creditors, or the court, whose duty is to take over all the property of the bankrupt person, sell the property for cash and distribute the resulting funds among the creditors.

Unoccupied dwelling which cannot be let separately

A dwelling in England and Wales is exempt if it is:
* unoccupied; *and*
* forms part of a single property which includes another dwelling; *and*
* cannot be let separately from that other dwelling without a breach of planning control.

An example of this exemption is an empty 'granny flat'.[25]

Other exempt dwellings

The following other occupied dwellings are also exempt:
- student halls of residence (see below);
- dwellings wholly occupied by students or school or college leavers (see below);
- armed forces accommodation (see p57);
- visiting forces accommodation (see p57);
- empty caravan pitches or houseboat moorings (see p58);
- dwellings wholly occupied by people under 18 (see p58);
- dwellings wholly occupied by people who are 'severely mentally impaired' (see p58);
- dwellings where at least one liable person has diplomatic, Commonwealth or consular privilege or immunity (see p58);
- one of at least two dwellings in a single property occupied by a dependent relative of a person living in another dwelling in the property (see p58).

Student hall of residence

A dwelling is exempt indefinitely if it is a hall of residence provided predominantly to accommodate students who would be disregarded for the purpose of a discount (see p95).[26] To qualify for the exemption the hall must be either:
- owned or managed by a prescribed educational institution (see p96); *or*
- the subject of an agreement allowing such an institution to nominate the majority of the people who are to occupy the accommodation.

This exemption also extends to halls of residence, predominantly for the accommodation of students, owned or managed by a body established solely for charitable purposes.[27]

A hall (or hostel) should be exempt even if some non-students (such as wardens, tutors or dependants) live there. Any separate, self-contained flat or house provided for a non-student, such as a caretaker, is not covered by this exemption. If a hall of residence is used for more than 140 days a year for commercial purposes, such as conferences, it may be subject to non-domestic rates.

Dwelling wholly occupied by students or 'relevant persons'

To be exempt under this heading the dwelling must be either:[28]
- occupied by one or more residents, all of whom are 'relevant persons' (see below); *or*
- occupied only by one or more 'relevant persons' as term-time accommodation.

A 'relevant person' is:[29]
- a student disregarded for discount purposes (see Chapter 8); *or*

- a student's spouse or dependant who is not a British citizen and who is prevented by the terms of her/his leave to enter or remain in the UK from working or claiming benefits; *or*
- a school or college leaver who is disregarded for discount purposes (see Chapter 8).

Students of nursing or midwifery who are studying academic courses at universities count as students.[30] If the dwelling has more than one resident, they all need to meet the qualifying conditions for the exemption to apply.

A dwelling is regarded as occupied by a relevant person as term-time accommodation during any vacation in which s/he:

- holds a freehold or leasehold interest in, or licence to occupy, the whole or any part of the dwelling; *and*
- has previously used, or intends to use, the dwelling as term-time accommodation.

Example
Three students rent a house as joint tenants. It is exempt from the council tax. The exemption ends when one of the students is dismissed from his course and, therefore, no longer qualifies for a status discount. The three joint tenants are now jointly liable for the council tax on the dwelling. There are three residents, but two of them are disregarded for the purpose of a discount. The bill should be reduced by 25 per cent because there is only one adult resident who is not disregarded.

Armed forces accommodation

Dwellings, either occupied or unoccupied, are exempt indefinitely if they are:[31]

- owned by the Secretary of State for Defence; *and*
- for the purposes of armed forces accommodation.

This includes, for example, armed forces barracks and married quarters. Contributions in place of the council tax are paid by the Ministry of Defence to local authorities. These contributions should broadly match the amount which would otherwise have been payable.[32]

Visiting forces accommodation

A dwelling is exempt indefinitely if at least one person who would be liable is a member (or dependant) of a visiting force and s/he is neither a British citizen nor ordinarily resident in the UK. A dwelling is exempt under this category 'even if not all of the liable persons have a relevant association with a visiting force'. So, for instance, a dwelling in which the liable persons are a visiting serviceman and his British wife would be exempt.[33]

Unoccupied pitch and mooring

A pitch or mooring not occupied by a caravan or boat is an exempt dwelling for council tax purposes.[34]

Dwelling wholly occupied by people under 18

A dwelling only occupied by a person or persons under 18 is exempt.[35]

Dwelling occupied by a 'severely mentally impaired' person

A dwelling is exempt if it is only occupied by a person(s) who is 'severely mentally impaired' as defined for the purposes of council tax discount (see Chapter 8).[36]

A dwelling is also exempt if it is occupied by at least one severely mentally impaired person and one or more students or relevant persons for the purpose of student exemption (see p95).[37]

People with diplomatic immunity

A dwelling is exempt if at least one liable person has diplomatic, Commonwealth or consular privilege or immunity and that person is not a permanent resident of the UK, a British citizen, British subject or British protected person. This exemption does not apply if that person has another dwelling in the UK which is her/his main residence or if her/his main residence is in the UK.

Dwelling occupied by a dependent relative

This exemption applies to a dwelling, which is one of at least two dwellings in a single property, occupied by a dependent relative of a person living in another dwelling in the property.[38]

A relative is a dependant if s/he is 65 or over, severely mentally impaired, or substantially and permanently disabled.[39] A relative is a person's spouse, parent, child, grandparent, grandchild, brother, sister, uncle or aunt, nephew or niece, great-grandparent, great-grandchild, great-uncle, great-aunt, great-nephew or great-niece, great-great-grandparent, great-great-grandchild, great-great-uncle, great-great-aunt, great-great-nephew or great-great-niece. A relationship by marriage (or by living together as husband and wife) is treated as a relationship by birth and any stepchild of a person shall be treated as her/his child.

From April 2005, the definition of relatives includes people linked by a civil partnership as well as by marriage.[40]

2. Exempt dwellings in Scotland

Unoccupied dwellings

In Scotland, an unoccupied dwelling (see p49) is exempt if:[41]
- it is recently erected and still unfurnished (see p59);

- it is undergoing, or has recently undergone, major repair work or structural alteration (see below);
- it was last used by a charity (see below);
- it is unfurnished (see p60);
- it was last occupied by, and remains the sole liability of someone in prison or someone living elsewhere to receive or provide care (see p60);
- it is owned by someone who has died (see p60);
- its occupation is prohibited by law (see p60);
- it is owned by a public sector housing authority prior to demolition (see p61);
- it is being kept for occupation by a minister of religion (see p61);
- it was last occupied by a student (see p61);
- it has been repossessed following a mortgage default (see p61);
- it was last occupied together with certain agricultural lands (see p61);
- it is part of the same premises as, or situated within the same curtilage as, another dwelling and is difficult to let separately (see p61);
- the sole liable person is a student (see p62).

Unoccupied new dwelling

A dwelling that is unoccupied and unfurnished is exempt for up to six months if:[42]

- less than six months have elapsed since the effective date of the first entry on the valuation list; *and*
- there was no entry on the valuation list immediately prior to that effective date.

Unoccupied dwelling undergoing structural repair, improvement or reconstruction

An unoccupied dwelling is exempt if it cannot be lived in because since the last occupation date it is undergoing or has undergone major repair work to make it habitable, or structural alteration.[43]

The lack of occupation must be because of the works being carried out. If the dwelling is occupied, it is not exempt. The exemption may last for 12 months after the dwelling was last occupied, or (if sooner) for six months after the work or alteration was substantially completed. The property may remain furnished.

Unoccupied dwelling owned by a charity

An unoccupied dwelling last occupied by a charitable body is exempt for up to six months if it was last occupied to further the charity's objectives.[44] 'Charitable' has the same meaning as in the Income Tax Acts. Any period of occupation for less than six weeks is disregarded.[45] This disregard is a device to avoid abuse of the exemption. Without the disregard, the liable person could ensure that the building is occupied for a few days near the end of the six-month period and thus trigger the exemption again for a further six months. The property may remain furnished.

Unoccupied and unfurnished dwelling

Unoccupied and unfurnished dwellings are exempt for up to six months from the end of the last period of six weeks or more during which the dwelling was occupied or furnished.[46]

Dwelling last occupied by someone in prison, or living elsewhere to receive or provide care

An unoccupied dwelling is exempt indefinitely if it was last occupied as the sole or main residence (see p71) of someone who continues to be liable for council tax and since the last day of occupation s/he is:

- disregarded for the purpose of a council tax discount because she is in prison or detention, or is in a hospital, care home or certain care hostels in Scotland, England or Wales (see Chapter 8); *or*
- receiving personal care elsewhere because of her/his old age, disablement, illness, past or present alcohol or drug dependence, or past or present mental illness or disorder; *or*
- providing personal care elsewhere to someone who needs it because of old age, disablement, illness, past or present alcohol or drug dependence, or past or present mental illness/disorder.[47]

Any period of occupation of less than six weeks since the last day of occupation is disregarded. The property may remain furnished.

Dwelling owned by someone who has died

To be exempt, the dwelling must be no one's sole or main residence (see p71). Additionally, any liability to pay council tax must fall under the estate of the deceased person.[48] In such cases the dwelling is exempt:

- indefinitely where no grant of confirmation to the estate of that person has been made; *and*
- for up to six months from the date such a grant is made.

The property may remain furnished.

Dwelling in which occupation is prohibited

If it is prohibited by law to occupy a dwelling, that dwelling is exempt indefinitely.[49] The property may remain furnished. The fact that such a property is actually occupied should not make it ineligible for the exemption.

It is also exempt if it is being kept unoccupied because legal action is underway to prohibit its occupation or to acquire it under a compulsory purchase order. In these circumstances, if the dwelling is actually occupied then it should not qualify for the exemption. The property may remain furnished.

Unoccupied dwelling owned by a housing body prior to demolition

A dwelling which is owned by a local authority or registered social landlord and is kept unoccupied pending demolition is exempt.[50] From 1 April 2002, properties owned by registered social landlords are also exempt.[51] The property may remain furnished.

Dwelling held for a minister of religion

A dwelling, such as a manse, which is no one's sole or main residence (see p71), is exempt indefinitely if it is being held by, or on behalf of, any religious body for the purpose of being available for occupation by a minister of religion as a residence from which to perform the duties of her/his office.[52] The property may remain furnished.

Student's unoccupied dwelling

An unoccupied dwelling which is a student's main residence and which was last occupied by a student or students is exempt for up to four months from the last day it was occupied for a period of six weeks or more.[53] This applies, for example, to the student's term-time accommodation during vacations if it remains unoccupied during that period. The property may remain furnished.

Dwelling repossessed by a mortgage lender

A dwelling which is no one's sole or main residence (see p71) is exempt indefinitely if it has been formally repossessed by a mortgage lender.[54] The property may remain furnished.

Dwelling last occupied with agricultural lands

An unoccupied and unfurnished dwelling is exempt indefinitely if it was last used and occupied with the land on which it is situated. The land must be:[55]
- agricultural or pastoral; *or*
- woodlands, market gardens, orchards, allotments or allotment gardens; *or*
- used for the purpose of poultry farming and exceeding one-tenth of a hectare.

Unoccupied dwelling difficult to let separately

An unoccupied dwelling, such as an empty 'granny flat' or staff accommodation, is exempt indefinitely if:[56]
- it forms part of premises which include another dwelling; *or*
- it is situated within the curtilage of another dwelling; *and*
- it is difficult to let separately from that other dwelling; *and*
- the person who would be liable for it has her/his sole or main residence in that other dwelling.

The property may remain furnished.

Unoccupied dwelling for which the sole liable person is a student

A dwelling which is no one's sole or main residence (see p71) is exempt indefinitely if the person who would be liable is a student for the purpose of a council tax discount (see Chapter 8).

In the case of joint owners/joint tenants they must all be students.[57] The property may remain furnished.

Occupied dwellings

An occupied dwelling is exempt if:[58]

- it is only occupied by one or more students, school or college leavers or under-18-year-olds (see below);
- it is occupied by a student or a student's spouse (see below);
- it is a housing association 'trial' property for older people or people with disabilities (see below);
- it is a students' hall of residence (see p63);
- it is armed forces accommodation (see p63);
- it is visiting forces accommodation (see p63);
- it includes garages, carports and storage sheds (see p63);
- it is held by a bankruptcy trustee (see p63);
- it is occupied by a 'severely mentally impaired' person (see p63);
- it is a property occupied or which could be occupied by persons who do not constitute a single household to which registered prescribed housing support is supplied (see p63).

Dwelling occupied only by students or under-18-year-olds

A dwelling is exempt indefinitely if it is not the sole or main residence (see p71) of anyone other than a student for the purpose of a council tax discount (see Chapter 8) or a person under 18, and it is occupied by at least one such person.[59] Also included is a student's spouse or dependant who is not a British citizen and who is prevented by the Immigration Rules from either claiming benefit or working in the UK.[60]

Temporary dwelling for older or disabled people owned by a housing association

A dwelling owned by a registered housing association is exempt indefinitely if:[61]

- it is not the sole or main residence (see p71) of any person; *and*
- it is for people over pension age or with a disability who are likely in the future to have their sole or main residences in other dwellings provided by the housing association.

Halls of residence

A dwelling is exempt if it is, or is part of, a hall of residence provided predominantly to accommodate students and which:[62]

- is owned and managed by a prescribed educational institution for the purpose of council tax discounts (see p96); *or*
- is the subject of an agreement allowing such an institution to nominate the majority of the people who are to occupy the accommodation.

Armed forces accommodation

An occupied or unoccupied dwelling is exempt indefinitely if it is:[63]

- owned by the Secretary of State for Defence; *and*
- held for the purposes of armed forces accommodation.

The local authority receives compensating payments for these dwellings.

Visiting forces accommodation

A dwelling is exempt indefinitely if a member of a visiting force or her/his dependant (but not a dependant who is a British citizen or is ordinarily resident in the UK) would be liable.[64]

Garages, carports and storage sheds

Certain garages, carports, car parking stances and premises used for storing domestic items, including cycles and similar vehicles, are considered to be dwellings (see Chapter 2). They are exempt indefinitely from council tax.[65]

Dwelling held by a trustee in bankruptcy

A dwelling which is no one's sole or main residence (see p71) is exempt indefinitely if the only person who would be liable is a bankruptcy trustee.[66]

Dwelling occupied by a 'severely mentally impaired' person

A dwelling is exempt if it is only occupied by a person(s) who is 'severely mentally impaired' as defined for the purposes of council tax discount (see Chapter 8).[67]

A dwelling is also exempt if it is occupied by at least one severely mentally impaired person and one or more students or relevant persons for the purpose of student exemption (see p95).[68]

Prescribed housing support accommodation

A dwelling is exempt if it falls into the category of 'prescribed housing support accommodation'.[69]

In order to be exempt:

- the dwelling must be the residence of one or more persons who are tenants, sub-tenants or who have a licence to occupy the dwelling;

- a registered prescribed housing support service must be provided to at least one licensee, tenant or sub-tenant of the dwelling; *and*
- all the residents must share the use of a kitchen, bathroom, shower-room or toilet-room, and these must also be shared with at least one other person who is not resident in the dwelling.

A dwelling is not exempt if each resident has exclusive use of a kitchen and a bathroom/shower-room (either containing a toilet or if there is a separate toilet which all the residents can use).

3. **How exempt dwellings are identified**

Local authorities must take reasonable steps each financial year to establish whether any dwellings in their area are exempt from council tax for any period during the year.[70] Most are likely to carry out periodic postal surveys and make use of other sources of information, such as the electoral roll and the local authority's benefit records. Most local authorities also carry out regular visits to unoccupied exempt dwellings.

If the local authority has no reason to believe that a particular dwelling will be or was exempt, it will assume it is a chargeable dwelling for council tax billing purposes.[71] Alternatively, if the local authority has reason to believe that a particular dwelling will be or was exempt for a period during the course of the year, it must make that assumption for council tax billing purposes.[72]

4. **Obtaining an exemption**

If the local authority has not awarded an exemption, you can write to it setting out the reasons why the dwelling should be exempt. Exemptions can be backdated to the date the qualifying conditions for the exemption were first met, the beginning of the scheme or when the particular exemption was first introduced, whichever is the latest. Unlike the provisions for backdating most social security benefits, there is no requirement to show 'good cause' for the backdating.

5. **Notification of exemption**

If the local authority has assumed that a dwelling is exempt, it must write to the person who would otherwise be liable, informing her/him of that fact.[73] The notification must be made as soon as is reasonably practicable.[74] The requirement does not apply in Scotland if:[75]

- the otherwise liable person is a housing body; *or*
- the dwelling is a separate garage, carport or storage shed.

The local authority should also supply a statement that:[76]
- shows the valuation band for the dwelling;
- summarises how people may make proposals for altering the valuation list;
- in Scotland, specifies for the financial year in question the amounts set by the local authority as council tax and Scottish Water charges;
- in England and Wales, specifies the local authority's estimate of the amount of council tax (or the actual amount if the year is over) which would have been payable disregarding any disability reduction, discount, transitional relief (in Wales) or council tax benefit that may have been awarded;
- summarises the most common classes of dwelling which are exempt;[77]
- in Scotland, summarises the individual's obligation to correct any incorrect assumptions the local authority may have made in awarding the exemption, and including the penalty which may be imposed if this obligation is not met (see below).

The above information need not be given if it was already provided when the scheme was introduced or on any bill ('demand notice').[78] If there is more than one potentially liable person, the local authority only needs to write to one of them.[79]

The duty to correct false assumptions

The person who has been notified that the dwelling is, or will be, exempt has a duty to notify the local authority if there is reason to believe that the dwelling is not exempt. The local authority should be notified in writing within 21 days of the person first having reason to believe a dwelling is not exempt, or will be or was exempt for a shorter period.[80]

If two or more people are jointly liable to pay council tax on a dwelling, they both have a duty to notify the local authority. Only one of them, however, has to supply the information for this obligation to be met.[81]

6. Penalties

The local authority has the discretion to impose a penalty of £70 (in England) or £50 (in Wales and Scotland) on a liable person who fails to notify it that her/his dwelling is no longer exempt. There are higher penalties for failing to supply information requested by the local authority for council tax purposes.[82]

Such penalties are not criminal convictions or punishments, but if unpaid can be recovered through the magistrates' court in the same way as unpaid sums of council tax.

Each time the local authority repeats the request and the person fails to supply the information, a further £280 penalty (in England) or £200 (in Wales and Scotland) can be imposed.[83]

You can appeal to a valuation tribunal against the imposition of a penalty (see Chapter 12),[84] although English and Welsh local authorities have the discretion to quash the penalty beforehand.[85] In England, you appeal directly to the Valuation Tribunal for England (see p206). In Wales, you should write directly to the appropriate valuation tribunal.

In Scotland, an appeal can be made to the valuation appeal committee by writing to the local authority. The local authority should pass the appeal on to the committee. A Scottish local authority may revoke the imposition of a penalty if the person upon whom it was imposed had a reasonable excuse for the failure.[86]

In England and Wales, an appeal to a tribunal must normally be made within two months of the penalty being imposed. The President of the tribunal has the discretion to allow an out-of-time appeal if you have failed to meet the time limit because of reasons beyond your control.

In Scotland, the appeal must be made within two months of the penalty being imposed. There is no power to consider out-of-time appeals. If an appeal has been made, the penalty need not be paid until the appeal has been decided.

7. Appeals

If the local authority decides that the dwelling is not exempt, you can appeal in writing to the local authority if you are an 'aggrieved person'.[87] There is no time limit for making such appeals. An **'aggrieved person'** is someone who would be liable to pay the tax if the dwelling were not exempt or s/he is the owner (if different). The appeal letter should give the reasons why the dwelling should be exempt. The local authority has two months in which to answer.[88] If an exemption is not granted, or if the local authority fails to answer within two months of receiving the appeal, a further appeal can be made.[89] The local authority may enforce payment of the original bill while the appeal is outstanding (see Chapter 11).

In England and Wales, a further appeal can be made by writing directly to the Valuation Tribunal for England/valuation tribunal. This should normally be made within two months of the date the local authority notified you of its decision, or within four months of the date when the initial written representation was made if the local authority has not responded. The President of the tribunal has the power to allow an out-of-time appeal if you have failed to meet the appropriate time limit because of reasons beyond your control.

In Scotland, a further appeal is made by writing again to the local authority. The local authority should pass the appeal on to the secretary of the relevant local valuation appeal committee. The appeal must be made within four months of the date on which the grievance was first raised with the local authority in writing. There is no power to consider an out-of-time appeal.

Notes

1 **EW** s4(2) LGFA 1992
   S s72(6)-(7) and Sch 11 para 7(2)-(3)
   LGFA 1992; CT(ED)(S)O 1992
2 **EW** s2(2)(a) LGFA 1992
   S s71(2)(a) LGFA 1992

1. Exempt dwellings in England and Wales
3 CT(ED)O
4 CT(ED)O
5 CT(ED)O
6 **E** Reg 2 CT(ED)O
   W CT(ED)(A)(W)O
7 Class A CT(ED)O
8 Class B CT(ED)O
9 Class C CT(ED)O
10 Class D CT(ED)O
11 s6 LGFA 1992
12 CT(ED)O
13 Class F CT(ED)O
14 Class G CT(ED)O; CT(ED)(A)(E)O
15 *Watson v Rhondda Cynon Taff BC* [2001] 913 (EWHC)
16 Class H CT(ED)O
17 Class H CT(ED)O
18 Class E CT(ED)O
19 Parliamentary Answer, given by Dr Alan Whitehead, Under Secretary of State for Transport, Local Government and the Regions, 24 January 2002
20 Class I CT(ED)O
21 Class J CT(ED)O
22 Class K CT(ED)O
23 Class L CT(ED)O
24 Class Q CT(ED)O
25 Class T CT(ED)O
26 Class M CT(ED)O
27 Class M CT(ED)O
28 Class N CT(ED)O
29 Class N CT(ED)O
30 para 28 Practice Note No.2

31 Class O CT(ED)O
32 para 30 Practice Note No.2
33 Class P CT(ED)O
34 CT(ED)O
35 Class S CT(ED)O
36 Class U CT(ED)O
37 CT(ED)O
38 CT(ED)O
39 CT(ED)O
40 Class W CT(ED)(A)(E)O 2005

2. Exempt dwellings in Scotland
41 CT(ED)(S)O 1997
42 Sch 1 para 1 CT(ED)(S)O 1997
43 Sch 1 para 2 CT(ED)(S)O 1997
44 Sch 1 para 3 CT(ED)(S)O 1997
45 Art 2 CT(ED)(S)O 1997
46 Sch 1 para 4 CT(ED)(S)O 1997
47 Sch 1 para 5 CT(ED)(S)O 1997
48 Sch 1 para 6 CT(ED)(S)O 1997
49 Sch 1 para 7 CT(ED)(S)O 1997
50 Sch 1 para 8 CT(ED)(S)O 1997
51 Reg 2(3) CT(ED)(S)O 2002
52 Sch 1 para 9 CT(ED)(S)O 1997
53 Sch 1 para 11 CT(ED)(S)O 1997
54 Sch 1 para 13 CT(ED)(S)O 1997
55 Sch 1 para 14 CT(ED)(S)O 1997
56 Sch 1 para 19 CT(ED)(S)O 1997
57 Sch 1 para 12 CT(ED)(S)O 1997
58 CT(ED)(S)(A)O 2006
59 Sch 1 para 10(a)(iii) and (iv) CT(ED)(S)O 1997; see also the Education (Graduate Endowment and Student Support) Act 2001
60 Sch 1 para 10(a)(ii) CT(ED)(S)O 1997
61 CT(ED)(S)O 2002
62 Sch 1 para 16 CT(ED)(S)O 1997
63 Sch 1 para 17 CT(ED)(S)O 1997
64 Sch 1 para 22 CT(ED)(S)O 1997
65 Sch 1 para 20 CT(ED)(S)O 1997
66 Sch 1 para 21 CT(ED)(S)O 1997

5

Chapter 5: Exempt dwellings
Notes

• •

67 Class U CT(ED)(S)O 1997
68 CT(ED)O
69 The CT(ED)(S)O 1997 was amended by
    the CT(ED)(S)(A)O 2006. Such a
    dwelling has the same meaning as
    accommodation defined by s91(8)
    Housing (Scotland) Act 2001 and the
    Housing Scotland Act 2001 (Housing
    Support Services) Regulations 2002,
    registered by the Scottish Commission
    for the regulation of care as a prescribed
    housing support service under the
    Regulation of Care (Scotland) Act 2001.

3. **How exempt dwellings are identified**
   70 **EW** Reg 8 CT(AE) Regs 1992
       S CT(ED)(S)O 1992
   71 **EW** Reg 9(1) CT(AE) Regs 1992
       S Reg 7 CT(AE)(S) Regs
   72 **EW** Reg 9(2) CT(AE) Regs 1992
       S Reg 8 CT(AE)(S) Regs

5. **Notification of exemption**
   73 **EW** Reg 10(1) CT(AE) Regs 1992
   74 **EW** Reg 10(2) CT(AE) Regs 1992
       S Reg 9 CT(AE)(S) Regs
   75 **EW** Reg 10 CT(AE) Regs 1992
       S Reg 9 CT(AE)(S) Regs
   76 **EW** Reg 10(3) CT(AE) Regs 1992
       S Reg 9 CT(AE)(S) Regs
   77 **EW** Reg 10 CT(AE) Regs 1992
       S Reg 9 CT(AE)(S) Regs
   78 **EW** Reg 10 CT(AE) Regs 1992
       S Reg 9 CT(AE)(S) Regs
   79 **EW** Reg 10 CT(AE) Regs 1992
       S Reg 9 CT(AE)(S) Regs
   80 **EW** Reg 11 CT(AE) Regs 1992
   81 **EW** Reg 11 CT(AE) Regs 1992
       S Reg 10 CT(AE)(S) Regs

6. **Penalties**
   82 Local Government Finance (Substitution
       of Penalties) Order 2008 No.981
   83 **EW** Sch 3 LGFA 1992
       S s97(4) and Sch 3 LGFA 1992
   84 **EW** s14(2) and Sch 3 LGFA 1992
       S s97(4) and Sch 3 LGFA 1992
   85 **EW** Sch 3 para 1 LGFA 1992
   86 **S** s97(4) and Sch 3 LGFA 1992

7. **Appeals**
   87 **EW** s16 LGFA 1992
   88 **EW** s16 LGFA 1992
       S s81 LGFA 1992
   89 **EW** s16 LGFA 1992
       S s81 LGFA 1992

Chapter 6

· ·

Liability

This chapter explains:
1. Who is liable (below)
2. Who is a resident (p71)
3. When the owner is always liable (p74)
4. Joint liability (p76)
5. Change of circumstances (p79)
6. Backdating of liability (p79)
7. How the liable person is identified (p79)
8. Appeals (p81)

---

1. **Who is liable**

Council tax is payable for any dwelling which is not exempt (see Chapter 5). Normally, the person liable to pay council tax is an adult resident of the dwelling. To be liable, the person must have their 'sole or main' residence in the dwelling and have a right to occupy the dwelling. To determine who is liable to pay council tax, it is necessary to consult the 'hierarchy of liability' which is set out in section 6 (section 75 in Scotland) of the Local Government Finance Act 1992. These sections list different possible categories of occupier, based upon security of occupancy, including owners, tenants, licensees and squatters. Normally, the person(s) whose sole or main residence is in a dwelling and who has the most secure interest in it will be the liable taxpayer(s) and the person to whom the council tax bill will be sent. The tables on p70 can be used to identify the person who is liable.

As soon as a description is reached which applies to someone in respect of the dwelling in question, that person is the liable person.[1] This will normally be an owner-occupier or a council, housing association or private tenant. A tenant is not liable, however, if the landlord lives in the same dwelling. If no one is solely or mainly resident (see p71) in the dwelling, the non-resident owner is liable. In certain instances, however, the owner is always liable (see p74). If more than one person fits the first description that applies, they will normally be jointly liable (see p76).

For the purpose of determining the liable person on any day, the state of affairs at the end of the day is assumed to have existed throughout that day.[2]

In certain cases, the liable person may also be a person who is disregarded for the purpose of a council tax discount (see Chapter 8). The rules on discounts are quite separate and do not affect liability, except in some cases where they affect 'severely mentally impaired' people who would otherwise be held jointly liable (see p78).

Asylum seekers are liable for council tax and a local authority will not be acting unreasonably if it pursues an asylum seeker for sums in tax. However, from 3 April 2000 council tax liability on dwellings occupied by some asylum seekers rests with the owner (see p76).[3]

Note: no one has to pay the tax unless a bill has been sent with her/his name on it (see Chapter 10), unless (in Scotland) s/he is jointly liable with someone who has been billed.

Hierarchy of liability in England and Wales
 – A resident with a freehold interest in the whole or any part of the dwelling.
 – A resident with a leasehold interest (including an assured tenancy or assured shorthold tenancy) in the whole or any part of the dwelling which is not inferior to another such interest held by another resident.
 – A resident and a statutory tenant (within the meaning of the Rent Act 1977 or the Rent (Agriculture) Act 1976) or a secure tenant (within the meaning of Part IV of the Housing Act 1985) of the whole or any part of the dwelling.[4]
 – A resident with a contractual licence to occupy the whole or any part of the dwelling.
 – A resident (including a squatter).
 – A non-resident owner – ie, the person who has the inferior (shortest) lease granted for a term of six months or more of the whole, or any part of, the dwelling. Where there is no such leaseholder, the freeholder is the owner.[5]

Scotland

Additionally in Scotland, Scottish Water charges are payable for any dwelling which is not exempt, except if:
 • Scottish Water does not provide a supply of water to the dwelling; *or*
 • the water is supplied by meter; *or*
 • Scottish Water is under an obligation to provide a supply free of charge.

Hierarchy of liability in Scotland
 – A resident owner of the whole or any part of the dwelling.
 – A resident tenant of the whole or any part of the dwelling.
 – A resident statutory tenant (within the meaning of the Rent (Scotland) Act 1984), resident statutory assured tenant (within the meaning of the Housing (Scotland) Act

1988) or resident secure tenant (within the meaning of Part III of the Housing (Scotland) Act 1987) of the whole or any part of the dwelling.[6]
- A resident sub-tenant of the whole or any part of the dwelling.
- A resident of the dwelling:
  - a sub-tenant of the whole or any part of the dwelling under a sub-lease granted for a term of six months or more;
  - a tenant, under a lease granted for a term of six months or more, of any part of the dwelling which is not subject to a sub-lease granted for a term of six months or more;
  - an owner of any part of the dwelling which is not subject to a lease granted for a term of six months or more.

Caravans and boats in England and Wales

The owner of a caravan or houseboat is liable for the council tax except for those days when a person other than the owner is resident and so becomes liable for those days.[7] The normal council tax definitions of 'resident' (see below) and 'owner' apply in the case of residential caravans or boats but the definition of **'owner'** is extended to include:[8]

- the person who has possession under any hire purchase or conditional sale agreement; *or*
- the person entitled to the property apart from any mortgage or bill of sale which applies to it.

2. Who is a resident

Council tax is usually payable by someone who is resident in the dwelling. If no one is resident then the non-resident owner is liable. To count as **'resident'** a person must:[9]

- be aged 18 or over; *and*
- be solely or mainly resident in the dwelling (see below).

If everyone who lives in the dwelling is aged under 18, the dwelling is exempt from the tax (see Chapter 5).

Sole or main residence

If a potentially liable person has more than one home, the local authority must decide which is her/his main residence. The concept of 'sole or main residence' is not defined in statute, but has been the subject of consideration by the courts.

The concept of sole or main residence was originally introduced by the community charge and the (then) Department of the Environment's Community Charge Practice Note No. 9 highlighted the *Oxford English Dictionary* definition of 'reside' as 'to dwell permanently or for a considerable time, to have one's settled or usual place of abode, to live in or at a particular place'. In relation to income tax and electoral law the courts have accepted that:

- residence implies a degree of permanence – temporary presence at an address does not necessarily make a person resident there, unless it is their sole residence for that period;
- temporary absence does not deprive a person of residence;
- the lawfulness or otherwise of occupying any home is irrelevant;
- in determining whether or not a person actually present at a given place is legally there it is necessary to establish whether that person intends to return, whether s/he is at physical liberty to return, and whether or not s/he could return without breaking any law or contract.

Originally, Council Tax Practice Note No. 2 (para 13) advised local authorities to bear in mind caselaw. Based on principles which applied for the poll tax or community charge, it pointed out that a person did not need to live in a dwelling all (or even most) of the time for it to be her/his main residence. The Practice Note advised local authorities that they should take into account all the relevant factors in each case, including the amount of time an individual spends at a dwelling, the place of residence of her/his immediate family, her/his security of tenure and the reason for occupying the dwelling – eg, whether it is occupied solely in relation to a job. This advice must now be read in light of the Court of Appeal decision in *R (Williams) v Horsham Borough Council* (see below).

Significantly, the length of time a taxpayer actually spends in a dwelling does not determine residence in itself. For instance, in *Bradford City Council v Anderton* the appellant was a seafarer who most of his life aboard ship. The Divisional Court ruled that he was solely or mainly resident in Bradford.[10] Similarly, in *Ward v Kingston Upon Hull City Council* an appellant who lived and worked abroad and spent only six weeks a year in the UK was nonetheless held to be resident for poll tax purposes.[11] As a result, sole or main residence in a dwelling could be found on the basis of the most tenuous of connections. Although the High Court stressed that tribunals were required to look at all the relevant facts, the possibility that the taxpayer might ultimately return to the dwelling at some point in the future was often held to be a crucial factor, even if the taxpayer had never actually lived in the dwelling. This approach is no longer correct.

Where does the taxpayer actually live?

Fortunately, the law has now been clarified to a greater extent by the Court of Appeal decision in *R (Williams) v Horsham District Council*.[12] The appellant and his wife occupied property provided by an employer between 1993 and 1997. During the same period, the couple also owned a cottage to which they intended to retire. No one was resident at the cottage in which they stored some belongings and they did not stay overnight. The couple claimed a backdated 50 per cent council tax discount for the four-year period. Horsham District Council refused the application and a valuation tribunal refused the appeal for the discount. The tribunal based its decision on the fact that the couple always intended to return to the cottage, that they enjoyed security of tenure and their absence for four-and-a-half years had been because of work.

The Court of Appeal held that the tribunal's view that local authorities were required to give particular weight to security of tenure and the fact that the couple intended to retire to the cottage was irrelevant. Referring to previous cases might be of assistance when identifying a person's main residence, but because a particular factor was significant in one decided case did not make it important in another.

The Court emphasised that the starting point for sole or main residence should be section 6(5) of the Local Government Finance Act 1992, where 'sole or main residence' refers to premises in which the taxpayer actually resides. Usually, a person's main residence would be the dwelling that 'a reasonable onlooker' with knowledge of the facts would regard as that person's home at the time. The test might not always be easy to apply and the answer would depend on the particular circumstances; it would be a matter of fact and degree. The establishment of a 'reasonable onlooker' principle sets up an objective test to be applied in every case. Thus, where a person is *actually* living in any financial year becomes key to determining residence, not hypothetical questions about the right to return in future years.

Following this case, it is clear that the starting point for any appeal is section 6 and the question of who is actually living in the dwelling. By emphasising section 6, the Court of Appeal has confirmed that resident tenants, licensees and even trespassers should normally be placed ahead of non-resident owners in terms of liability for the tax. Factors such as voter registration and registration for medical treatment have often been details used by valuation tribunals to determine sole or main residence. However, the key question following the *Williams* case is: 'Where does the taxpayer actually live?' Hypothetical questions such as where a person might move or remain in the event of job loss or serious illness or where s/he might live were tenants to move out are not in themselves determinative.

The establishment of an objective 'reasonable onlooker' greatly assists people at the tribunal stage. What a 'reasonable onlooker' may think is an objective test. This may well differ from what the local authority or even a particular valuation tribunal would conclude (unless it happens to coincide with what the 'reasonable onlooker' would think).

The judgment in *Williams* is of particular importance to anyone who has let their principal home to tenants or to someone who normally lives or works abroad. In the case of *Parry v Derbyshire Dales District Council*, the taxpayer lived in Spain and let his cottage to tenants.[13] The High Court held that the taxpayer was resident in Spain for local tax purposes and the fact that the tenant left did not mean that Mr Parry ceased to reside in Spain. The Court followed the approach of the Court of Appeal in the *Williams* case and confirmed section 6 of the Local

Government Finance Act 1992: setting out a hierarchy of liability based upon who is actually resident in the dwelling rather than security of tenure is crucial to determining the liable person for council tax purposes.

Following *Williams*, a person letting a dwelling out to tenants should ensure that the calculation of a bill should relate to when s/he actually moves out of a dwelling, *not* necessarily when tenants move in.

When determining daily liability, any residence which existed at the end of a particular day will be treated as having existed throughout the day in question.

Example

Mr and Mrs Shah live in a house with their 17-year-old daughter. Mrs Shah is the joint owner of the property with her sister, who frequently comes to stay and has a bedroom of her own, but who has her main home elsewhere. At the moment Mr and Mrs Shah are liable for the council tax. The non-resident joint owner would not be liable.

If the couple were to separate and Mr Shah leave the dwelling, Mrs Shah would be liable by herself, but Mr Shah would remain jointly liable for any amount that accrued while living as a couple.

If Mrs Shah were also to leave the dwelling, leaving the daughter as the only one living there, the dwelling may be considered as exempt as it is the sole residence of someone under the age of 18. On the daughter's 18th birthday she would become the sole liable person as the only resident of the dwelling.

Main residence in Scotland

The same approach to residence taken in the *Williams* case (see p72) has been applied in Scotland. In this case, a taxpayer lived during the week and some weekends in a dwelling closer to his job rather than in the dwelling occupied by his wife and family.[14] The Court of Session ruled that the valuation appeal committee was entitled to find that the dwelling where the appellant spent most of his time during the week was his sole or main residence.

3. When the owner is always liable

If there are no residents in the dwelling, the non-resident owner is liable. Additionally, the Secretary of State has power to specify circumstances in which, even if there are residents, the owner is always liable.[15] The owner (not the residents) is liable for the council tax in:

- care homes and certain hostels providing care and support (see p75);
- houses of religious communities (see p75);
- houses in multiple occupation (see p75);
- second homes with domestic servants (see p76);
- residences of ministers of religion (see p76);

- school boarding accommodation in Scotland (see p76);
- accommodation occupied by asylum seekers under section 95 of the Immigration and Asylum Act 1999 (see p76).

Care homes and hostels

An owner is liable to pay council tax on care homes and certain hostels providing care and support that are registered under the Care Standards Act 2000.[16]

Religious communities

For the owner to be liable, the dwelling must be inhabited by a religious community whose principal occupation consists of prayer, contemplation, education, the relief of suffering, or any combination of these.[17] Monasteries and convents come within this description. Members of such communities may qualify to be disregarded for the purpose of a council tax discount (see Chapter 8).

Houses in multiple occupation

A dwelling is classed as a house in multiple occupation if:[18]
- it was originally constructed, or subsequently adapted, for occupation by more than one household; or
- each person who lives in it is either:
  – a tenant or licensee able to occupy only part of the dwelling; or
  – a licensee liable to pay rent or a licence fee on only part of the dwelling.

Examples include some bedsits, hostels, nurses' homes and long-stay wards in hospitals where they are classed as dwellings. In England and Wales, this class can include a dwelling occupied by only one person if the above conditions are met, so long as the dwelling was originally constructed, or subsequently adapted, for occupation by multiple households. From 2003 in Scotland, a dwelling need not have been constructed or adapted for multiple occupation; the fact that the tenant or licensee has the right to occupy or pay rent or a fee for only part of the dwelling is the crucial factor.

The term 'tenant' includes a secure tenant or a statutory tenant and includes those leaseholders whose interest is granted for six months or more. In England and Wales, the normal definition of an owner applies in the case of a house in multiple occupation, except that where someone has a leasehold interest it must be an interest in the whole of the dwelling. If this is not the case, the liability falls upon the person who has a freehold interest in the whole or any part of the dwelling.[19] In deciding the status of residents and the degree of exclusive possession, the valuation tribunal can look beyond the tenancy or licence agreement and examine the actual facts of the relationship.[20]

Second homes with domestic servants

A dwelling fits into this category if it is:[21]

- occupied from time to time by the employer who does not live in it as her/his main residence; *and*
- all the residents are either employed in domestic service in the dwelling or are their family members.

Ministers of religion

The dwelling must be inhabited by a minister of religion (of any faith) as a residence from where s/he performs her/his duties of office. If the dwelling is owned by the minister, then it is the minister who is liable. The one exception to this rule is where an English or Welsh dwelling is owned by a minister of the Church of England who is in receipt of a stipend. In such a case the liability is transferred to the Diocesan Board of Finance.[22]

School boarding accommodation

In Scotland, the owner of school boarding accommodation which is specifically included within the definition of a dwelling (see Chapter 2) is liable for the council tax.[23]

Accommodation occupied by asylum seekers

Asylum seekers occupying accommodation under section 95 of the Immigration and Asylum Act 1999 are not liable for council tax. The owner is liable.[24]

---

4. Joint liability

If two or more people fall into the liable category (eg, joint owners, joint tenants or simply joint residents), they are jointly and severally liable, except if one is severely mentally impaired or, since 1 April 2004, a student (see p78).[25]

Additionally, the liable person's partner is jointly liable if s/he is:[26]

- married to or in a civil partnership with the liable person; *or*
- living with her/his partner as husband and wife or as if in a civil partnership; *and*
- a resident of the dwelling.

This applies whether or not the partner has a legal interest in the dwelling. The definition of '**couple**' used to establish joint liability for council tax is almost the same as that which applies for many social security benefits. Under the social security rules, however, to be a couple both partners must reside in the same *household*. In the case of council tax it is only necessary to show that they reside in the same *dwelling*. As it is possible for a single dwelling to contain more than one separate household, there will be some situations where the two definitions do not exactly coincide. An obvious case arises where a married couple are estranged and continue to live in the same house, but have completely separate households. For council tax purposes they are still classed as a jointly liable couple since they remain married and both continue to reside in the same *dwelling*. But they are not a couple for council tax benefit purposes since, despite being married, they reside in different *households*. This means that both partners are jointly liable, but each can make a separate claim for council tax benefit based on an apportioned (50 per cent) share of council tax liability (see Chapter 9) and their own individual circumstances.

The expression 'living together as husband and wife' uses exactly the same form of words for both council tax and social security purposes, but is not defined in the legislation in either case. However, there is a substantial body of social security caselaw on the various criteria that must be considered when attempting to establish whether two people are living together as husband and wife (see Chapter 9) and, arguably, this will be highly persuasive in council tax cases also. The above discrepancy between the council tax and social security definitions of a 'couple' is unlikely to occur in the case of *unmarried* couples, therefore, since in this case the council tax rules require the parties to be living together as husband and wife *and* to reside in the same dwelling. It is difficult to see how the local authority could conclude that two unmarried people are living together as husband and wife unless they were, in fact, members of the same household (as opposed to merely being resident in the same dwelling). This is because, according to established caselaw, two unmarried people must be members of the same household in order for the local authority to conclude that they are living together as husband and wife.

Practice Note No. 2 (para 20) points out that, in polygamous marriages, all partners resident in the dwelling are jointly liable.

The significance of joint liability

The local authority has the option of addressing the council tax bill to any one or more of the jointly liable people, or all of them. In Scotland, someone who is jointly liable with the person(s) named on the bill, but whose name is not included, is still liable to make the required payments (see Chapter 10). In England and Wales, no payment can be required from a liable person until s/he has been billed. Practice Note No. 2 (para 22) advises English and Welsh local authorities to include the names of as many liable people as possible on their bills. This allows the local authority to take recovery action against any or all of them. If the local authority wants to recover the council tax from someone who is jointly liable but not named on the original bill, a fresh bill (a joint taxpayers' notice) must be issued.[27] In practice, local authorities tend to pursue the first two named persons on a bill.

To be eligible for council tax benefit, the claimant also has to be liable for the council tax. If someone other than the claimant's partner is jointly liable for the tax, council tax benefit is worked out on the claimant's apportioned share, even though the local authority may be seeking to recover all of the council tax due from one person (see Chapter 9). If the claimant is in receipt of council tax benefit, the late identification of retrospective joint liability may mean an overpayment has been made, and could raise the possibility of a late claim for benefit from the newly identified jointly liable person (see Chapter 9).

Joint liability and severe mental impairment

A person who is disregarded for the purpose of working out a discount because of a 'severe mental impairment' (see Chapter 8) is not held jointly liable if there is someone else with the same status and legal interest in the property who is not severely mentally impaired.[28] However, a severely mentally impaired person is liable for the tax if:

- s/he is the only liable person; *or*
- s/he is the only owner, tenant or contractual licensee even if her/his partner is not severely mentally impaired; *or*
- all the jointly liable people are severely mentally impaired.

Dwellings in which all the occupants are severely mentally impaired are exempt (see p58).[29]

Example

A couple are joint owners of a house. The man counts as severely mentally impaired and is disregarded for the purpose of a council tax discount. Normally the couple, as joint owners and residents, would be liable but as the man is severely mentally impaired his wife is liable. If she were no longer to reside in the dwelling, it would become exempt.

Students

From 1 April 2004, a student who is disregarded for the purpose of working out a discount (see p95) is not held jointly liable if there is someone else with the same status and legal interest in the property who is not a student. Dwellings occupied solely by students or occupied as term-time accommodation are exempt from council tax (see Chapter 5). If a dwelling is occupied by a student and a non-student, the student is disregarded for the purpose of a discount, attracting a 25 per cent reduction on the amount of council tax payable by the non-student (see Chapter 8).

Before 1 April 2004, a student could have been liable for council tax if s/he occupied a property with a non-student and either had an equal legal interest in the dwelling or was married to or living together as husband and wife with a non-student resident.

5. **Change of circumstances**

A change of circumstances may alter or change the tax liability during the year. For example, a liable owner may sell the dwelling or a liable tenant may move to live elsewhere. Liability for the council tax arises on a daily basis and the state of affairs at the end of the day is assumed to have lasted all that day.[30] Consequently, the liable person is liable for the first day of residence in the dwelling but not the last. If a liable person dies there is no liability for any part of the day on which s/he dies.

6. **Backdating of liability**

Liability may be backdated to previous years. The relevant date is the day a person became liable – ie, had her/his sole or main residence in the dwelling, not the date the local authority informed the taxpayer.[31] However, a local authority which delays serving demand notices may find its right to recover sums limited if it seeks to enforce the demand through the magistrates' court (see Chapters 10 and 11). One problem is that council tax benefit (see Chapter 9) can only be backdated by 52 weeks (or three or six months depending on your status).

7. **How the liable person is identified**

In order to establish liability, the local authority has a variety of powers that require people and organisations to provide information. It is also able to use its own information obtained for other purposes. If the local authority is unable to identify a liable person by name, it may serve a bill on 'The Council Tax Payer'. The residents of the dwelling will then need to decide who has to pay the tax.

The local authority's own information

A local authority may use information obtained under any other enactment in England and Wales provided that it was not obtained in its role as a police authority and, in Scotland, that it is not information obtained through social work activities, unless it consists solely of names and addresses.[32] Thus, local authorities were able to use their community charge and other records to establish an initial database of liable people. Practice Note No. 5 (para 2.2) reminds local authorities, however, to bear in mind data protection law when considering using information held digitally.

Information from residents, owners or managing agents

The local authority has the power to write to anyone who appears to be a resident, owner or managing agent of a particular dwelling, requesting information it requires to identify the liable person or the person who would be liable if the dwelling were not exempt.[33] A **'managing agent'** means any person authorised to arrange lettings of the dwelling concerned. If you receive a written enquiry, you must supply the required information within 21 days if it is in your possession or control.

Penalties

From 1 May 2008, a local authority in England has the discretion to impose a penalty of £70 on someone who fails to respond to a request for information needed to identify the liable person.[34] In Wales and Scotland the penalty is £50. An English or Welsh authority may quash such a penalty. A Scottish authority may revoke the imposition of such a penalty if the person upon whom it was imposed had a reasonable excuse for failing to supply it.[35] Each time the local authority repeats the request and the person fails to supply the information, another £280 penalty (£200 in Wales and Scotland) can be imposed.[36]

An appeal may be made against the imposition of a penalty (see Chapter 12).[37] This should be done by writing to the Valuation Tribunal for England (in England) or directly to the valuation tribunal (in Wales). In Scotland an appeal can be made to the valuation appeal committee by writing to the local authority, which should pass the appeal on to the committee. In England and Wales an appeal to a tribunal must normally be made within two months of the penalty being imposed. The President of the tribunal has the discretion to allow an out-of-time appeal if you have failed to meet the time limit because of reasons beyond your control. In Scotland the appeal must be made within two months of the penalty being imposed. There is no power to consider out-of-time appeals.[38] If an appeal has been made, the penalty need not be paid until the appeal has been decided.

Information from other public bodies

The local authority has the power to request information from:
- any billing authority;
- any levying authority;
- the electoral registration officer for any area in Great Britain.

In Scotland, information may also be requested from the assessor.[39]

The authority cannot, however, request information from an organisation if it obtained it in its capacity as:
- a police authority; *or*
- a constituent council of a police authority; *or*
- an employer.

The local authority can only request the following details:
- name;
- address;
- any past or present place of residence of any person;
- the dates during which that person is known, or is thought, to have resided there.

Information following a death

Within seven days of the registration of the death of any person aged 18 or over, the registrar of births and deaths for the area in which the death occurred must supply the appropriate authority with the name of the deceased, the date of her/his death and her/his usual address.[40]

8. Appeals

An appeal can be made against a local authority's decision on liability by writing to the authority.[41] There is no time limit for making an appeal. In order to appeal you must be an 'aggrieved person' – ie, the person considered liable to pay the tax or the owner (if different). The appeal letter should give the reasons why you believe the local authority has come to the wrong decision. The local authority has two months in which to answer.[42] In the initial appeal letter, it is advisable to refer to the right to take an appeal to a valuation tribunal if the local authority does not accept the appeal.

If the local authority refuses to alter its decision or fails to answer within two months of receiving the appeal, a further appeal can be made (see Chapter 12).[43] This is done by writing to the Valuation Tribunal for England (in England) or directly to the valuation tribunal (in Wales). In Scotland a further appeal is made by writing again to the local authority. The local authority should pass the appeal on to the secretary of the relevant local valuation appeal committee. If an appeal is served on the local authority, it is advisable to send a copy to the valuation tribunal for it to be placed on file, in case the letter to the local authority goes astray.

In England and Wales, an appeal to a tribunal must normally be made within two months of the date the local authority notified you of its decision; or within four months of the date when the initial written representation was made, if the local authority has not responded. The President of the tribunal has the power to allow an out-of-time appeal if you have failed to meet the appropriate time limits for reasons beyond your control.

In Scotland, the appeal must be made within four months of the date on which the grievance was first raised with the local authority in writing. There is no power to consider an out-of-time appeal.[44]

The local authority may enforce payment of the original bill while the appeal is outstanding, but if recovery proceedings (whether for a liability order or committal to prison) have been commenced through the magistrates' court (or a sheriff's court in Scotland), you should seek an adjournment of any hearing, pending the outcome of an appeal (see Chapter 11).[45]

Notes

1. Who is liable
1 **EW** s6(2) LGFA 1992
  S s75(2) LGFA 1992
2 **EW** s2(2)(c) LGFA 1992
  S s71(2)(c) LGFA 1992
3 *R v Hackney LBC ex parte Adebiri and other appeals* [1997], *The Times*, 4 November 1997; CT(LO) Regs; Council Tax (Liability of Owners) (Amendment) (Scotland) Regulations 2000 No.715
4 **EW** s6(6) LGFA 1992
5 **EW** s6(5) LGFA 1992
6 **S** s75(5) LGFA 1992
7 **EW** ss6-7 LGFA 1992
8 **EW** ss6-7 LGFA 1992

2. Who is a resident
9 **EW** s6(5) LGFA 1992
  S s99(1) LGFA 1992
10 *Bradford City Council v Anderton* [1991] RA 45 (HC)
11 *Ward v Kingston Upon Hull City Council* [1992] RA 71
12 *R (Williams) v Horsham District Council* [2004], *The Times*, 29 January 2004 (CA)
13 *Parry v Derbyshire Dales District Council* [2006] RA 25
14 *Highland Council v Highland and Western Isles Region Valuation Committee* [2008] RA 311 Sc

3. When the owner is always liable
15 **EW** s8(1) LGFA 1992
  S s76(1) LGFA 1992
16 **E** CT(LO)(A)(E) Regs
  W CT(LO)(A)(W) Regs
17 **EW** CT(LO) Regs
  S CT(LO)(S) Regs
18 **EW** CT(LO) Regs
  S CT(LO)(S) Regs
19 **EW** CT(LO) Regs

20 *Norris and Norris v Birmingham City Council* [2001] RVR 89
21 **EW** CT(LO) Regs
  S CT(LO)(S) Regs
22 **EW** CT(LO) Regs
23 **S** CT(LO)(S) Regs
24 **EW** Reg 2 CT(LO) Regs
  S CT(LO)(S) Regs

4. Joint liability
25 **EW** s6(3)-(4) LGFA 1992, as amended by s74 LGA 2003
  S s75(3)-(4) LGFA 1992
26 **EW** s9 LGFA 1992
  S s77 LGFA 1992
27 **EW** Reg 28 CT(AE) Regs 1992
28 **EW** ss6(4) and 9(2) LGFA 1992
  S ss75(4) and 77(2) LGFA 1992
29 **EW** CT(ED)O

5. Change of circumstances
30 **EW** s2 LGFA 1992
  S s71 LGFA 1992

6. Backdating of liability
31 *Hammersmith and Fulham Billing Authority v Butler* [2001] RVR 197

7. How the liable person is identified
32 **EW** Reg 6 CT(AE) Regs 1992
  S Reg 5 CT(AE)(S) Regs
33 **EW** Regs 3 and 12 CT(AE) Regs 1992
  S Reg 2 CT(AE)(S) Regs
34 **EW** s14(2) and Sch 3 LGFA 1992
  S s97(4) and Sch 3 LGFA 1992
35 **EW** s14(2) and Sch 3 LGFA 1992
  S s97(4) and Sch 3 LGFA 1992
36 **EW** s14(2) and Sch 3 LGFA 1992
  S s97(4) and Sch 3 LGFA 1992
37 **EW** s14(2) and Sch 3 LGFA 1992
  S s97(4) and Sch 3 LGFA 1992

38 **EW** Reg 36(3) VCCT(Amdt) Regs
39 **S** Reg 3 CT(AE)(S) Regs
40 **EW** Reg 5 CT(AE) Regs 1992
   S Reg 4 CT(AE)(S) Regs

8. Appeals
41 **EW** s16 LGFA 1992
   S s81 LGFA 1992
42 **EW** s16 LGFA 1992
   S s81 LGFA 1992
43 **EW** s16 LGFA 1992
   S s81 LGFA 1992
44 **EW** Reg 36 VCCT(Amdt) Regs
45 See *R v Ealing Justices ex parte Coatsworth*
   [1980] 126 *Solicitors Journal 128*

7

Chapter 7

Disability reduction

This chapter explains:
1. Conditions for a disability reduction (below)
2. Who can obtain the reduction (p87)
3. How an application is made (p87)
4. How the reduction is made (p88)
5. Change in circumstances (p89)
6. Appeals (p89)

Disability reduction schemes apply in England and Wales,[1] and in Scotland.[2] The basic amount of the council tax and, in Scotland, Scottish Water charges,[3] may be reduced if:

- a disabled person lives in the dwelling; *and*
- the dwelling has certain features that are essential, or of major importance, to the disabled person because of her/his disability; *or*
- the disabled person uses a wheelchair in the home.

A reduction can be made on residential care or nursing homes as well as any other dwelling.

In addition to the disability reduction scheme, the value of fixtures (such as a lift or specially designed kitchen units) designed to make the dwelling suitable for use by a physically disabled person should have been ignored in the valuation of the dwelling if they added to its value (see Chapter 3). Where fixtures designed to make the dwelling suitable for use by a physically disabled person reduce the value of the dwelling, they should have been taken into account in the valuation process and, therefore, reflected in the dwelling's banding.[4]

1. Conditions for a disability reduction

The person with a disability

For the reduction to be awarded, the dwelling must be the sole or main residence (see p71) of at least one person with a disability. No additional reduction is made if more than one disabled person lives in the dwelling.

To count as disabled for the purpose of the reduction, a person must be 'substantially and permanently disabled' (whether by illness, injury, congenital deformity or otherwise). This means that a person with a learning difficulty or a mental health problem may qualify as well as a person with a physical disability. The disabled person may be an adult or a child. S/he need not be a person liable to pay the council tax on the dwelling.

Social services departments in England and Wales and social work departments in Scotland have a duty to maintain a register of, and provide various services to, people in their area who are substantially and permanently disabled. They have considerably more skills and experience in making assessments of disability than their counterparts in council tax administration. If a person is on the disabled person's register this should be sufficient to satisfy the criteria of 'substantially and permanently disabled' for the purposes of a disability reduction (although non-inclusion on the register should not lead to the opposite conclusion, since such registers are not comprehensive and registering as disabled is not compulsory).

The dwelling

The dwelling must have at least one of the following features:
- a room, but not a sole bathroom, a kitchen or a lavatory, which is predominantly used (whether for providing therapy or otherwise) by the person with a disability; *or*
- an additional bathroom or kitchen within the dwelling which is necessary for meeting the needs of the person with a disability; *or*
- sufficient floor space to permit the use of a wheelchair.

To qualify, however, the feature must be essential, or of major importance to the disabled person's well-being because of the nature of her/his disability.

Practice Note No. 2 (para 40) advises local authorities that in deciding whether these conditions apply they should consider whether, if the room or feature were not available:
- the disabled person would find it physically impossible or extremely difficult to live in the dwelling; *or*
- her/his health would suffer or the disability would be likely to become more severe.

However, it should be noted that this is guidance only and is not contained in the legislation. The High Court has ruled that there must be an appropriate causative link between the disability in question and the need to use the room. Relevant factors to be considered include the nature and extent of the person's disability and whether the use of the room is essential or of major importance to her/him.[5]

A sole bathroom or kitchen, even if specially adapted to meet the needs of a person with a disability, is not sufficient to qualify. Additionally, a wheelchair is not considered to be required for meeting the disabled person's needs if s/he does not need to use it in the living accommodation in the dwelling concerned. A reduction may be awarded, for example, if the dwelling has an extension used for dialysis equipment.

Three High Court cases during 2006 further clarified the law on rooms attracting a reduction the meaning of 'major importance'. These were *South Gloucestershire Council v Titley, South Gloucestershire Council v Clothier*[6] and *Hanson v Middlesborough Council*.[7]

In the case of *Titley*, the taxpayer was a profoundly deaf man living alone in a two-bedroom house. His living room was fitted with a hearing loop box enabling him to hear the television and to converse with visitors to his home. In the case of *Clothier*, there were two bedrooms occupied by two adults with Down's syndrome who were being looked after by their parents. Both bedrooms were used for therapy and periods of relaxation which enabled the adult children to cope with their conditions. The High Court ruled that a disabled reduction was not to be awarded in either case. The Court held it was necessary to consider whether a room was specifically required for meeting the needs of a disabled person.

Importantly, the Court stressed that having a disabled resident in a property was not enough. To attract the reduction, the dwelling has to have a room that would not be required but for the presence of a disabled person.

In neither case could the rooms be said to be additional, since they would have been essential or of major importance to almost any household. In the case of *Titley*, the taxpayer would have been using the living room whether or not he was disabled. Similarly in *Clothier*, the rooms were not additional; the two adult children would have required a bedroom whether or not they were disabled.

However, in *Hanson* the appellant succeeded. She was a disabled woman registered as partially sighted. She had a bedroom converted into an en-suite bathroom in 1996, a few months after she moved into the property, also in 1996, and 19 months before she was registered as blind. In 2004 she became aware of the right to a disability reduction for council tax but was refused. This decision was upheld by Teeside Valuation Tribunal, who rejected her appeal on the basis that the bathroom was not essential to her needs.

The High Court, however, upheld her appeal, as the correct test was that the adaptation was essential *or* of major importance to the wellbeing of the disabled person by reason of the nature and extent of her/his disability. Teeside Valuation Tribunal had failed to apply a test of major importance and had wrongly equated it with a test of 'extreme difficulty without', which is not in the legislation. The Court concluded that an en-suite bathroom was of major importance to a disabled person in the position of the applicant because it reduced the risk of tripping or slipping.

Thus, the cases indicate that, to attract a disability reduction, the room used or adapted for a disabled person must be:

- extra or additional to what a person would ordinarily need, whether disabled or not;
- essential or of major importance to the welfare of the disabled person.

Example

A bungalow with one bathroom is occupied by a married couple. One partner becomes seriously disabled and needs a separate bedroom and a specially adapted en-suite bathroom, which is added to the property as an extension. The room qualifies the dwelling for council tax reduction as it is extra or additional to the property *and* is needed for meeting the needs of the disabled person.

2. Who can obtain the reduction

The person entitled to the reduction is the person liable to pay the council tax on the dwelling. S/he may be solely liable or jointly liable. Where there is joint liability, an application made by one of the liable people is treated as having been made on behalf of both of them. None of the liable people need have a disability.

The local authority may also award a disability reduction to someone who will become liable for the council tax on the dwelling perhaps, for example, following work on it to meet the needs of a disabled person.

3. How an application is made

The local authority cannot award a reduction without a written application for each financial year (April to March) from the liable person or someone acting on her/his behalf. The local authority will normally require a copy of a written authorisation to act on behalf of that person or a copy of a Power of Attorney if you are completing the application for someone else. Most local authorities have standard application forms for this purpose. An annex to Practice Note No. 2 contains a model form that local authorities may use.

Backdating and repeat applications

The fact that a written application must be made for each financial year does not prevent a person from making an application for previous years – ie, backdated to when the qualifying conditions were met. The year/s in question must, however, be identified on the application.

Once a written application has been made, a repeat application is required each financial year. It is hoped that local authorities will send people receiving the reduction a repeat application form, and a reminder, at the appropriate time each year. There is, however, nothing in the regulations that requires this, although the reduction may be backdated once the application is received. Practice Note No. 2 (para 52) suggests that local authorities should not generally require a full application in a second or subsequent year. It will often be sufficient to seek the liable person's confirmation that the circumstances have not changed since the original application.

Information required by the local authority

When considering whether or not the reduction applies, an English or Welsh local authority may make a written request for information it reasonably requires at any time and to anyone. It may also require that person to respond within a specified period, but must give her/him at least 21 days to answer. The local authority will often, for example, require a supporting letter from a doctor, occupational therapist or social worker confirming that the disabled person needs the particular qualifying feature of the dwelling because of her/his disability. There is no statutory requirement to seek such letters and local authorities should consider on a case-by-case basis whether verification of a person's disability, or its effect, is necessary. The majority of local authorities also send an officer to visit the dwelling.

4. **How the reduction is made**

If a disability reduction is awarded, the liable person's council tax bill is reduced to that of a dwelling in the valuation band immediately below the band to which the dwelling has been allocated on the valuation list.

The reduction applies for each day that the qualifying conditions are met.

From 1 April 2000, the amount payable on a dwelling that qualifies for a disability reduction in Band A is reduced by the same proportion of the bill as dwellings in valuation Bands B, C and D, being equivalent to one-ninth of Band D.

Example

The liable person's dwelling is shown as being in Band C on the valuation list. Following the award of a disability reduction, the bill that must be paid should be the same as that of someone liable for the tax on a Band B dwelling.

The disability reduction does not alter the actual valuation of the dwelling nor its banding on the valuation list. The liable person's bill should show both the dwelling's actual band and the reduction.

In Wales, if a dwelling qualifies for transitional relief, the banding reduction for disability is applied after the transitional reduction is taken into consideration – ie, it lowers the transitional band for the year by a further band.

The effect of the reduction on other forms of help

Someone entitled to a disability reduction may also be entitled to a discount or council tax benefit. These other forms of help are calculated on the basis of the council tax liability after the disability reduction has been made. Consequently, the retrospective award of a disability reduction may result in a recoverable council tax benefit overpayment.

5. Change in circumstances

If there is a change in circumstances – eg, if the disabled person moves to alternative accommodation, the liable person may no longer be entitled to a disability reduction. If the liable person believes that s/he has ceased to be eligible for the reduction, s/he must notify the local authority. This obligation extends to all those who are jointly liable for the tax on the dwelling in question.

6. Appeals

If the local authority refuses to award a disability reduction, an appeal can be made in writing to the local authority.[8] There is no time limit for making an appeal. An appeal can be made if you are liable to pay the tax or if you are the owner of the property (if different). The appeal letter should give the reasons why you believe the local authority has come to the wrong decision. The local authority has two months in which to answer.[9] If no disability reduction is awarded, or if the local authority fails to answer within two months of receipt of the appeal, a further appeal can be made (see Chapter 12).[10] The local authority may enforce payment of the original bill while the appeal is outstanding (see Chapter 11), but it may agree to a suspension until the matter is resolved by the valuation tribunal. Alternatively, the magistrates' court (sheriff's court in Scotland) may agree to an adjournment of any proceedings which may be issued if an agreement to suspend recovery is not reached.

A further appeal can be made by writing to the Valuation Tribunal for England (in England) or directly to the valuation tribunal (in Wales). The appeal should normally be made within two months of the date the local authority notified you of its decision, or within four months of the date when the initial representation was made, if the local authority has not responded. The President of the tribunal has the power to allow an out-of-time appeal if you have failed to meet the appropriate time limits for reasons beyond your control.[11]

In Scotland, a further appeal can be made by writing again to the local authority. The local authority should pass the appeal on to the secretary of the relevant local valuation appeal committee. The appeal must be made within four months of the date on which the grievance was first raised with the authority in writing. There is no power to consider an out-of-time appeal.

Notes

1 **EW** s13 LGFA 1992; CT(RD) Regs and CT(RDTA)(W)(A) Regs
2 **S** s80(1)-(4) and (6)-(7) LGFA 1992; CT(RD)(S) Regs
3 **S** CT(RD)(S) Regs
4 **EW** Reg 6 CT(SVD) Regs

1. Conditions for a disability reduction
4 **S** Reg 2 CT(VD)(S) Regs
5 *Sandwell Metropolitan District Council v Perks* [2003] RVR 317 Admin 1749 (HC)
6 *South Gloucestershire Council v Clothier* [2006] EWHC 3117 (Admin), CO/1064/2005, 7 December 2006
7 *Hanson v Middlesborough Council* [2006] RA 320 (HC)

6. Appeals
8 **EW** s16 LGFA 1992
  S s81 LGFA 1992
9 **EW** s16 LGFA 1992
  S s81 LGFA 1992
10 **EW** s16 LGFA 1992
  S s81 LGFA 1992
11 **EW** Reg 36 VCCT(Amdt) Regs

Chapter 8

Discounts

This chapter explains:
1. When a discount is granted (below)
2. Who is ignored for the purpose of a discount (p92)
3. Who is disregarded for the purpose of a discount (p92)
4. How discounts are obtained (p106)
5. Reduced discounts (p108)
6. Energy efficiency rebates (p110)
7. Miscellaneous discounts (p111)
8. Appeals (p111)

---

1. When a discount is granted

From its beginning in 1992, the council tax scheme has included a system of discounts, available for certain categories of taxpayer and in certain circumstances.

The council tax and, in Scotland, Scottish Water charges payable on a dwelling is initially based on the assumption that there are at least two adults living in it. The bill does not increase if there are more than two, but should be reduced by:

- 25 per cent if there is only one person solely or mainly resident in the dwelling; *or*
- up to 50 per cent in England and Scotland if no one is solely or mainly resident (this is also normally the case in Wales, but special rules apply in some cases – see below).

Certain people, however, are ignored or 'discounted' by authorities when deciding how many people are solely or mainly resident in the dwelling.

For the purpose of deciding whether the council tax is subject to a discount for any day, the state of affairs at the end of the day is assumed to have existed throughout that day.[1]

Discounts can apply to empty dwellings or second homes. However, following concerns about the growth of second homes in certain areas, the English and Scottish governments granted new powers to local authorities to reduce the amount of discount applied at local level for certain classes of unoccupied properties. Certain empty dwellings are exempt from the tax (see Chapter 5). A discount may follow at the end of an exemption.

Example

An unoccupied and unfurnished (vacant) dwelling qualifies for a six-month exemption. If the dwelling is still unoccupied at the end of the six-month period it no longer qualifies for the exemption, but the full tax bill may be reduced by a 50 per cent discount.

Discounts and other forms of help

The liable person may be granted a discount in addition to any disability reduction, transitional relief or council tax benefit. The discount is applied to the tax after granting a disability reduction, but before calculating main council tax benefit. Second adult rebate is worked out on the basis of the council tax liability, ignoring any discount that has been granted (see Chapter 9).

2. **Who is ignored for the purpose of a discount**

Only adults solely or mainly resident in the dwelling count for the purpose of working out whether or not a discount applies. Consequently, people under 18 and those solely or mainly resident elsewhere are ignored.[2]

Example

Petra and her 15-year-old daughter live in a property. Thus, there is only one person aged 18 or over residing in the dwelling. A 25 per cent discount is granted.

Petra's friend comes to stay with her but keeps a home elsewhere. If it is decided that the friend is mainly resident elsewhere, the discount should continue. If it is decided that the friend is mainly resident in Petra's house, the discount no longer applies from the day she moved in.

3. **Who is disregarded for the purpose of a discount**

In addition to those who are ignored for the purposes of a discount (see above), certain categories of people are disregarded.[3] They are sometimes described as 'having a status discount', or more simply as 'invisible'. They are:
• people aged 18 for whom child benefit is payable (see p94);
• recent school and college leavers under 20 (see p94);

- students under the age of 20 studying up to A level, Higher Scottish Certificate of Education or equivalent (see p95);
- full-time students attending a college or university (see p96);
- foreign language assistants (see p95);
- student nurses (see p95);
- a person who has diplomatic, Commonwealth or consular privilege or immunity;
- spouses or dependants of foreign students (see p95);
- apprentices (see p101);
- National Traineeship trainees (see p101);
- people in prison and other forms of detention (see p101);
- people who are severely mentally impaired (see p102);
- certain carers (see p103);
- hospital patients (see p104);
- people in care homes and hostels providing a high level of care (see p104);
- members of international headquarters and defence organisations and their dependants (see p105);
- members of visiting forces (see p105);
- members of religious communities (see p105);
- in England and Wales, residents in certain hostels and night shelters and other accommodation for those with no fixed abode (see p106).

Status discounts and tax bills

If someone is disregarded for the purpose of a discount, it does not necessarily mean that the tax bill is reduced. A discount is only awarded if there are fewer than two adults in the dwelling, not counting any who are disregarded. A liable person may be disregarded for the purpose of a discount, but is still liable for the council tax. The exceptions to this last rule concern liable people who are considered to be severely mentally impaired and students (see Chapter 6).

Examples

Two adult women are joint owner-occupiers. One is a full-time student and disregarded for the purpose of a discount. The other is in full-time work and is not disregarded. As there are only two residents and one of them is disregarded, a 25 per cent discount should be granted. Although they are both joint resident owners, the student is not jointly liable for the reduced amount of council tax with the one in full-time work (see p78).

A couple in their fifties are joint owner-occupiers of a house. Their daughter lives with them. She is aged 20 and a full-time student. Their son, aged 17, also lives with them. He is in full-time work. The daughter, as a full-time student, is disregarded for the purpose of a discount and the son, as someone under 18, is ignored. Nevertheless, no discount is awarded because two adults (the joint owner-occupiers) live in the house and are not ignored or discounted.

A pensioner couple are liable joint tenants. No one else lives with them. One of the couple has Alzheimer's disease and receives the care component of disability living allowance. He is considered to be severely mentally impaired. In these circumstances, a 25 per cent status discount is awarded because there are only two people solely or mainly resident in the dwelling and one of them is disregarded for the purpose of a discount. In this instance, only the joint tenant who is not severely mentally impaired is liable for the tax.

An adult carer, introduced by a charity, comes to live with the above couple. The couple provides free accommodation plus £50 a week to the carer. In these circumstances, the couple lose their discount as there are now two adults living in the dwelling who are not disregarded for the purpose of a discount. If the carer had received £44 a week or less, however, the discount would have continued as there would still have been only one adult living in the dwelling who was not disregarded for discount purposes.

18-year-olds for whom child benefit is payable

A person falls into this category if s/he is aged 18 and someone is entitled to child benefit for her/him, or would be if s/he were not in local authority care.[4]

The conditions of entitlement to child benefit are described in CPAG's *Welfare Benefits and Tax Credits Handbook*. A child ceases to qualify for child benefit the week after turning 19 or on the Sunday after the first of the following dates after leaving school or college:
- first Monday in January;
- first Monday after Easter Monday;
- first Monday in September.

School and college leavers

A person who is under the age of 20, and has left school or college on or after 1 May in any year after undertaking a qualifying course of education (ie, one no higher than A level, Higher Scottish Certificate of Education or equivalent) or additionally, in England and Wales, full-time education (see p96), should be disregarded for the purpose of working out a discount during the period 1 May to 31 October in the same year.[5] School and college leavers continue to be disregarded if they go on to some other form of further or higher education (see p95).

Future changes
There may be further changes that affect school and college leavers when the Education and Skills Act 2008 comes into force. This will raise the school-leaving age to 18 in 2012 and extend education, work and training schemes to all young people.

Students

A person is disregarded for the purposes of discount if s/he is a student.[6] Dwellings occupied only by students are exempt (see Chapter 5).

A person counts as a **'student'** if s/he is:[7]

- under 20, studying for more than three months and for at least 12 hours a week for any qualification up to A level or Higher Scottish Certificate of Education or equivalent;
- undertaking a college, polytechnic or university course lasting at least one academic year or, in Scotland, a specified course which takes at least 24 weeks a year and involves at least 21 hours of study a week during term time;
- a foreign language assistant.

Nursing and midwifery students, including those on pre-registration undergraduate courses and post-registration health visitor training, count as students.[8] For discount purposes, a student nurse means a person undertaking a course which, if successfully completed, would lead to a first registration under the Nurses, Midwives and Health Visitors Act 1997.[9]

Student nurses undertaking 'traditional' hospital-based training do not count as students.

Students under 20 on a qualifying course

A student must be undertaking a qualifying course of education.[10] A **'qualifying course of education'** is one which:[11]

- lasts for more than three calendar months;
- is at, or below, the following standards or equivalent: A level, Higher Scottish Certificate of Education, National Certificate of the Scottish Vocational Educational Council or Scottish Vocational Qualification Level III;
- is not a correspondence course;
- is not undertaken as a result of the person's office or employment;
- in terms of tuition, supervised exercises, experiments, project or practical work, is normally carried out between 8am and 5.30pm (to the extent that such activities have to be carried out at a particular time).

The person is considered to be undertaking such a course on a particular day if:

- s/he is under the age of 20; *and*
- the relevant number of hours per week for that course, or where two or more such courses are being taken at the same establishment, the combined number of hours per week, exceeds 12 (excluding any vacation period).[12]

A person is treated as undertaking such a course throughout both term time and vacations from the date the course begins to the date s/he completes, abandons or is dismissed from it. The person is no longer considered to be undertaking such a course if s/he becomes an apprentice or a National Traineeship trainee.[13]

Full-time students

To be treated as a full-time student, a person must be enrolled on a course with a 'prescribed educational establishment' and undertaking a full-time course of education. In Scotland, the course must be a specified course.[14]

The educational establishments are the same as those that apply for the purpose of student hall of residence exemptions (see p56).

Prescribed educational establishments
 – a university, including a constituent college, school or other institution of a university;
 – a central institution or college of education in Scotland within the meaning of s135(1) Education (Scotland) Act 1980;
 – a college of education in Northern Ireland within the meaning of Article 2(2) Education and Libraries (Northern Ireland) Order 1986;
 – a theological college;
 – any other institution in England or Wales established solely or mainly for the purpose of providing courses of further or higher education within the meaning of the Further and Higher Education Act 1992 and the Education Act 1996;
 – any other institution in Scotland or Northern Ireland established solely or mainly for the purpose of providing courses of further education;
 – an institution accredited by the Teacher Training Agency or the Higher Education Funding Council for Wales under regulations in force under ss218(2) and (2A) Education Reform Act 1988;[15]
 – a college of nursing and midwifery or a college of health, established by a health board or by a regional or district health authority;
 – an institution of a research council established by Royal Charter under section 1 of the Science and Technology Act 1965.

A Ministry of Defence training establishment for the armed forces does not count as an educational establishment for this purpose.[16]

Full-time course of education

A '**full-time course of education**' is one which:
- lasts for at least one academic year of the educational establishment concerned or, if the establishment does not have academic years, for at least one calendar year; *and*
- normally requires attendance (either at the establishment or elsewhere) for periods of at least 24 weeks in each academic or calendar year throughout its duration; *and*
- normally requires an average of at least 21 hours a week study, tuition or work experience, or a combination of such periods during periods of attendance.

In addition, in Scotland the course must be a 'specified course'.[17]

Specified courses in Scotland[18]

Courses at first degree and diploma level
– a course at undergraduate level leading to:
   – a degree, certificate, diploma or licentiateship from a university or theological college; *or*
   – a degree, certificate or diploma granted by a designated institution, a central institution or any other institution for the provision of any form of further education.

Courses in further education
– a course in further education leading to an award of the Scottish Certificate of Education, the General Certificate of Education, the General Certificate of Secondary Education or the International Baccalaureate;
– a course in further education leading to the National Certificate, the Higher National Certificate or Higher National Diploma of the Scottish Vocational Education Council, or a Scottish Vocational Qualification, or any other course in further education leading to a comparable award;
– a course in further education required by an educational establishment to be undertaken prior to any other course mentioned in this table being undertaken.

Training for teaching, social work or youth and community work
– a course at undergraduate or postgraduate level for the initial training of teachers, social workers or youth and community workers.

Vocational courses at postgraduate level
– a course at postgraduate level leading to a certificate or diploma in professional studies or to any other comparable award.

Courses at higher degree level
– a course leading to the award of the degree of Doctor of Philosophy, a Master's degree or any other comparable award.

A course does not count as full time if the combined periods of work experience normally required to be undertaken as part of it exceed the combined periods of study or tuition. This does not apply in the case of a course for the initial training of teachers in schools.[19]

People are treated as undertaking work experience if, as part of the curriculum of the course, they are:[20]
• at their workplace providing services under a contract of employment; *or*
• at a place where a trade, business, profession or other occupation which is relevant to the subject matter of the course is carried out for the purposes of gaining experience of that trade.

For the purpose of working out the number of weeks of attendance in the year, the following rules apply.

If the course starts at the beginning of an academic year:

- the first calendar year of the course is treated as beginning on the day on which the course begins; *and*
- subsequent calendar years (if any) are treated as beginning on the anniversary of that day.

If the course begins part-way through an academic year:
- the academic year is treated as beginning at the start of the term in which the course begins; *and*
- subsequent academic years (if any) are treated as beginning at the start of the equivalent terms in those years.

The final part of a course which lasts (or is treated as lasting) for other than a number of complete academic or calendar years is disregarded.[21]

A person is treated as a full-time student from the date the course begins to the date s/he completes, abandons or is dismissed from it.

There has been little caselaw on what constitutes a qualifying course for the purposes of student status under council tax legislation.

In *Birmingham City Council v Birmingham VCCT and Adamson* the High Court considered the question in the context of the now repealed community charge legislation.[22] The Court decided that the phrase 'normally required to undertake' was a common sense expression and:

... that as far as the amount of study or tuition is concerned, the timetable will provide the *prima facie* structure against which one justifies whatever conclusion one reaches, supplemented by whatever evidence may be put before the tribunal which establishes that which can properly be considered as the normal expectation of those undertaking the course on the one hand and those providing the course on the other, as to what over and above that which is timetabled should be considered as the requirement of the course for the purpose of its being successfully completed.

This judgment suggests that a limited amount of extra study outside the full-hours timetable may be taken into account when assessing whether the course constitutes 21 hours or more. However, it is clear that the High Court expects tribunals to scrutinise such claims and distinguish between how many weeks a student is actually required to attend a place of study and not simply consider how long a course lasts in calendar terms.[23] The 'common sense' approach would also suggest that a student who has special arrangements for her/his course because of illness, disability or childcare arrangements will also come within the definition of a full-time student 'normally required to undertake' the prescribed hours and periods.

Postgraduate students

A High Court decision in 2008 has restricted the availability of discounts and exemptions for students writing up PhDs away from college. In the case of *R (on the application of Fayad) v London South East Valuation Tribunal*, the applicant undertook a PhD at Imperial College London.[24] He argued that he was entitled to be exempt from council tax as a full-time student between March 1998 and February 2006. Although his student exemption certificate expired in 2003, he contended that an exemption should apply for a longer period as he had been granted five years by the college to write up his thesis. He also maintained that an asylum and immigration tribunal had recognised him as a student. The applicant was refused student status by the local authority and he appealed to the High Court when the valuation tribunal dismissed his appeal. The High Court upheld the tribunal's decision and refused an application for judicial review. It held that attendance meant physical attendance at an educational establishment of at least 24 weeks of study in the academic year and with an average of at least 21 hours a week in those 24 weeks.

This meant the student had to attend some identifiable place. As Imperial College did not impose a requirement of attendance, he was not exempt from paying council tax. Following this decision, it appears that students who are not required to attend at 'some identified place' for the statutory period are not entitled to a student exemption. Thus, many PhD students and others (eg, students permitted to work from home, perhaps with childcare responsibilities) could be potentially liable for council tax. At a time when increasing numbers of courses are being delivered online, this could have major implications, unless physical attendance is also interpreted as interaction with a physical place – ie, the college or educational institution. However, it may also be maintained that the terms of a number of PhD courses which give a year for writing-up time after a two-year course also require qualifying attendance if the student receives supervision and guidance.

Condensed courses

Full-time students on condensed courses of study are also likely to fall outside the definition of a student for discount purposes, following the High Court decision in *Merseyside Valuation Tribunal and Wirral Borough Council v Farthing*.[25] The student was pursuing a course of education that had been condensed from a one-year course taught between October and June as the academic year to a course taught between January and June. The Court ruled that a full-time condensed course fell outside the criteria for a student exemption.

Students overseas

Students who undertake part of their course at an educational institution outside the UK should seek exemption on the basis that they do not have their sole or main residence in the UK (see p71).

Spouse of foreign student

A foreign student's spouse or dependant who is prevented from working or claiming benefit may be disregarded for discount purposes or may be exempt.[26] To qualify the spouse/dependant must not be a British citizen and must be 'prevented by the terms of her/his leave to enter or remain in the UK from taking paid employment or from claiming benefits'.

This was subject of a tribunal ruling in *Oladehin v Redbridge Council* [2008] in a case of a spouse who was able to work but was not entitled to claim benefits. The tribunal chose to interpret the word 'or' literally, so as to exclude from the exemption a spouse who had no access to public funds, but was not prevented from working.

Arguably, the interpretation of the tribunal is wrong – one of the principles of statutory interpretation, known as 'the golden rule', provides for a statute or regulation to be normally interpreted literally unless this would be absurd.

In such situations then, the exemption should not be interpreted so as to defeat the purpose of the exemption. The regulation must be read as a whole, in conjunction with the intention of Parliament under the Local Government Finance Act 1992. It was the intention of Parliament that an exemption should exist for the foreign spouse of a student. It should also be emphasised that this is only a tribunal decision and is not binding on other tribunals.

Evidence of student status

When considering whether someone can be disregarded as a student, the local authority may ask for a student certificate. With the exception of foreign language assistants, prescribed educational institutions (see p96) are required to provide certificates when requested to do so by a student or student nurse.[27] Certificates need not be supplied, however, if the person making the request stopped following a course at that institution more than a year previously. The former Office of the Deputy Prime Minister issued an advice note, reproduced as Annex E in Practice Note No. 2, advising authorities that educational institutions are required, if requested, to provide students and student nurses with certificates, which they may use as evidence of entitlement to student discounts. However, it is for authorities to decide what evidence they need.

The certificate should include the following information:[28]
- the educational establishment's name and address;
- the full name of the person to whom it is issued;
- the student's date of birth if this is known to the establishment and if the person is, or was, a student under 20 studying a course no higher than A level or equivalent;
- a statement certifying that the person is following, or has followed, a course of education as a student or student nurse;

- the date when the person became a student or a student nurse at the establishment and the date when her/his course came, or is expected to come, to an end;
- in Scotland, the student's home address if different to her/his term-time one.

Apprentices

An apprentice is someone:
- employed for the purpose of learning a trade, business, profession, office, employment or vocation;
- undertaking a programme of training leading to an accredited qualification;
- receiving a salary or allowance (or both) which, in total, is no more than £190 per week before any deductions for income tax and national insurance.[29] Guidance to local authorities advises that when calculating earnings, any overtime or bonuses should be ignored.

Youth trainees

Youth trainees are disregarded for the purpose of a discount if s/he is:[30]
- under the age of 25; *and*
- receiving training in line with an individual training plan under section 2 of the Employment and Training Act 1973, funded by the Learning and Skills Council for England.

Trainees are usually aged 16 to 21, but the council tax definition includes those under the age of 25 as some trainees – eg, those with disabilities, may need extra time to complete the training or may start training plans late. The trainee is regarded as undertaking training from the day on which the course or programme begins to the day s/he completes, abandons or is dismissed from it.

People in prison and other forms of detention

In many cases, people in prison or some other form of detention are considered no longer solely or mainly resident in a dwelling and should therefore be ignored for the purpose of a discount. Dwellings left empty by those in detention are exempt from council tax (see Chapter 5). In certain instances, however, the period of detention may be for such a short period that the person in detention is still considered mainly to occupy the dwelling. In such circumstances, a disregard for the purpose of a discount applies if s/he is:[31]
- detained in a prison, a hospital or any other place by a British court;
- detained under the deportation provisions of the Immigration Act 1971;
- detained under the Mental Health Act 1983 or the Mental Health (Scotland) Act 1984;
- imprisoned, detained or in custody (but not in custody under open arrest for the purposes of Queen's Regulations) for more than 48 hours under the Army Act 1955, the Air Force Act 1955 or the Naval Discipline Act 1957.

A person who is in police custody before her/his first court appearance, or who is detained for non-payment of council tax in England or Wales, or non-payment of a fine is not treated as detained for the purpose of a discount.[32] A prisoner on temporary release is treated as being detained.

People who are severely mentally impaired

For council tax purposes, someone is considered **'severely mentally impaired'** if s/he has a severe impairment of intelligence and social functioning (however caused) which appears to be permanent.[33] This includes people who are severely mentally impaired as a result of a degenerative brain disorder such as Alzheimer's disease, a stroke or other forms of dementia. To count as severely mentally impaired, the person concerned must have a certificate of confirmation from a registered medical practitioner. Certificates of severe mental impairment issued before the introduction of council tax are acceptable, provided they do not include any information that should only be used for some other purpose – eg, exemption from the community charge. Doctors must issue certificates free of charge.

In addition, to qualify for the discount the person must be entitled to (though not necessarily in receipt of) one of the following benefits:
- short-term or long-term incapacity benefit (IB);
- employment and support allowance;
- attendance allowance (AA);
- severe disablement allowance (SDA);
- the highest or middle rate care component of disability living allowance (DLA);
- an increase in disablement pension for constant attendance;
- the disability element of working tax credit;
- unemployability supplement (this was abolished in 1987 but existing claimants remain entitled);
- constant attendance allowance payable under the industrial injuries or war pension schemes;
- unemployability allowance payable under the industrial injuries or war pension schemes;
- income support which includes a disability premium because of incapacity for work.

A person who would have been entitled to one of the above benefits, except for the fact that s/he has reached pensionable age, still qualifies for the discount.[34]

A person also qualifies if s/he is the partner of a person in receipt of income-based jobseeker's allowance (JSA) which includes a disability premium or higher pensioner premium because:[35]
- s/he gets the long-term rate of IB; *or*
- s/he was either in receipt of long-term IB up to pension age and is still alive or is entitled to AA/DLA but has been in hospital for more than 28 days.

Carers

A carer is disregarded for the purpose of a discount if s/he is providing care or support (or both):[36]

- to another person on behalf of a local authority or charitable body (see below); *or*
- to another person, is employed by the person being cared for and was introduced by a charitable body (see below); *or*
- to someone in receipt of certain benefits (see below).

Carers providing care on behalf of a local authority or charitable body

The carer must be:

- providing the care or support in question on behalf of a local authority, the Common Council of the City of London, the Council of the Isles of Scilly, a government department or a charitable body, and be resident in premises provided by, or on behalf of, that organisation, so that the best care can be provided; *and*
- engaged or employed for at least 24 hours a week; *and*
- from 1 April 2007 is paid no more than £44 a week.

Carers introduced by a charitable body

The carer must:

- be employed to provide care or support by the person who needs the care for at least 24 hours a week; *and*
- be earning not more than £36 a week from this employment; *and*
- have been introduced to the person by a charitable body; *and*
- be resident in premises provided by, or on behalf of, the person being cared for to enable the best care to be provided.

Caring for someone in receipt of certain benefits

The carer must:

- be resident in the same dwelling as the person being cared for; *and*
- be providing care for at least 35 hours a week on average; *and*
- not be the partner of the person being cared for, or, if the person needing care is a child under 18, not be the child's parent; *and*
- be caring for someone entitled to:
  - higher rate AA; *or*
  - the highest rate care component of DLA; *or*
  - an increase in constant attendance allowance under the industrial injuries or war pensions scheme; *or*
  - the highest rate of constant attendance allowance payable on top of full rate disablement benefit paid for an industrial injury.

More than one person living in the same dwelling can count as a carer.

Example

Mr and Mrs Evans have a son aged 21. He is severely mentally impaired and gets DLA care component at the highest rate. Both parents care for their son for at least 35 hours a week so they both should be disregarded. As their son is also disregarded, their council tax bill should be reduced by 50 per cent. All three occupiers are disregarded, but cannot claim an exemption.

A dwelling left empty by a carer is exempt, whether or not the carer meets any of the above definitions. A dwelling left empty by someone who has moved to receive care elsewhere is also exempt (see Chapter 5).

For more information on the position of carers and council tax in England and Wales, including sample application letters, see www.carersuk.org. In Scotland, see www.carerscotland.org.

Hospital patients

If someone has a short stay in hospital it has no effect on council tax liability or the amount of tax that must be paid. If the patient has been, or is likely to be, in a hospital for so long that s/he can no longer be considered to be solely or even mainly resident in her/his home, s/he should be ignored for the purpose of a discount. A dwelling left empty by someone who is solely or mainly resident in hospital is exempt from the council tax (see Chapter 5).

Most hospitals are subject to non-domestic rates, but some types of long-stay hospitals can be considered dwellings for council tax purposes. Patients who are solely or mainly resident in such a hospital are disregarded for the purposes of a discount.[37] In this context, and for the purpose of exemptions, a '**hospital**' means:[38]

- an NHS hospital including any NHS trust hospital; *and*
- a military, air force or naval unit or establishment in which medical or surgical treatment is provided.

People in care homes and hostels

The owners, rather than the residents, of these types of accommodation are liable for the council tax (see Chapter 6). The owners may be eligible for a disability reduction (see Chapter 7). A person solely or mainly resident in such accommodation is disregarded for the purposes of a discount if receiving care or treatment (or both) in the home or hostel.[39] If a resident has left her/his own home empty it may be exempt from the council tax (see Chapter 5).

For the purposes of a discount, a '**care home**' is:

- a care home within the meaning of the Care Standards Act 2000 – ie, if it provides accommodation with nursing or personal care to:
  - people who have been ill;
  - people who have had a mental disorder;

- people with a disability or infirmity;
- people dependent on alcohol or drugs; *or*
- a building, or part of a building, in which residential accommodation is provided under section 21 of the National Assistance Act 1948.

In England and Wales, a **'hostel'** refers to bail and probation hostels and hostels that provide:[40]

- mainly communal residential accommodation; *and*
- personal care for people who need it because of old age, disablement, past or present alcohol or drug dependence, or past or present mental disorder.

In Scotland, a **'hostel'** is an establishment in which residential accommodation is provided and whose sole or main function is to provide personal care or support to people who have their sole or main residence there.

'Personal care' includes providing appropriate help with physical and social needs and **'support'** refers to counselling or other help provided as part of a planned programme of care. To qualify, the hostel must be:[41]

- managed by a registered housing association or a voluntary organisation within the meaning of section 94(1) of the Social Work (Scotland) Act 1968; *or*
- operated other than on a commercial basis and in respect of which funds are provided wholly or in part by a government department or agency, or a local authority.

Members of international headquarters and defence organisations

A member (or dependant) of certain international headquarters or defence organisations listed in section 1 of the International and Defence Organisations Act 1964 is disregarded for discount purposes.[42]

Members of visiting forces

Members of visiting forces and any of their dependants who are neither British citizens nor ordinarily resident in the UK are disregarded for the purposes of a discount.[43] A dwelling is exempt from council tax if one of the liable people has a relevant association with a visiting force (see Chapter 5). Consequently, this disregard only applies where none of the liable people have a relevant association. This would be the case, for example, if a member of a visiting force lodges with a British citizen.

Members of religious communities

A person is a member of a religious community if:[44]

- the principal occupation of the community consists of prayer, contemplation, education, the relief of suffering, or any combination of these; *and*

- s/he has no income or capital of her/his own and is dependent on the community to provide for her/his material needs.

In considering whether or not the individual has any income, the local authority should disregard any pension(s) from former employment.

The owner, rather than the residents, is liable for the tax on a dwelling occupied by a religious community (see Chapter 6).

Residents in hostels and night shelters for homeless people

In England and Wales, a person is disregarded for the purposes of discount if s/he is living in a hostel for homeless people, such as those run by the Salvation Army or Church Army. Most of the accommodation must be communal (ie, not divided into self-contained units) and most agreements to occupy the accommodation must be under licences which do not constitute tenancies. The disregard applies to resident staff as well as residents, so long as the accommodation is predominantly provided for those with no fixed abode on the terms and conditions specified.

4. How discounts are obtained

Before calculating the council tax liability of any dwelling in its area, a local authority should take reasonable steps to establish whether any discount should be granted.[45]

If the local authority has reason to believe that a discount applies, this should be assumed when calculating the council tax liability for the dwelling.[46] Practice Note No. 2 (para 70) points out that a local authority may have reason to believe that a discount applies (and hence may be required to apply one) even if it does not have conclusive evidence.

Applications for discounts

To enquire about discounts available in a particular area, you should first contact your local authority taxation office. If the local authority has not granted a discount, the liable person may write and request one on the council tax bill. Any relevant evidence supporting the request should be included. In the case of a student, a student's certificate may prove useful but is not necessary. In the case of someone who is severely mentally impaired, a certificate from a GP is required. Practice Note No. 2 (para 74) reminds authorities that anyone who presents information which they know to be false in order to reduce their council tax bill may be subject to a civil penalty. It advises authorities to pass any evidence of such deception to the police.

Backdating discounts

Many authorities have claim forms for council tax discounts. While filling in such a form may speed up the award of a discount, you can obtain a discount without making a claim. Authorities must therefore grant discounts for a past period if the appropriate conditions were met. Unlike the provisions for backdating most social security benefits, there is no requirement for 'good cause' to be shown before a discount is backdated. If a discount should not have been granted for a past period, it may be withdrawn. The Government has not issued any guidance on whether it considers that a six-year time limit on backdating discounts is imposed by the Limitation Act 1980. As a result, you can apply for a discount, backdated for more than six years.

The duty to correct false assumptions

If a discount has been granted, the local authority must inform the liable person in writing, normally on the tax bill. If that person, or any jointly liable person, has reason to believe that the discount should not have been awarded, s/he should write and advise the local authority within 21 days of first having reason to believe the discount was incorrect.[47] This obligation only arises before the end of the financial year following the financial year in respect of which the local authority's assumption about the discount was made.[48]

Penalties

The local authority has the discretion to impose a penalty of £70 (in England) and £50 (in Wales or Scotland) on a liable person who fails to notify the local authority of her/his belief that a discount should not have been granted.[49] An English or Welsh authority may quash such a penalty. A Scottish authority may revoke the imposition of such a penalty if the person upon whom it was imposed had a reasonable excuse for the failure.[50] Each time the local authority repeats the request and the person continues to fail to supply the information, a further £280 penalty in England or a further £200 penalty in Wales or Scotland can be imposed.[51]

An appeal against the imposition of a penalty may be made (see Chapter 12).[52] This is done by writing to the Valuation Tribunal for England (in England) or directly to the valuation tribunal (in Wales). In Scotland an appeal can be made to the valuation appeal committee by writing to the local authority. The local authority should pass the appeal on to the committee. An appeal should be made within two months of the imposition of the penalty. If someone appeals, the penalty need not be paid until the appeal has been decided.

5. **Reduced discounts**

From 1 April 2004, local authorities in England and Wales can reduce the amount of discount awarded for certain classes of unoccupied dwellings – ie, in which no one has sole or main residence (see Chapter 5). A discount may be reduced to less than 50 per cent, but not less than 10 per cent if the dwelling falls within special prescribed classes (see below). In some cases, this will mean that an empty property attracts a bill equivalent to 90 per cent of that appropriate for the valuation band. However, no reduction is given in Scotland for Scottish Water charges.

A discount may be reduced to 10 per cent of the annual council tax bill payable on a property if it falls into one of the following classes.

- **Class A.** Dwellings which are unoccupied and are furnished, but occupation of which is prevented by a planning condition for at least 28 days a year – eg, holiday chalets.
- **Class B.** Dwellings which are unoccupied and furnished and which are not subject to a planning condition restricting occupancy for at least 28 days – eg, potential second homes.

A discount may be reduced to 0 per cent of the annual council tax bill payable on a property if it falls into:

- **Class C.** Dwellings which are unoccupied and substantially unfurnished. **Note:** dwellings in Class C are those which have been substantially unfurnished and unoccupied for more than six months. If substantially unfurnished and unoccupied for *less* than six months, they will normally be exempt from council tax (see Chapter 5).

This leaves 100 per cent of the bill payable.

As well as increasing the amount of revenue for local authorities, the reduction in discount serves to encourage property owners who own more than one dwelling to let out a second home. For some taxpayers who do not want to let out a dwelling on a commercial basis, it may be an option to allow a relative (such as a son or daughter over 18) to occupy the property, thus qualifying the property for a 25 per cent discount. If the person occupying the property is under 18, the property will be exempt (see Chapter 5).

Local authorities cannot reduce the amount of discount applicable to properties which fall outside the definitions in Classes A and B. These dwellings continue to receive a discount of 50 per cent.

Dwellings not included in Class A or B include those which consist of a pitch occupied by a caravan or a mooring occupied by a boat, job-related dwellings, and unoccupied dwellings left empty because a person is required to occupy another dwelling because of her/his job.

Job-related dwellings and discounts

A job-related dwelling for reduced discount purposes is defined as one provided to a person or her/his spouse because of her/his employment and which:
- is necessary in order to do the job properly; *or*
- has been provided in order for her/him to perform her/his duties better and where it is customary for employers to provide dwellings to employees; *or*
- s/he lives in as part of special security arrangements.

Job-related dwellings include any dwelling provided as a second home to a person as part of her/his employment – eg, a live-in teacher or caretaker, and dwellings owned as second homes by people who are required by their employment to occupy another dwelling – eg, the second home of a publican who is required to live in other licensed premises as a tenant of a brewery.

If a person also has a second home in England on which council tax is payable, the local authority in which the second home is situated is prevented from reducing the 50 per cent discount.

Company directors and partnerships

If the dwelling is provided by a company and the employee is either a director (as defined by sections 67 and 69 or the Income Tax Earnings and Pensions Act 2003) of it or an associated company, the local authority may reduce the discount unless:[53]
- s/he is employed as a full-time director; *or*
- the company is non-profit making; *or*
- the company is established for charitable purposes.

Ministers of religion

From 22 April 2004, ministers of any religious denomination who are required to live in premises in England to perform their duties of office come within the definition of those with a job-related dwelling. This means that if a minister of religion also has a second home in England on which council tax is chargeable, the local authority is prohibited from reducing the council tax discount from 50 per cent.[54]

Wales

Originally in Wales most classes of unoccupied dwelling qualified for a 50 per cent discount, but each Welsh local authority could decide that a 25 per cent discount, or no discount at all, applied if a furnished dwelling had been no one's sole or main residence for six months. Following changes introduced by the Local Government Act 2003, the Welsh Assembly Government now has wider powers to change the amount of discount available on an unoccupied property – eg, a second home.[55] Local authorities in Wales may reduce the amount of discount for dwellings of a particular class by at least 10 per cent or remove the discount altogether. Such a decision lasts for one financial year.

If the local authority makes a decision using the new power, it must apply it to all such dwellings in its area. It cannot, however, apply it to a pitch occupied by a caravan or a mooring occupied by a houseboat. Additionally, it does not apply if:[56]

- someone is liable for the tax on a dwelling only in her/his capacity as a personal representative (ie, the executor of a will) and either no grant of probate or letters of administration has been made, or less than 12 months have elapsed since the day on which such a grant was made; *or*
- the liable person is also a liable person of another job-related dwelling.

If a Welsh authority has made a decision to alter the discounts available on second homes, it must publicise it in at least one newspaper circulating in its area within 21 days of the decision. Failure to comply with this requirement, however, does not make the decision invalid.[57] If such a decision has been made for any financial year, it may be varied or revoked at any time before the beginning of that year.

A Welsh authority's decision about applying a discount to a class of dwelling cannot be appealed. It may, however, be challenged via judicial review.[58] A person may appeal in the normal way (see p111) against the local authority's decision that a dwelling is within a prescribed class.

6. Energy efficiency rebates

A number of local authorities are currently giving rebates on council tax bills to householders who introduce certain energy efficiency measures in their homes, with funding from Centrica.

Councils with energy efficiency rebates

Babergh, Braintree, Breckland, Conwy, Croydon, Dartford, Daventry, Derbyshire Dales, Ellesmere Port and Neston, Fareham, Forest Heath, Ipswich, Kettering, Redditch, Runnymede, St Edmundsbury, Salford, Sefton, Slough, Solihull, South Cambridgeshire, South Derbyshire, South Hams, South Norfolk, South Norhamptonshire, South Shropshire, Suffolk Coastal, Tameside, Tamworth, Taunton Dean, Test Valley, Uttlesford and Wear Valley.[59]

Note, however, that adopting energy efficiency measures in dwellings in other local authorities does not attract a discount or generally affect the size of a bill. The only exception is where adaptations are made to a dwelling that materially increase its value and the alterations are sufficient to result in a change in banding.[60]

7. **Miscellaneous discounts**

Local authorities have the power to give discretionary discounts.[61] In a Parliamentary Answer given in the House of Commons by John Healy, Minister for Local Government on 2 February 2009, at least 23 local authorities were mentioned as having granted some kind of discount in particular cases. These included discounts for:

- people over pension age;[62]
- hard-to-sell property;
- newly unfurnished property;
- property affected by a wind turbine;
- occupied and unoccupied property without the benefit of mains services – eg, beach chalets;
- problems with a chalk mine;
- property that is no one's sole or main residence and where access was restricted;
- single occupiers called up for 28 days or more as members of the reserve forces;
- taxpayers who cannot comply with the council's mooring policy;
- members of the RAF whose redundancy was delayed because of events abroad.

Precise details of which authorities had awarded which discounts were not given, however, on the grounds that individual properties or individual taxpayers might be identified. You should, therefore, check with your local authority whether additional discounts are available.

In Scotland, the water authority, Scottish Water, has allowed a reduction to be granted to households receiving council tax benefit (CTB) who are not in receipt of any discounts. The reduction is equal to the level of CTB.[63]

8. **Appeals**

If the local authority refuses to grant a discount, you can appeal in writing if you are an 'aggrieved person'.[64] There is no time limit for making such an appeal. You are an aggrieved person if you are liable to pay the council tax or the owner (if different). The appeal letter should give the reasons why the discount should be granted. The local authority has two months in which to answer.[65] If no discount is granted, or if the local authority fails to answer within two months of receiving the appeal, you can make a further appeal (see Chapter 12).[66]

In a case where a local authority reduces the amount of discount available and a person experiences hardship, an application may be made to reduce the amount of council tax payable. The local authority must consider the application to reduce the sum on an individual basis.

The local authority may enforce payment of the original bill while the appeal is outstanding (see Chapter 11). The local authority may be prepared to agree to suspend recovery action while awaiting the decision of the tribunal. Alternatively, an adjournment may be sought from the magistrates' court if recovery proceedings are commenced.

The further appeal is made by writing to the Valuation Tribunal for England (in England) or directly to the valuation tribunal (in Wales). The appeal should normally be made within two months of the date the local authority notified you of its decision, or within four months of the date when the initial representation was made if the local authority has not responded. The President of the tribunal has the power to allow an out-of-time appeal if you have failed to meet the appropriate time limit because of reasons beyond your control.

In Scotland, the further appeal is made by writing again to the local authority. The local authority should pass the appeal on to the secretary of the relevant local valuation appeal committee. The appeal must be made within four months of the date on which the grievance was first raised with the local authority in writing. There is no power to consider an out-of-time appeal.

Notes

1. **When a discount is granted**
   1 **EW** s2(2)(d) LGFA 1992
     S s71(2)(d) LGFA 1992

2. **Who is ignored for the purpose of a discount**
   2 **EW** s6 LGFA 1992
     S s99(1) LGFA 1992

3. **Who is disregarded for the purpose of a discount**
   3 **EW** s11 and Sch 1 LGFA 1992;
     CT(DD)O; CT(APDD) Regs
     S CT(D)(S)O; CT(D)(S) Regs; CT(D)(S)
     Amdt Regs; CT(D)(S) Amdt O
   4 **EWS** Sch 1 para 3 LGFA 1992
   5 **EW** CT(APDD) Regs
     S CT(D)(S)CAO
   6 **EWS** Sch 1 para 4 LGFA 1992
   7 **EW** CT(DD)O
     S CT(D)(S)O
   8 para 28 Practice Note No.2

9 **EW** CT(DD)O
  S CT(D)(S)CAO
10 **EW** CT(DD)O
  S CT(D)(S)CAO
11 **EW** CT(DD)O
  S CT(D)(S)CAO
12 **EW** CT(DD)O
  S CT(D)(S)CAO
13 **EW** CT(DD)O
  S CT(D)(S)CAO
14 **EW** CT(DD)O
  E CT(DD)(A)(E)O
  W CT(DD)(A)(W)O
  S CT(D)(S)CAO
15 **EW** CT(DD)O
16 **EW** CT(DD)O
17 **S** CT(D)(S)O
18 **S** Schs 3 and 4 CT(D)(S)CAO; The
  Education (Recognised
  Bodies)(Scotland) Amendment Order
  2009 No.61
19 **EW** CT(DD)O

20 **EW** CT(DD)O
21 **EW** CT(DD)O
22 *Birmingham City Council v Birmingham VCCT and Adamson* [1993] CO365/92 (QBD)
23 *R (Carmarthenshire CC) v West Wales Valuation Tribunal* [2004] 223 (HC)
24 *R (on the application of Fayad) v London South East Valuation Tribunal* [2008] EWHC 2531 (Admin), 10 October 2008
25 *Merseyside Valuation Tribunal and Wirral Borough Council v Farthing* [2008]
26 CT(DDED)(A)O, as amended. See also CT(ED)(S)O 1995 and CT(D)(S)(A) Regs; The Council Tax (Discounts)(Scotland) Amendment Regulations 1995 No.597
27 CT(D)(S)CAO
28 **EW** CT(DD)O
   S Reg 9 CT(D)(S)CAO
29 **E** Amended by Art 2(2) CT(DD)(A)(E)O
   W Amended by CT(DD)(A)(W)O
   S CT(D)(S)CAO
30 **E** CT(DD)O, as amended by CT(DD)(A)(E)O
   EW Reg 3 CT(EDDD)(A)O
   S CT(D)CAO
31 **EWS** Sch 1 para 1 LGFA 1992
   EW CT(DD)O
   S Reg 3 CT(D)(S)CAO
32 **EWS** Sch 1 para 1 LGFA 1992
   EW CT(DD)O
33 **EWS** Sch 1 para 2 LGFA 1992
   EW CT(DD)O
   S CT(D)(S)CAO
34 **EW** CT(DD)O
35 **EW** CT(DD)O
   S CT(D)(S)O
36 **E** CT(APDD) Regs, amended by The Council Tax and Non-Domestic Rating (Amendment) (England) Regulations 2006 No.3395
   W The Council Tax (Additional Provisions for Discount Disregards) (Amendment) (Wales) Regulations 2007 No.581
   S The Council Tax (Discounts) Scotland Amendment Order 2007
37 **EWS** Sch 1 para 6 LGFA 1992
38 **EWS** Sch 1 para 6 LGFA 1992
39 **EWS** Sch 1 paras 7-8 LGFA 1992
40 **EW** CT(DD)O
41 **S** CT(D)(S)O

42 **EWS** Sch 1 para 11 LGFA 1992; The European Union Military Staff (Immunities and Privileges) Order 2009 No.887; The International Organisations (Immunities and Privileges) Order 2009 No.44
   EW CT(APDD) Regs
   S CT(D)(S) Regs
43 **EW** CT(APDD) Amdt Regs
   S CT(D)(S) Amdt Regs
   See also The Visiting Forces and International Headquarters (Application of Law)(Amendment) Order 2009 No.705 and The European Union Military Staff (Immunities and Privileges) Order 2009 No.887
44 **EW** CT(APDD) Regs
   S CT(D)(S) Regs

4. How discounts are obtained
45 **EW** Reg 14 CT(AE) Regs 1992
   S Reg 12 CT(AE)(S) Regs
46 **EW** Reg 15 CT(AE) Regs 1992
   S Reg 13 CT(AE)(S) Regs
47 **EW** Reg 16 CT(AE) Regs 1992
   S Reg 15 CT(AE)(S) Regs
48 **EW** Reg 16 CT(AE) Regs 1992
   S Reg 15 CT(AE)(S) Regs
49 **EW** s14(2) and Sch 3 LGFA 1992
   S s97(4) and Sch 3 LGFA 1992
50 **EW** s14(2) and Sch 3 LGFA 1992
   S s97(4) and Sch 3 LGFA 1992
51 **EW** s14(2) and Sch 3 LGFA 1992
   S s97(4) and Sch 3 LGFA 1992
52 **EW** s14(2) and Sch 3 LGFA 1992
   S s97(4) and Sch 3 LGFA 1992

5. Reduced discounts
53 Sch paras 2 and 3 CT(PCD)(E) Regs
54 Regs 2 and 6 CT(PCD)(E) Regs
55 **W** s12 LGFA 1992 as inserted by s75 LGA 2003
56 **W** CT(PCD)(W) Regs
57 **W** s12 LGFA 1992 as inserted by s75 LGA 2003
58 **W** s66 LGFA 1992

6. Energy efficiency rebates
59 Parliamentary Answer from Phil Woolas, Minister for Local Government and Parliamentary Answer by Ruth Kelly, Minister for Communities and Local Government, given on 19 March 2007

7. **Miscellaneous discounts**
   61 s13A LGFA 1992, as inserted by LGA
      1992
   62 A further answer indicated that special
      discounts for pensioners had been
      recognised by Bury, Hillingdon, Kirklees
      and Wirral Councils
   63 The Water and Sewerage Charges
      (Exemption and Reduction)(Scotland)
      Regulations 2006, SSI 2006/71

8. **Appeals**
   64 **EW** s16 LGFA 1992
      S s81 LGFA 1992
   65 **EW** s16 LGFA 1992
      S s81 LGFA 1992
   66 **EW** s16 LGFA 1992
      S s81 LGFA 1992

Chapter 9

• •

Council tax benefit

This chapter explains:
1. Who is entitled to main council tax benefit (p116)
2. How main council tax benefit is calculated (p119)
3. Who is entitled to second adult rebate (p131)
4. How second adult rebate is calculated (p133)
5. Claiming and getting paid (p136)
6. Challenging decisions (p142)
7. Discretionary housing payments (p142)

Council tax benefit (CTB) is paid to people on low incomes to help pay their council tax. It is paid by local authorities, although it is a national scheme.

There are two types of CTB: main CTB and alternative maximum CTB, which is known as second adult rebate. If you are eligible for both, you are paid whichever is the higher.

Main CTB is based on your council tax liability and your (and any partner's and dependants') assumed needs and resources (see p122). If you are entitled to income support, income-based jobseeker's allowance, income-related employment and support allowance or the guarantee credit of pension credit, you automatically qualify for maximum CTB (see p120). Otherwise, your CTB is calculated using a special formula.

Second adult rebate is a form of CTB, but it is not based on your needs or resources. Rather, it is based on the circumstances of certain other adults ('second adults') living with you (see p131).

If you are a member of a couple and are jointly liable for council tax, one of you must claim CTB for both of you.[1] All references to 'couples' and 'partners' include same-sex partnerships, whether registered or not.

The rules for CTB are often the same as for housing benefit.

In addition to CTB, discretionary housing payments may also be available if you are in financial need (see p142).

This chapter gives an overview of the rules for claiming and calculating CTB. For more detailed information, see *CPAG's Welfare Benefits and Tax Credits Handbook*.

1. **Who is entitled to main council tax benefit**

You qualify for main council tax benefit (CTB) if:[2]
- you are liable for council tax (see p69) in respect of the home where you are 'resident' (see below); *and*
- you are aged 18 or over; *and*
- your income is low enough (see p125); *and*
- unless you or your partner are getting the guarantee credit of pension credit (PC), your savings and other capital are worth £16,000 or less (see p124). There is no capital limit if you or your partner are getting the guarantee credit of PC;[3] *and*
- you satisfy the 'right to reside test' and the 'habitual residence test' and you are not a 'person subject to immigration control' for benefit purposes; *and*
- you are not a full-time student (although there are certain limited exceptions) (see p117). This rule does not apply if you are 60 or over and neither you nor your partner are getting income support (IS), income-based jobseeker's allowance (JSA) or income-related employment and support allowance (ESA).

Where you are resident

For CTB purposes, you are a resident in the home where you have your 'sole or main residence'.[4] This is the same criterion as for liability for council tax (see Chapter 6), so any decision on your sole or main residence should be the same for CTB purposes.[5]

Owners not resident in a dwelling, or those whose main residence is elsewhere – eg, second home owners, are not entitled to CTB. **Note:** you cannot qualify for CTB if you are a prisoner on temporary release.[6]

Temporary absence from home

If you are temporarily away from your normal home, have not rented it out and intend to return, your CTB can continue to be paid for a certain period.[7] You can try to argue that you count as temporarily absent from home even if you have not yet stayed there – eg, you move your furniture and belongings in but then have to go into hospital.[8]

You can get CTB for 13 weeks for your normal home while you are away, whatever the reason. You must be unlikely to be away for longer than this.

You can get CTB for 52 weeks for your normal home if you are unlikely to be away for longer than this (or in exceptional circumstances, unlikely to be away for substantially longer than this) and:
- you are a remand prisoner held in custody pending trial or sentence;
- you are required to live in an approved bail hostel or an address away from your normal home as a condition of bail;
- you are resident in a hospital or similar institution as a patient;

- you, your partner or a dependent child under 16 are undergoing medical treatment or medically approved convalescence in the UK or abroad, other than in residential accommodation;
- you are providing (or, other than in residential accommodation, receiving) 'medically approved' care (or you are caring for a child under 16 whose parent or guardian is away from home receiving medically approved care or medical treatment) in the UK or abroad;
- you are undertaking a training course in the UK or abroad which is provided or approved by, or on behalf of, a government department, the Secretary of State, Skills Development Scotland, Scottish Enterprise or Highlands and Islands Enterprise;
- you are a student;
- you are in residential accommodation for short-term respite care;
- you are away from home because of fear of violence.

Note: if you are not living in your normal home because you are in prison, in a care home or in hospital, the property may be exempt from council tax (see Chapter 5).

Council tax benefit for more than one home

There are no rules for when you can and cannot get CTB for more than one home. However, if you occupy more than one property as a home (eg because you have a large family) and you are liable for council tax on both, you can argue that you are resident in, and qualify for CTB for, both properties.[9] However, if you choose to split your time between two homes (eg, your normal home and a holiday home), you can only get CTB for the property that is your main residence.

Students

Most students are not liable for council tax and do not, therefore, need to claim CTB. If you are a full-time student (unless you are one of those listed on p118) you cannot qualify for main CTB. However, you can qualify for second adult rebate if you satisfy the qualifying conditions (see p131). If you are a part-time student you can qualify for main CTB and second adult rebate.

The definition of a student for CTB purposes is different from that for council tax purposes and mirrors the provision for housing benefit. For CTB a 'student' is someone who is attending a course of study at an educational establishment or a qualifying course for JSA purposes. Once a course has started you count as a student until:[10]

- the last day of the course (ie, the end of the final academic term of the course);
  or
- until you abandon or are dismissed from it.

You count as a student even during periods when you temporarily suspend attendance – eg, because of sickness or for personal reasons.

A 'full-time student' is a person attending or undertaking a full-time course of study, or a course which:[11]

- in England and Wales, is funded wholly or partly by the Learning and Skills Council (LSC) or the Welsh Ministers and involves more than 16 guided learning hours a week;
- in Scotland, is funded by the Scottish Ministers at a college of further education and involves:
  - more than 16 hours a week of classroom or workshop-based programmed learning under the direct guidance of teaching staff; *or*
  - 16 hours or less a week of classroom or workshop-based programmed learning, but involves additional hours using structured learning packages supported by the teaching staff where the combined total of hours exceeds 21 per week.

A 'learning agreement', provided by the college, is used to provide proof of the number of hours. **Note:** 'Full-time student' includes a student on a sandwich course.

For higher education (eg, university) courses or other courses not funded as described above (eg, courses funded by the European Social Fund) there is no definition of 'full time'. Local authorities normally decide on the basis of advice from the educational establishment concerned.

Students on full-time parts of modular courses are regarded as full-time students.[12]

Students who can claim main council tax benefit

Even if you are a full-time student you can qualify for main CTB if you:[13]

- are at least the qualifying age for PC (currently 60, but increasing gradually to 65 from April 2010); *or*
- are on IS, income-based JSA or income-related ESA; *or*
- are entitled to:
  - disability premium (see p122), or would be if not disqualified from incapacity benefit; *or*
  - severe disability premium (see p122); *or*
- are a lone parent; *or*
- have been (or have been treated as) incapable of work for at least 196 days; *or*
- have had (or have been treated as having) limited capability for work for at least 196 days; *or*
- have a partner who is also a full-time student and one of you is treated as responsible for a child or young person – ie, someone for whom child benefit is payable; *or*

- are single but fostering a child formally placed with you by a local authority or voluntary agency; *or*
- are aged under 21 and not in higher education – ie, on a course up to and including A level standard (so long as you started the course when under 19); *or*
- count as a child or 'qualifying young person' for child benefit purposes, eg, someone under 20 in full-time education or approved training who started (or was enrolled or accepted on) the course or training when under 19; *or*
- are a deaf student and qualify for a disabled student's allowance because of your deafness; *or*
- are waiting to return to your course after having taken approved time out because of illness or caring responsibilities.

The following people may also qualify for main CTB:
- the non-student partner of a full-time student;
- employment trainees in receipt of a training allowance;
- people on other training courses which do not take place at an educational establishment – eg, student nurses following hospital-based training.

Example

Two brothers are the joint tenants of the property in which they live. The older brother, Sam, is a full-time student. He is disregarded for the purpose of a council tax discount (see Chapter 8). The younger brother, Nick, is in low-paid employment.

Their sister, Jessica, lives with them. For the last six months they have also put up Jessica's friend, Paula, a lone parent on IS with a child aged two.

Nick is liable for council tax and eligible for main CTB. Jessica and Paula are not liable for council tax, and consequently neither is eligible for CTB. As a student who shares with a non-student who is at the same level in the hierarchy of liability (see p70), Sam is not liable for council tax.

Nick moves out and Sam becomes the sole tenant. Sam is solely liable for the council tax, but he is not eligible for main CTB. He is eligible for second adult rebate.

Sam and Paula become a couple. Paula's name is added to the tenancy. She is now jointly liable for the council tax. She can claim main CTB.

2. How main council tax benefit is calculated

The amount of main council tax benefit (CTB) you get depends on:
- your 'maximum CTB' (see p120); *and*
- your 'applicable amount' (see p122). This is made up of personal allowances as well as premiums and components for any special needs; *and*

- how much income and capital you have (see p124).

If you are getting income support (IS), income-based jobseeker's allowance (JSA), income-related employment and support allowance (ESA) or the guarantee credit of pension credit (PC), you are automatically passported to maximum CTB (once you have made a claim). You do not, therefore, need to work out applicable amounts, income or capital. CTB = maximum CTB (see below).

If you are not on IS, income-based JSA, income-related ESA or the guarantee credit of PC:

- **Step one:** check that your capital is not too high (see p124).
- **Step two:** work out your maximum CTB (see below).
- **Step three:** work out your applicable amount (see p122).
- **Step four:** work out your income (see p125).
- **Step five:** calculate CTB:
  - If your income is less than or equal to your applicable amount, CTB = maximum CTB.
  - If your income is greater than your applicable amount, work out the difference. CTB = maximum CTB minus 20 per cent of the difference between your income and your applicable amount.[14]

Example

Arfan is aged 45. He lives with his daughter, Gulshun, who is 25 and earns £100 a week. Arfan's weekly council tax liability is £10. His weekly net income is £79.95 and his applicable amount is £64.30.

Maximum CTB = £10 – £2.30 non-dependant deduction (see p128) = £7.70

Arfan's income is more than his applicable amount.

The difference = £15.65 x 20% = £3.13

Arfan is entitled to £4.57 CTB (£7.70 – £3.13).

Maximum council tax benefit

Maximum CTB is your net weekly liability for council tax after deducting:[15]
- any disability reduction, discount or transitional relief;
- any non-dependant deductions (see p128).

Note:
- If the local authority awards a reduction for a lump-sum payment at the beginning of the financial year (see Chapter 10), CTB is calculated on the basis of your council tax liability disregarding any such reduction.
- If your council tax bill has been increased to recover an overpayment of council tax, any such increase is also ignored for the purpose of working out CTB.

- If an award of a disability reduction or a discount is delayed and you have already been awarded CTB, an overpayment may have been made. This can be recovered by the local authority.[16]

Your net weekly council tax liability is assessed by dividing your annual council tax liability by the number of days in the financial year (365 or 366) and then multiplying this by seven.[17]

Example
Cara's net council tax liability is £805
Divide this by 365 = £2.205479
Multiply this by 7.
Cara's net weekly liability = £15.438355

Department for Work and Pensions' guidance recommends that the figures should not be rounded until the final annual amount of CTB is worked out, and that calculations should usually be done to six decimal places.[18] When notifying you of your CTB a rounded figure can be specified.[19]

Joint council tax liability

If you are a member of a couple and are jointly liable for council tax, one of you must claim CTB for both of you.[20] If you are also jointly liable with one or more other residents, you can claim on a two-person share of the bill.

If you are (or count as) a single person and are jointly liable for council tax, the local authority calculates your maximum CTB by dividing the total net liability for council tax by the number of liable people. Any liable person who is a student not entitled to CTB is ignored.[21]

Example
Ravi, Maxine and Bill share a flat. They are jointly liable for a net annual council tax bill of £600.
£600 divided by 3 = £200.
Ravi and Maxine are a couple. Either of them can make a claim for CTB on £400 liability (a two-person share), with Bill making a separate claim on £200 liability (a one-person share).
Bill becomes a full-time student and is excluded from entitlement to CTB. Ravi and Maxine can now claim CTB on the full £600 liability.

Under the council tax rules, a person who is jointly and severally liable for council tax can be held responsible for the full amount of council tax due on the property while receiving CTB only on her/his share. Note, however, that students who share with non-students are not jointly and severally liable for council tax with the non-students (see p78).[22]

Who is included in the claim

Your claim for CTB includes you and your 'family'. This means your partner and any dependent children and qualifying young people. In deciding whether you have a partner, a similar test applies to that used to determine joint liability for council tax (see p76).

Applicable amount

Your applicable amount is a figure that represents your weekly needs and those of your family (see above) for the purpose of calculating your entitlement to CTB. It is made up of:[23]

- personal allowances. This is an amount the law says you and your family need for living expenses;
- premiums. These are amounts included for certain extra needs;
- components. These are amounts included if you or your partner have (or are treated as having) limited capability for work.

The amounts change each year.

Applicable amounts 2009/10

Personal allowances

Claimant:

– entitled to main phase ESA	£64.30
– aged 18–24	£50.95
– aged 25–59	£64.30
– aged 60–64	£130.00
– aged 65 or over	£150.40
Lone parent aged 18 or over	£64.30
Couple at least one aged 18 or over	£100.95
Couple at least one aged 60–64	£198.45
Couple at least one aged 65 or over	£225.50
Children under 20	£56.11

Premiums

Family:

– ordinary	£17.30
– higher	£27.80
– some lone parents	£22.20
Disabled child	£51.24

Disability:

– single/lone parent	£27.50
– couple	£39.15

Severe disability:

– single/one partner qualifies	£52.85
– couple (both qualify)	£105.70

Enhanced disability:

– single	£13.40
– couple (one or both qualify)	£19.30
Child	£20.65

Carer:

– single/one partner qualifies	£29.50
– couple (both qualify)	£59.00

Components

Work-related activity	£25.50
Support	£30.85

Qualifying conditions for premiums

Premium	*Main conditions*
Family:	
Ordinary rate	Claimant is responsible for a child or qualifying young person.
Higher rate	Family includes a child under one year.
Lone parent rate	Claimant was entitled, or treated as entitled, to lone parent rate on 5 April 1998 and retains transitional protection.
Disabled child	Child or qualifying young person gets disability living allowance (DLA) or is blind. A premium is included for each disabled child or young person.
Disability	Claimant does not have (or is not treated as having) limited capability for work (eg, s/he is not claiming ESA) and:

- claimant has been incapable of work for 364 days (196 days if terminally ill); *or*
- claimant or partner is registered blind or was registered within the previous 28 weeks; *or*
- claimant or partner receives:
  - incapacity benefit (IB) paid at long-term rate (or short-term rate if terminally ill) or was getting this when s/he reached pension age; *or*
  - attendance allowance (AA); *or*
  - DLA; *or*
  - attendance or mobility supplements under the War Pension Scheme; *or*
  - disability or severe disability element of working tax credit (WTC); *or*
  - an NHS allowance for an invalid trike or private car allowance for a disability.

Severe disability	Claimant receives AA or DLA care component (highest or middle rate) or if a couple, they both receive one of those benefits, or one does and the other is registered blind or treated as blind and
	– no one receives carer's allowance (CA) for looking after her/him (or if a couple, for looking after both of them); *and*
	– there are no non-dependants living in the household.
Enhanced disability	Child receives DLA care component (highest rate).
	Claimant or partner is under 60, and receives DLA care component (highest rate), or claimant has (or is treated as having) limited capability for work-related activity.
	Note: claimant can get a premium for each child who qualifies as well as a premium if s/he or her/his partner qualifies.
Carer	Claimant or partner is entitled to CA (even if it is not being paid).
	Note: couples can get a double premium if each partner qualifies.

Qualifying conditions for components

Component	Main conditions
Both components	Claimant or partner has claimed ESA and claimant is not entitled to a disability premium
Work-related activity	Claimant or partner has (or is treated as having) limited capability for work.
Support	Claimant or partner has (or is treated as having) limited capability for work-related activity.

Capital

Whose capital counts

If you are a member of a couple your partner's capital is also included. Any capital that belongs to your child(ren) does not count. Certain capital, however, such as the claimant's home and personal possessions, is disregarded.

Capital limit

The amount of your lower or upper capital limit depends on whether you or your partner are under or over the qualifying age for PC. This is currently age 60, but is due to begin increasing gradually to 65 from April 2010.

Claimants aged under 60

The capital limit is:
- £6,000 lower (£10,000 if you live in a care home);
- £16,000 upper.

If you or your partner get IS, income-based JSA or income-related ESA all of your and your partner's capital is ignored.

In any other case, if you have more than £16,000 capital you are not entitled to main CTB. Any capital below the lower limit is ignored. You are assumed to have a 'tariff income' of £1 a week for every £250, or part of £250, of capital you have over the lower limit.[24]

Note that for second adult rebate, all of your capital is ignored.[25]

Claimants aged 60 or over

If you or your partner are getting the guarantee credit of PC, all of your and your partner's capital is ignored.

In any other case, the capital limit is:

- £6,000 lower (£10,000 if you live in a care home). **Note:** from 2 November 2009 the lower limit is 10,000 for all claimants;
- £16,000 upper.

If you have more than £16,000 capital you are not entitled to main CTB. Capital below the lower limit is ignored. You are treated as having £1 a week 'tariff income' for every £500, or part of £500, of capital you have above the lower limit.[26] Note that for second adult rebate all of your capital is ignored.[27]

Income

Note: if you or your partner are at least the qualifying age for PC (currently 60) and neither of you are getting IS, income-based JSA or income-related ESA, more generous rules on income apply.

Whose income counts

If you are a member of a couple, your partner's income is added to yours.

The income of any dependent child or qualifying young person does not affect the amount of CTB you receive.

What income counts

Income includes both earned and unearned income.[28]

If you get IS, income-based JSA, income-related ESA or the guarantee credit of PC, all your income is ignored for CTB.

If you do not get IS, income-based JSA, income-related ESA or the guarantee credit of PC, all your income counts, unless it is disregarded.

Earnings

Your (and any partner's) weekly net earnings are taken into account. For self-employed people, weekly earnings are averaged out over an 'appropriate period', usually based on the previous year's trading accounts.

The following earnings are disregarded:[29]

- £25 for lone parents;
- £20:
  - if you or your partner qualify for a carer premium; *or*
  - if you or your partner are an auxiliary coastguard, part-time firefighter, part-time member of a lifeboat crew or member of the Territorial Army; *or*
  - if you are under 60 and you or your partner qualify for a disability premium, severe disability premium, work-related activity component or support component; *or*
  - if you are at least the qualifying age for PC (currently 60) and you or your partner:
    - are in receipt of ESA which includes a work-related activity or support component, long-term IB, severe disablement allowance (SDA), AA, DLA, mobility supplement or the disability or severe disability element of WTC; *or*
    - are registered or certified as blind; *or*
    - are, or are treated as, incapable of work and have been for at least 364 days (196 days if terminally ill); *or*
    - have, or are treated as having, limited capability for work or limited capability for work-related activity; *or*
    - previously had an earnings disregard of £20 in your housing benefit (HB) or CTB when you (or your partner) turned 60, or in the period of up to eight weeks before then. The employment must have continued after the end of the previous award of HB or CTB;
- £5 (£10 if you are a member of a couple) if no other disregard applies.

Note: from April 2010, the Government intends to introduce an additional (higher) disregard for those doing 'permitted work' – ie, work you may do while claiming contributory ESA, incapacity benefit or severe disablement allowance.
  In addition to the above disregards, £16.85 is disregarded if:[30]
- you or your partner receive the 30-hour element as part of your WTC;
- you or your partner are aged 25 or over and work 30 hours or more a week on average;
- you or your partner work 16 hours a week or more on average and your CTB includes a family or disability premium or the work-related activity or support component;
- you are a lone parent and work 16 hours or more a week on average;
- you or your partner qualify for a 50+ element in WTC.

An allowance is deducted from earnings for childcare costs of up to £175 a week for one child or up to £300 per week for two or more children if you are:[31]
- a lone parent working 16 hours or more a week; *or*

- a member of a couple, both of whom work 16 hours or more a week, or one works 16 hours or more a week and the other is incapacitated, or in hospital or prison.

The childcare allowance only applies if you have children aged under 15 (16 if disabled) for whom you are paying charges for childcare provided by a registered childminder or certain other childcare providers.

Benefits and tax credits

Benefits and tax credits are generally taken into account as income, unless they are disregarded. **Note:** child benefit and child tax credit (CTC) are taken into account as income (unless you are at least the qualifying age for PC – currently 60). However, child benefit will be ignored in all cases from November 2009.

Unclaimed or unawarded tax credits are not taken into account as income. They only count as income from the date they are awarded.

Benefits that are ignored completely include:
- AA;
- constant attendance allowance, exceptionally severe disablement allowance or severe disablement occupational allowance paid because of an injury at work or a war injury;
- DLA care component and mobility component;
- guardian's allowance;
- mobility supplement under the War Pensions Scheme;
- pensioner's Christmas bonus;
- any extra-statutory payment to compensate for non-payment of IS, income-based JSA, income-related ESA, mobility supplement, AA or DLA;
- social fund payments (also disregarded as capital indefinitely);
- certain payments to war widows, widowers or surviving civil partners for pre-1973 service;
- any increase for adult or child dependants who are not members of your family if you are getting IB, maternity allowance, SDA, widowed mother's allowance, widowed parent's allowance, retirement pension, industrial injuries benefits (including unemployability supplement), CA or a service pension;
- IS, income-based JSA, income-related ESA and the guarantee credit of PC;
- any payment in consequence of a reduction in liability for council tax.

Benefits that have £15 ignored:
- widowed mother's allowance and widowed parent's allowance.

Benefits that have £10 ignored:
- war disablement pension;
- war widow's or widower's or surviving civil partner's pension;

- guaranteed income payments under the Armed Forces and Reserve Forces Compensation Scheme;
- an extra-statutory payment made instead of the above pensions;
- similar payments made by another country;
- a pension from Germany or Austria paid to the victims of Nazi persecution.

Even if you have more than two payments which attract a £10 disregard, if you or your partner are under 60 only £20 in all can be disregarded.

Local authorities are given a limited discretion to increase the £10 disregard on certain war pensions when assessing income for CTB.[32] Some local authorities disregard the full amount of these pensions, and some do not increase the disregard at all, so you should check your own local authority's policy on this issue. It has been held that a local authority must at least consider the nature and purpose of such pensions when deciding whether or not to disregard them, and the courts have indicated that it may be appropriate to apply a disregard to retrospective awards.

Other income

Most other income, such as an occupational pension, is taken into account in full, but some other income is disregarded in full or in part.[33] These include the following.

- Maintenance. For lone parents or couples with children:
  - child maintenance is ignored if it is paid by the child's parent (who is not your partner);
  - £15 of any other maintenance payments paid by your (or your partner's) former partner is disregarded.
- Adoption allowance, residence order allowance, special guardianship allowance. For claimants under 60, these are taken into account up to the amount of the child's personal allowance and disabled child premium.
- Fostering allowance. If the child is boarded out with you by the local authority or a voluntary organisation under specific legal provisions, the child does not count as a member of your family, so you get no benefit for her/him, but the fostering allowance is disregarded. Money from a private fostering allowance is treated as maintenance.
- Voluntary, charitable and personal injury payments from trust funds. These are disregarded.
- Income from tenants living in your home without board. £20 is disregarded.
- Boarders. The first £20 is disregarded and half the remaining balance is taken into account as income.

Non-dependant deductions

If other people normally live with you in your home who are not part of your family for benefit purposes (see p122)) and are not liable for council tax (called 'non-dependants'), a set deduction is usually made from your CTB.[34] This is because it is assumed the non-dependant makes a contribution towards your outgoings, whether or not s/he does so. Examples of non-dependants are adult sons or daughters, or elderly relatives who share your home. You may, therefore, need to ask your non-dependant(s) for a contribution.

A person can only be treated as living with you if s/he shares some accommodation with you. A person does not normally live with you if s/he has not been there long enough to regard your home as her/his normal home.

People who are not non-dependants

The following people do not count as non-dependants, and no non-dependant deduction is made for them, even if they normally live with you:[35]

- a member of your family for benefit purposes (see p122);
- if you are in a polygamous marriage, a partner of yours and any child or qualifying young person in your household for whom you or a partner are responsible;
- a child or qualifying young person living with you who is not a member of your household;
- someone who is employed by a charitable or voluntary organisation as a resident carer for you or your partner and who you pay for the service. This can also apply if a public body pays on your behalf;
- someone who is jointly liable to pay council tax in respect of your home;
- someone who is liable to pay rent on a commercial basis to you or your partner. However, although no non-dependant deduction can be made for her/him, the rent s/he pays can count as your income (see p128).

If the person comes within the last two categories above, s/he can still be treated as your non-dependant if s/he is a close relative of yours or your partner or the agreement to pay rent or council tax is not a commercial one.

When no non-dependant deduction is made

No non-dependant deduction is made if you (or your partner):[36]

- are registered as blind or, having been registered, have regained your eyesight within the last 28 weeks; *or*
- receive AA (or equivalent benefits paid because of injury at work or a war injury) or the care component of DLA.

Example
Denise looks after her pensioner husband who receives the care component of DLA. Their three sons, who are all working full time and earning over £650 each a week, are aged 22, 24 and 26. No non-dependant deduction is made.

No non-dependant deduction is made for any non-dependant who is:[37]

- on IS, income-based JSA, income-related ESA or PC; *or*
- staying with you but whose normal home is elsewhere; *or*
- receiving a training allowance in connection with a youth training scheme under specific provisions; *or*
- a full-time student; *or*
- in hospital for more than 52 weeks. Separate stays which are not more than 28 days apart are added together when calculating the 52 weeks; *or*
- under 18 years old; *or*
- a person who is disregarded for the purpose of a council tax discount – ie:
  - under-20-year-olds for whom child benefit is payable;
  - recent school and college leavers under 20 years;
  - student nurses;
  - foreign language assistants;
  - apprentices;
  - people who are 'severely mentally impaired' (see p102);
  - people in detention;
  - certain carers;
  - members of visiting armed forces, members of international headquarters and defence organisations and their dependants;
  - foreign spouses or dependants of students.

The amount of deductions

If you have a non-dependant living with you who is 18 or over and for whom a deduction must be made, a fixed amount is deducted from your CTB whatever s/he pays you. Unless your non-dependant is in full-time paid work, a £2.30 deduction is made each week. If your non-dependant is in full-time paid work, the amount of the deduction depends on her/his gross weekly income as follows.[38]

Circumstances of the dependant	Deduction
Aged 18 or over and in full-time paid work with a weekly gross income of:	
£382 or more	£6.95
£306 – £381.99	£5.80
£178 – £305.99	£4.60
Below £178	£2.30
Others aged 18 or over (for whom a deduction is made)	£2.30

The above income bands only apply to non-dependants in full-time paid work. This means work of 16 hours a week or more.[39] Remember:
- a non-dependant who is not in (or treated as in) full-time paid work does not attract the higher levels of deduction, even if her/his income exceeds £178;

- if someone is on IS, income-based JSA or income-related ESA for more than three days in a benefit week, s/he does not count as in full-time paid work in that week. This means no deduction is made.[40]

'Gross income' includes both earned and unearned income, but any DLA and AA are disregarded, as are payments from certain trusts and funds.

Your CTB can be assessed using the income and capital of a non-dependant, instead of your own, if you are trying to take advantage of the CTB scheme.

Non-dependant couples

Only one deduction is made for a non-dependant couple (or the members of a polygamous marriage). The deduction made is the highest that would have been made if they were treated as individuals, based on their joint income, even if only one of them is in full-time paid work.[41]

Non-dependants of joint occupiers

If you share liability for the council tax with others, the amount of the non-dependant deduction is divided equally between you, even if the others are not claiming CTB.[42] However, if the local authority thinks that the non-dependant deduction only belongs to one of you, the whole deduction is made from that person's CTB. If you are a member of a couple and share liability with someone, your CTB is reduced by two-thirds of the non-dependant deduction.

Example
Lincoln and Jane are joint tenants. Their son Luke, aged 25, works part time and earns £100 a week gross. A non-dependant deduction of £2.30 is made from Lincoln's weekly net council tax liability for the purpose of calculating maximum CTB.
Luke marries Marcia and the couple live in Lincoln's household. Marcia has a gross weekly income of £95 a week. Only one non-dependant deduction is made, but it is based on the couple's combined gross income. A £4.60 deduction is made from Lincoln's net weekly council tax liability for the purpose of calculating his maximum CTB because Luke and Marcia's combined gross income is between £178 and £305.99.

3. **Who is entitled to second adult rebate**

Alternative maximum council tax benefit (CTB), known as 'second adult rebate', is designed to help you if you share your home with anyone on a low income who does not share liability for council tax with you and who does not pay rent to you (referred to as 'second adults').

You qualify for a second adult rebate if:[43]

- you are liable for council tax in respect of the home where you are 'resident' (see p69); *and*
- you are the only person liable for the council tax on the home (with certain exceptions – see p69); *and*
- no one living in your home pays you rent (with certain exceptions) *and*
- you have one or more 'second adults' (see below) living with you who are on a low income; *and*
- you satisfy the 'right to reside test' and the 'habitual residence test' and are not a 'person subject to immigration control' for benefit purposes.

Note: second adult rebate is based on the circumstances of the 'second adult(s)' living with you. The whole of *your* income and capital is ignored. Therefore you can get second adult rebate even if you have a high income and/or capital worth more than £16,000.[44]

For second adult rebate, it does not matter if you are a student.

Example
Lorraine owns her own home and earns £40,000 a year. She is liable for council tax of £750 a year. Lorraine's adult son Barry, who receives income support, moves in with her. Lorraine loses her 25 per cent single person's discount and her council tax liability is now £1,000. Barry is a second adult. Lorraine is entitled to a second adult rebate of £250.

Second adult rebate is an alternative type of CTB that can be paid instead of, but not as well as, main CTB. Whenever you claim CTB the local authority must assess you for both types and award whichever is the greater.[45]

Who counts as a second adult

A 'second adult' is someone who is resident with you. In practice, residents classified as second adults are mainly the same people as those treated as non-dependants for main CTB purposes (see p128). However, someone residing with you does not count as a second adult if:[46]

- s/he is aged under 18;[47] *or*
- s/he has a status discount – ie, s/he is disregarded for council tax purposes (see p92);[48] *or*
- s/he is your partner with whom you are jointly liable for council tax;[49] *or*
- s/he is jointly liable to pay the council tax on the dwelling with you – eg, because s/he is a joint owner or tenant. Although you cannot get second adult rebate for her/him, s/he may be able to claim main CTB for her/his own share of the bill – see p116).[50]

No one who resides with you counts as a second adult (and you therefore cannot get second adult rebate) if:

- you are a member of a couple or polygamous marriage, unless both you and your partner (or in the case of polygamous marriages, at least two of you) have status discounts;[51] *or*
- you:[52]
  - are living with one or more other people, all of whom are jointly liable for council tax with you (eg, as joint owners or tenants); *and*
  - at least two of those of you who are jointly liable do *not* have status discounts.

Examples

Jason's elderly widowed mother lives with him. Jason is liable for council tax and can claim second adult rebate as his mother is a second adult.

Dorinda is the tenant of a three-bedroom house. She lives with her partner, who is a full-time student and is disregarded for the purpose of a council tax discount. Their 20-year-old daughter and 25-year-old son live with them. The daughter is unemployed and in receipt of income-based jobseeker's allowance. The son is in low-paid employment. Dorinda may claim the second adult rebate as the adult daughter and son are second adults.

Phoebe is a lone parent who lives with her two children aged 10 and 14. She is not entitled to second adult rebate as there are no second adults in the dwelling.

You cannot qualify for second adult rebate if a second adult who lives with you is liable to pay you rent in respect of her/his occupation of your home. Any people paying you rent who do not count as second adults are ignored for these purposes.[53] Some local authorities think you are not entitled to second adult rebate if *any* resident is liable to pay you rent. You should argue that if a person paying you rent does not come within the description of a second adult, s/he does not prevent you receiving second adult rebate.

4. **How second adult rebate is calculated**

The amount of second adult rebate you get is a percentage of your council tax liability based on the gross income of the second adult.[54]

Income of second adult(s)	Second adult rebate
Second adult (or all second adults) on income support (IS)/ income-based jobseeker's allowance (JSA)/income-related employment and support allowance (ESA)/pension credit (PC)	25 per cent

Second adult(s) total gross weekly income:

Below £175	15 per cent
£175–£227.99	7.5 per cent
£228 or more	Nil

Student dwellings

Occupiers are either students excluded from entitlement to main   100 per cent
council tax benefit (CTB) or on IS/income-based JSA/income-
related ESA/PC. At least one must be a student and at least one
on IS/income-based JSA/income-related ESA/PC.

For the 100 per cent rebate, someone counts as a student excluded from entitlement to main CTB if s/he would be excluded if s/he were under the qualifying age for PC (currently 60).

Unless you qualify for a 100 per cent rebate, the maximum second adult rebate you can get is always 25 per cent of your council tax liability, even if you would have received a 50 per cent discount, or would have been exempt altogether, were it not for the presence of two or more second adults in your home.

Examples

Liam is a student who lives alone in a home he owns, so he is exempt from paying council tax. His friend Brian who is on IS comes to lodge with him, so Liam is now liable for council tax. Liam claims second adult rebate. This is 100 per cent of his council tax liability.

Ravi is the tenant of his flat. He is in a very well paid job so lets his friend Carl stay with him without charging him rent. Carl earns £190 per week. Ravi's second adult rebate is 7.5 per cent of his council tax liability.

Council tax liability used for a second adult rebate

Second adult rebate is based on your gross council tax liability, after any disability reduction and, in the case of 100 per cent rebate, any discounts, have been applied.[55] Note that this is not the same figure as is used for main CTB. However, the procedure for converting annual to weekly amounts is the same (see p121). Any reduction in council tax liability from a discount (see Chapter 8) is ignored for the purpose of second adult rebate. In other words, if a discount has been granted it must be added back on to the net amount of council tax to arrive at the figure used in the second adult rebate calculation. The discount itself is still granted.

Assessment of second adult income

To obtain a second adult rebate, you must give the local authority details of the gross income of any second adults living with you. If there is more than one second adult, their combined gross income is used.[56]

Gross income includes the second adult's:
- earnings;
- non-earned income, including social security benefits;
- actual income from capital (as opposed to, for example, 'tariff income'). The capital itself is ignored.

Gross income does *not* include:[57]
- any income of a second adult on IS, income-based JSA, income-related ESA or PC;
- any attendance allowance or disability living allowance;
- certain payments from the MacFarlane Trusts, the Eileen Trust, the Skipton Fund, the London Bombings Relief Charitable Fund, the Fund and the Independent Living Fund (2006);
- the income of any person with a status discount (see p92), except where that person has a partner who is not ignored for discount purposes (in which case the gross income of both partners, less disregarded income, is taken into account).

A basic problem with second adult rebate is that it involves looking at the income of someone who may not always wish to give you that information. If you have difficulty establishing the income of your second adults you may find that the local authority automatically assumes the highest income and that you are not entitled to CTB. If you cannot persuade your second adults to give details of their income to you, they may be prepared to tell the local authority directly. Failing this, you could try finding out the going rate for the type of work they do, or social security benefits they receive, and ask the local authority to make a reasonable estimate based on that. The local authority should not assume the worst. It should assess what the likely level of your second adult's earnings are on the evidence available.[58]

Second adult rebate and jointly liable claimants

In contrast to main CTB, if there is more than one resident liable for the council tax in your dwelling, any second adult rebate is always calculated on the (pre-discounted) liability for your dwelling as a whole. Any second adult rebate arising is then apportioned equally between all the liable residents (except if the claimant is jointly liable with only a partner).[59] Unless you are jointly liable with your partner, every jointly liable person must make her/his own separate claim in order to get a share of the second adult rebate. However, if you are jointly liable with your partner, one of you claims on behalf of both and receives the entire second adult rebate (or if you are sharing with other liable residents, a couple's share).[60]

5. **Claiming and getting paid**

You should claim council tax benefit (CTB) as soon as you think you might be entitled or you may lose benefit. The rules about backdating are explained on p139.

If you want to claim discretionary housing payments, you must claim separately. See p142 for further information.

Making a claim

All claims for CTB must be made in writing on a properly completed claim form, unless you are allowed to claim by telephone or are claiming income support (IS), income-based jobseeker's allowance (JSA), income-related employment and support allowance (ESA), incapacity benefit (IB) or pension credit (PC) by telephone. You must provide any information and evidence required on the claim form. You can claim in some other written form (eg, by letter) so long as the written information and evidence you provide is sufficient.[61] Claim forms are available from your local authority. If your local authority has authorised it, you can also claim by electronic communication – eg online or by email.[62]

In addition, if you are claiming:

- IS, income-based JSA or PC on a written claim form, you are given a CTB (and housing benefit (HB)) claim form with your IS/JSA/PC form. This is also available from the Department for Work and Pensions (DWP) website. You should complete this and return it to the local authority. The local authority may ask you to complete its own form. You should do this as soon as possible. It should not ask you to complete its own form if you claim CTB when you claim PC;
- IS, income-based JSA or IB via a contact centre, your CTB (and HB) claims are usually completed at the same time. The DWP takes your details over the telephone and sends you a statement of your circumstances to check, sign and return to the Jobcentre Plus office, along with evidence to support your claim. The Jobcentre Plus office forwards your claim, to the local authority. When you claim ESA via a contact centre you are issued with a CTB (and HB) claim form to complete and return to the local authority. At some point in the future, you will be able to complete your claim for CTB (and HB) at the same time as your claim for ESA.
- IS, JSA, ESA, IB or PC by telephone, if the DWP agrees, you can also claim CTB (and HB) by telephone to the number specified by the DWP for this purpose. You can do this at any time before a decision is made on your claim for IS, JSA, ESA, IB or PC. You may be asked for further information (see p138). The local authority or DWP may provide a written statement of your circumstances. For your claim to be valid, you must approve this statement.

If the DWP agrees, you can claim CTB (and HB) when you are providing evidence or information that is required, or notifying a change of circumstances, in connection with your claim for IS, JSA, ESA, IB or PC. You can do this at any time before a decision is made on the award of benefit to which the evidence, information or change of circumstances relates. Although the rules do not say so, the intention is that you can make your claim for CTB (and HB) by telephone in this situation. You may be asked to provide further information (see p138).

If you are claiming CTB in writing, send your claim in as soon as you can so you do not lose benefit. Keep a copy of your claim in case queries arise.

If you have:[63]

- not completed the claim form properly, the local authority can return it to you to do so or ask you for further information or evidence. However, if you sent or gave your claim form to the DWP, it can ask you to provide the local authority with information needed to complete the form; *or*
- claimed by letter, the local authority can send you a claim form to complete properly or ask you for further information or evidence; *or*
- claimed CTB by telephone to the local authority, it must give you an opportunity to provide the information required; *or*
- claimed CTB by telephone to the DWP, the DWP can give you an opportunity to provide the information required. However, if the DWP does not do so, the local authority *must* give you an opportunity to provide the information, unless it thinks it already has sufficient information.

If you return the form properly completed or provide the information or evidence within one month, your claim is treated as though it was received on the date of your original claim.[64] The local authority can allow you longer than one month if it thinks this reasonable. Note that if you claimed CTB by telephone to the DWP and you do not provide the information within the time limit, the local authority can treat your claim, as though it was received on the date of your original claim, if it thinks it already has sufficient information.

You might be able to complete a shortened CTB claim form – known as 'rapid reclaim' – if you are also making a rapid reclaim for IS, incapacity benefit, ESA or JSA.

Remember:

- you can claim CTB even if you have already paid your council tax bill in advance;
- if you are in arrears with your council tax bill, this does not affect your right to claim CTB. You may even be able to get your claim backdated (see p139).

Where to make your claim

If you claim **in writing**, you must usually send or give your claim to:[65]

- your DWP office or the local authority's designated office if you or your partner are claiming IS, JSA, ESA, IB or PC. If you send your form to the DWP, it must forward it to the local authority within two working days of the date your CTB claim was received or as soon as practicable after that; *or*

- if you are at least the qualifying age for PC (currently 60), any office nominated by the DWP and authorised by the local authority to receive your claim.

Keep a copy of your claim form wherever possible. Ask for confirmation that you have delivered it to the relevant office.

If your local authority has authorised it, and you are claiming **by electronic communication**, check the correct address for this with your local authority.

If you are allowed to claim **by telephone**, you must make your claim to the telephone number published for this purpose.[66]

Information to support your claim

Where possible, your claim should be accompanied by all the information and evidence needed to assess it, but you should not delay your claim just because you do not have all the evidence ready to send. Even if you provide all the information required with your claim, the local authority might ask you for further evidence or information. You must then supply this within one month.[67] You can ask for a longer period and local authorities can allow this if they think it reasonable.

You and your partner must usually satisfy the national insurance (NI) number requirement. If you have claimed CTB in association with a claim for IS, JSA, ESA, IB or PC and the DWP has accepted that you satisfy the NI number requirement, the local authority can accept that it is also satisfied for CTB purposes.

Who should claim

If you are a single person or a lone parent, you make a claim for CTB on your own behalf. If you are one of a couple, you can decide between you who should claim. See p122 for who counts as a couple. The choice of claimant may affect the level of CTB you receive – eg, if one of you is a full-time student and not entitled to CTB (see p117).

If a person is either temporarily or permanently unable to manage her/his own affairs, the local authority must accept a claim made by someone formally appointed to act legally on her/his behalf.

If no one has been formally appointed to look after a claimant's affairs, the local authority can decide to make someone aged over 18 an appointee who can act on her/his behalf. For the purpose of the claim, an appointee has the responsibility of exercising all rights and duties as though s/he were the claimant.

The date of your claim

Your date of claim is important because it affects the date from which your CTB begins. In some cases, you can claim in advance and in some cases your claim can be backdated (see p139).

Your 'date of claim' is usually the earliest of:[68]
- the date you first notify a designated office, DWP office or authorised office (or county council office, if the local authority has arranged for claims there) that you want to claim CTB (eg, by telephone or in person or where someone does this on your behalf), if a properly completed claim form is received in one of those offices within one month. The one-month period can be extended if the local authority thinks it is reasonable; *or*
- the date your valid claim is received by the designated office, DWP office or authorised office (or county council office, if the local authority has arranged for claims there).

There are exceptions to the rule.[69]

Backdating

It is very important to claim in time. A claim for CTB can be backdated:
- if you are at least the qualifying age for PC (currently 60) and neither you nor your partner are on IS, income-based JSA or income-related ESA, for up to three months. You only need to show that you qualified for CTB during that period;[70] *or*
- in all other cases, for up to six months. However, you must show that you qualified for CTB during that period *and* prove you have continuous 'good cause' for your failure to claim throughout the whole time for which you want to claim.[71] **Note:** the Government may reduce backdating to three months at some point in the future.

Any backdated CTB is calculated based on your circumstances and the CTB rules as they were over the backdating period.

You must ask for your CTB to be backdated for this to be considered. CTB can only be backdated from the date of your request for backdating, not from the date of your original claim for CTB.

There is a special rule if your local authority has not set its council tax rate by the beginning of the financial year.[72] As long as you claim within one month of the council tax being set or imposed, your claim is backdated to 1 April or the date you first became entitled to CTB if that is later.

When your entitlement begins and ends

Your entitlement to CTB starts:[73]
- if you became liable for council tax in the first of the weeks for which you are claiming, from the Monday of that week; *or*
- in all other cases, from the Monday following your date of claim (or following the date from which you are claiming if your claim is backdated).

Your entitlement to CTB ends if your circumstances change in a way that means you no longer satisfy the rules described in this chapter. **Note:** if you stop claiming IS, income-based JSA or income-related ESA, your entitlement to CTB continues without you having to make a fresh claim, but your new circumstances could affect the amount of CTB you get.

Continuing payments

There are two situations when your CTB can continue to be paid even though your entitlement may otherwise have changed. If you stop claiming:

- IS, income-based JSA, or income-related ESA because you or your partner are moving onto PC, you may qualify for continuing payments of CTB for four weeks pending the assessment of the claim for PC;[74]
- IS, income-based JSA, ESA (either contributory or income-related), IB or severe disablement allowance (SDA) because of moving into work or increasing your hours or earnings, you may be entitled to extended payments of CTB (and HB) – see below.

Getting paid

There is no minimum entitlement to CTB. This means you are paid CTB however low your entitlement is.

Payment is normally made by making a reduction to your annual council tax bill. If your CTB cannot be used to reduce your bill – eg, if you have already paid your council tax, payment can be made directly to you.

Extended payments

If you or your partner have been on IS, income-based JSA, ESA, IB or SDA for at least 26 weeks and entitlement to that benefit ends because you (or s/he) start full-time work or because of increased hours or earnings, you can qualify for extended payments of CTB for up to four weeks. If the amount of CTB you received before the entitlement to IS, income-based JSA, ESA, IB or SDA ended was higher than your CTB entitlement based on your new circumstances, you may be entitled to continue to receive the higher amount of CTB.[75] If you pay rent, you may also be entitled to extended payments of HB.

Overpayments

The local authority may recover overpaid CTB ('excess benefit') except where:[76]

- it was caused by official error; *and*
- no 'relevant person' caused the official error; *and*
- no 'relevant person' could reasonably have been expected to be aware that it was an overpayment at the time of payment or the receipt of any notification relating to the payment.

The local authority must notify you of the overpayment, the reasons for it, the amount, how it was calculated, what benefit weeks it relates to and how recovery is to be made. It must also notify you of your right to ask for a written explanation and your right to appeal.

The local authority usually recovers overpaid CTB by debiting a claimant's council tax account and should, therefore, advise you of your increased liability.

Suspension of benefit

A local authority may suspend payment of CTB wholly or in part where:[77]
- an appeal by the local authority is pending;
- a question has arisen about your entitlement;
- it looks as if your award should be superseded or revised;
- you are not living at the last notified address;
- a recoverable overpayment may have occurred.

A local authority may also suspend benefit if a claimant fails to provide information needed to determine CTB entitlement.[78] A person in this situation must either:
- supply the requested information within one month or such period as the local authority sets to comply with the requirement; *or*
- satisfy the relevant authority that it is not possible for her/him to obtain the information or evidence required.

Change of circumstances

It is your duty to report any change in circumstances which you might reasonably be expected to know might affect your right to, or the amount of, CTB. You should do this promptly in writing (although in individual cases, notification might be accepted in a form other than in writing). If your local authority allows you to claim CTB by telephone, you can also report a change in circumstances by telephone (unless it says you must do this in writing). If your local authority authorises it, you can also report changes by electronic means. However, for fraud purposes, you must report changes in writing. It is always best to report a change in writing and to keep a copy in case of a dispute in the future.

If you do not report a change promptly in writing, any resulting overpayment may be recoverable from you. If you are considered to have deliberately acted falsely or dishonestly, you may also be guilty of an offence.

A change in circumstances normally affects your CTB from the Monday after it occurs.

6. Challenging decisions

The main ways to change a decision on your council tax benefit (CTB) are:
- **within a month** of the date you are sent or given a decision:
  - by revision on any grounds;
  - by appeal on any grounds. You can appeal against an original decision, a revision, a refusal to revise where this was requested within a month or a refusal to supersede (see below).

  In limited circumstances, you can ask for a revision, or appeal, outside the one-month period;
- **at any time:**
  - by supersession, on specific grounds – eg, because your circumstances have changed or there was a mistake about the facts of your case;
  - by 'any time' revision on specific grounds, including official error.

In practice, local authorities often refer to these ways of changing decisions as 'reconsiderations'. However, you should use the proper term wherever possible. Any request for your CTB award to be looked at again in any of these ways must be made in writing, and you must sign a request for an appeal. Appeals are heard by the First-tier Tribunal.

7. Discretionary housing payments

Discretionary housing payments (DHPs) are extra payments that can be paid by the local authority to help meet your council tax liability if:[79]
- you are entitled to housing benefit (HB) or council tax benefit (CTB); *and*
- you appear to require some financial assistance in addition to your HB or CTB to meet your housing costs (this includes council tax).

Local authorities have discretion whether to pay you, what amount to pay you (within certain limits) and over what period to pay you.[80] DHPs are not taxable.

Payments not met by discretionary housing payments

DHPs cannot be made to you if your need for financial assistance arises as a consequence of:[81]
- ineligible services charges under the HB scheme;
- water and sewerage charges;
- council tax liability if you are entitled to HB but not CTB;
- liabilities that can be met by HB if you are entitled to CTB but not HB;
- council tax liability if you are only entitled to second adult rebate and are not, or would not otherwise have been, entitled to CTB;

- your rent payments being increased to cover arrears of rent, service charges or other unpaid charges;
- a reduced benefit decision because you refused to co-operate in pursuing maintenance for your child(ren);
- your benefit being reduced because you refused to attend a work-focused interview;
- your jobseeker's allowance being stopped or reduced because you left your work voluntarily or you lost your job because of misconduct;
- your benefit being suspended;
- a reduction in the amount of your HB or CTB because an overpayment is being recovered;
- your benefit being restricted because a court has decided that you failed to comply with a community order without reasonable excuse or under the 'loss of benefit for benefit offences' rules.

The amount of discretionary housing payments

DHPs are normally paid in weekly amounts. It is up to the local authority to decide for how long you can be paid and how far your payments can be backdated.[82] However, the local authority can only pay DHPs for periods during which you are (or were) entitled to HB or CTB (or both). You cannot be paid more than your weekly council tax liability.[83]

Claims

A claim for a DHP is separate from your claim for CTB. You claim from the local authority and you should ask it how to make a claim. The local authority may accept a claim from you, or from someone acting on your behalf, as long as you are entitled to HB or CTB.[84] Your local authority does not have to insist that your claim is made in writing, but it decides what 'form or manner' your claim should take.[85]

You must provide grounds for your claim and provide any other information that the local authority specifies.[86] If you want your claim to be backdated, tell the local authority.

Getting paid

You must be given written notice of the local authority's decision on your claim and the reasons for its decision as soon 'as is reasonably practicable'.[87] It can pay you or, if reasonable, someone else where appropriate.[88]

Change of circumstances

As with CTB, it is your duty to report any changes in circumstances which you might reasonably be expected to know might affect your right to, the amount of, or payment of your benefit.

Challenging a decision

You do not have the right of appeal to the First-tier Tribunal against a DHP decision. You can ask the local authority for a review of its decision.[89] Judicial review may be available if a local authority has wrongly exercised its discretion.[90]

Notes

1   Reg 57(4) CTB Regs; reg 40(4) CTB(SPC) Regs

1. Who is entitled to main council tax benefit
2   s131(1)(a) and (3)-(5) SSCBA 1992
3   Reg 16 CTB(SPC) Regs
4   s131(11) SSCBA 1992; s6(5) LGFA 1992
5   R(H) 3/08
6   Reg 8(5) and (6)(c) CTB Regs; reg 8(5) and (6)(c) CTB(SPC) Regs
7   s131(3)(b) SSCBA 1992; reg 8 CTB Regs; reg 8 CTB(SPC) Regs
8   R(H) 9/05
9   R(H) 3/08
10 Reg 43(2) CTB Regs
11 Reg 43 CTB Regs, definition of 'full-time course of study' and 'full-time student'
12 Reg 43(2)-(4) CTB Regs
13 Reg 45(3), (3A) and (7) CTB Regs

2. How main council tax benefit is calculated
14 Reg 59 CTB Regs; reg 43 CTB(SPC) Regs
15 Reg 57(1) and (2) CTB Regs; reg 40(1) and (2) CTB(SPC) Regs
16 Regs 82 and 83 CTB Regs; regs 67 and 68 CTB(SPC) Regs
17 Reg 57(1) CTB Regs; reg 40(1) CTB(SPC) Regs
18 A5 Annex B GM
19 Sch 8 paras 9-10 CTB Regs; Sch 7 paras 9-10 CTB(SPC) Regs
20 Reg 57(4) CTB Regs; reg 40(4) CTB(SPC) Regs
21 Reg 57(3) CTB Regs; reg 40(3) CTB(SPC) Regs
22 **EW** ss6(4) and 9(2) LGFA 1992
    S Sch 1 para 4(2) LGFA 1992
    EWS Sch 1 para 4(2) LGFA 1992. Note that the definition of student is different from that for CTB.

23 Regs 12 and 13 and Sch 1 CTB Regs; reg 12 and Sch 1 CTB(SPC) Regs
24 Reg 42 CTB Regs
25 Sch 5 para 46(1) CTB Regs
26 Reg 19(2) CTB(SPC) Regs
27 Sch 4 para 26A CTB(SPC) Regs
28 Part 4 CTB Regs; part 4 CTB(SPC) Regs
29 Regs 26 and 28 and Sch 3 CTB Regs; reg 23(8) and Sch 2 CTB(SPC) Regs
30 Sch 3 para 16 CTB Regs; Sch 2 para 9 CTB(SPC) Regs
31 Regs 17 and 18 CTB Regs; regs 20 and 21 CTB(SPC) Regs
32 s139 SSAA 1992
33 Reg 30 and Sch 4 CTB Regs; regs 19 and 23 and Sch 3 CTB(SPC) Regs
34 Regs 3 and 57 CTB Regs; regs 3 and 40 CTB(SPC) Regs
35 Reg 3(2) CTB Regs; reg 3(2) CTB(SPC) Regs
36 Reg 58(6) CTB Regs; reg 42(6) CTB(SPC) Regs
37 Reg 58(7) CTB Regs; reg 42(7) CTB(SPC) Regs
38 Reg 58 (1), (2) and (9) CTB Regs; reg 42(1), (2) and (9) CTB(SPC) Regs
39 Reg 6 CTB Regs; reg 6 CTB(SPC) Regs
40 Reg 6(6) CTB Regs; reg 6(6) CTB(SPC) Regs
41 Reg 58(3) and (4) CTB Regs; reg 42(3) and (4) CTB(SPC) Regs
42 Reg 58(5) CTB Regs; reg 42(5) CTB(SPC) Regs

3. Who is entitled to second adult rebate
43 s131(1)(b), (3) and (6) SSCBA 1992
44 Sch 5 para 46(1) CTB Regs; reg 16 and Sch 4 para 26A CTB(SPC) Regs
45 s131(9) SSCBA 1992; CH/48/2006
46 s131(7) SSCBA 1992
47 s6(5) LGFA 1992
48 Sch 1 LGFA 1992

49 Reg 63(a) CTB Regs; reg 47(a) CTB(SPC) Regs
50 Reg 63(c) CTB Regs; reg 47(c) CTB(SPC) Regs
51 Reg 63(b) CTB Regs; reg 47(b) CTB(SPC) Regs
52 Reg 63(d) CTB Regs; reg 47(d) CTB(SPC) Regs
53 s131(6)(a) and (7) SSCBA 1992

4. How second adult rebate is calculated
54 Reg 62 and Sch 2 para 1 CTB Regs; reg 46 and Sch 6 para 1 CTB(SPC) Regs
55 Reg 62 and Sch 2 para 1(2) CTB Regs; reg 46 and Sch 6 para 1(2) CTB(SPC) Regs
56 Reg 62 and Sch 2 para 1 CTB Regs; reg 46 and Sch 6 para 1 CTB(SPC) Regs
57 Sch 2 paras 1, 2 and 3 CTB Regs; Sch 6 paras 1, 2 and 3 CTB (SPC) Regs
58 CH/48/2006
59 Reg 62(2) CTB Regs; reg 46(2) CTB(SPC) Regs
60 Reg 62(3) CTB Regs; reg 46(3) CTB(SPC) Regs

5. Claiming and getting paid
61 Reg 69(1) and (9) CTB Regs; reg 53(1) and (9) CTB(SPC) Regs
62 Reg 69A and Sch 9 CTB Regs; reg 53A and Sch 8 CTB(SPC) Regs
63 Reg 69(4D), (4DA) and (7) CTB Regs; reg 53 (4E), (4EA) and (7) CTB(SPC) Regs
64 Reg 69(4E), (4F), (8) and (8A) CTB Regs; reg 53(4F), (4G), (8) and (8A) CTB(SPC) Regs
65 Reg 69 CTB Regs; reg 53 CTB(SPC) Regs
66 Reg 69(4A) and (4AA) CTB Regs; reg 53(4A) and (4AA) CTB(SPC) Regs
67 Reg 72(1) CTB Regs; reg 57(1) CTB(SPC) Regs
68 Reg 69(5)(d) and (e) CTB Regs; reg 53(5)(d) and (e) CTB(SPC) Regs
69 Reg 69(5)(a)-(c) CTB Regs; reg 53(5)(a)-(c) CTB(SPC) Regs
70 Regs 53(1ZA) and 56 CTB(SPC) Regs
71 Reg 69(14) CTB Regs
72 Reg 69(11) CTB Regs; reg 53(11) CTB(SPC) Regs
73 Reg 64 CTB Regs; reg 48 CTB(SPC) Regs
74 Reg 45(3)-(5) CTB(SPC) Regs
75 Regs 60-61D CTB Regs; regs 44-44D CTB(SPC) Regs
76 Reg 83 CTB Regs; reg 68 CTB(SPC) Regs
77 Reg 11 HBCTB(DA) Regs
78 Reg 13 HBCTB(DA) Regs

7. Discretionary housing payments
79 s69 CSPSSA 2000; reg 2(1) DFA Regs
80 Reg 2(2) DFA Regs
81 Reg 3 DFA Regs
82 Reg 5 DFA Regs
83 Reg 4 DFA Regs
84 Reg 6 DFA Regs
85 Reg 6(1)(a) DFA Regs
86 Reg 7 DFA Regs
87 Reg 6(3) DFA Regs
88 Reg 6(2) DFA Regs
89 Reg 8 DFA Regs
90 *R(on the application of Gargett) v London Borough of Lambeth* [2008] EWCA 1450, 18 December 2008

Chapter 10

∙∙

Bills and payments

This chapter explains:
1. Who has to pay the bill (below)
2. When bills should be issued (p147)
3. How the bill is calculated (p149)
4. How bills are served (p150)
5. Information the bill should contain (p150)
6. Appeals against the amount of the bill (p152)
7. Payment arrangements (p152)
8. Estimates based on incorrect assumptions (p158)
9. Incorrect payments (p158)
10. Penalties (p159)

---

1. Who has to pay the bill

Chapter 6 identified the people who are liable for council tax, but in most cases no one need actually pay the tax until a bill has been issued.[1] If the name of a liable person cannot be established after reasonable enquiries have been made by the local authority, the bill may be addressed to 'The Council Tax Payer'.[2]

Local authorities should seek to ensure that their computer systems do not issue bills in the name of taxpayers who have died. These should normally be sent to the 'personal representatives of . . . deceased' or the 'executors of the deceased'.

In Scotland, a bill need not be issued if the only liable person is a housing body (ie, a local council, new town development corporation or Communities Scotland) or an owner who has agreed with the local authority that a bill need not be served.[3]

The liable person's spouse or unmarried partner, and anyone who has the same degree of legal interest in the dwelling, is jointly liable for the bill (see Chapter 6). In Scotland, but not England and Wales, someone who is jointly liable with the person(s) named on the bill but whose name is not included on the bill is still liable to make any payments required.[4]

In England and Wales, no payment can be required of someone who is jointly liable if s/he has not been included on the bill, until a 'joint taxpayers' bill' has been issued.[5] This must be served within six years of the first day of the financial year to which it relates. It is up to the liable people themselves to determine how exactly they share out responsibility for the bill.

Joint liability means that both or all jointly liable taxpayers can be held individually or collectively liable to pay the whole amount.

2. **When bills should be issued**

Each financial year the local authority should serve a council tax bill on each chargeable dwelling. In England and Wales this should be done 'as soon as practicable' (see below) after the local authority first sets a council tax for the year.[6] In Scotland, a local authority should serve the bill as soon as practicable after it has first set a council tax and knows the water charge for the year.[7]

Separate bills have to be sent for different financial years and for different dwellings, even if the same person is liable for both.[8] In England and Wales, however, one council tax bill may also cover the current and preceding financial years if it is in respect of the same dwelling.[9]

Local authorities will want to ensure that bills are produced promptly to maximise their cash flows. Most local authorities aim to send out council tax bills in mid-March with the payment falling due from 1 April. People paying by direct debit may be given several dates in April on which to make their first payment. In Scotland, local authorities now have two options for starting annual billing. The established method of 10 annual instalments can be used, or the local authority may select April as the first instalment date and end in January.

Late service of bills

A local authority must issue a bill 'as soon as reasonably practicable'. In cases where there has been a delay of years, the local authority may not be able to recover the money if it has been in breach of this requirement. In one case, the local authority delayed seven years before serving demand notices for the years 1990–1997 under analogous provisions for non-domestic rates.[10] When the ratepayers failed to pay, the local authority obtained liability orders. The High Court, however, quashed the liability orders as the delay in serving the demand notices was 'inexcusable'. A common sense approach should be taken when deciding whether a local authority has acted as soon as reasonably practicable.

The High Court has recently indicated, however, that late bills may be valid, even if they are sent several years after the tax fell due. In *Regentford Ltd v Thanet District Council*, a company which had been pursued for an earlier financial year sought to quash a liability order obtained in its absence by the local authority on 20 January 2003 in respect of council tax for 1996/97.[11] The council tax had been set on 22 February 1996, but the local authority had not sent out a bill to the company until 2 October 2002.

The High Court considered that the bill only became payable when it was served. Although the enforcement regulations place a six-year limitation period on the initiation of recovery proceedings, this is different to the requirement to serve a bill. Time began to flow from the date of the demand notice. This must be served before a final notice, after which an application could be made to the magistrates' court.

This is a surprising decision given the length of time between setting the.tax and serving the demand. However, the High Court indicated that magistrates have a discretion to refuse an application for a liability order where a taxpayer may suffer 'prejudice'.

In *Regentford*, the Court may have taken a more rigid approach because the taxpayer was a limited company rather than, for example, an individual who might have been entitled to a discount or benefit and might reasonably be expected to have difficultly in recalling her/his precise financial circumstances in earlier years.

It might be possible to argue that difficulties may arise for individuals who are sent council tax bills in respect of previous financial years not accounting for any council tax benefit (CTB) entitlement that might have existed at the time. Indeed, any application for CTB in respect of earlier financial years will be thwarted by the benefit backdating rules (see p139). Following *Regentford*, it appears the Court expects a person to contest liability order proceedings involving a late bill in the hope of magistrates dismissing the application. Arguably, prejudice is caused to anyone who effectively loses a right to claim CTB which might have covered the total liability for the year concerned. Any challenge against the late issue of bills must be made before a liability order is issued by a magistrates' court[12] and it may be necessary for a taxpayer to argue that s/he has been 'prejudiced' by the late service of the bill. In the case of a person entitled to CTB, this may be relatively easy to do as entitlement cannot be backdated by more than three/six months (see Chapter 9).

Another remedy might be to lodge an appeal with a valuation tribunal or valuation appeal committee under section 16 (section 81 in Scotland) of the Local Government Finance Act 1992, which allows appeals on 'any calculation' in respect of a sum of council tax. The right to appeal arises as soon as the taxpayer becomes aware of the bill.

In an unreported decision in *Hardy v Sefton*, the High Court again endorsed the power of magistrates to reject an application for a liability order where 'prejudice' had been caused to the taxpayer as a result of late billing.[13]

Reducing council tax if a bill is served late

A local authority has the power to reduce an individual council tax bill (see Chapter 4). In cases where a bill is served late, perhaps years after the original liability arose, an application to the local authority should be made to reduce the sum concerned.

Late service of a bill may amount to maladministration (see Chapter 13) and cause hardship. While the bill being served late does not automatically make it invalid, a local authority would be expected to act sympathetically and reasonably to anyone prejudiced through official error, including giving her/him time to pay. A failure to respond properly if a late bill causes hardship to a vulnerable person may amount to maladministration. If a council has an anti-poverty strategy, it is expected to act in accordance with it.

3. **How the bill is calculated**

Liability for council tax is calculated on a daily basis. However, the bill issued at the beginning of the financial year is for the full year. The local authority is required to use certain assumptions in estimating what it thinks the council tax will be for the whole year.

The local authority must estimate the 'chargeable amount' by taking the relevant amount of council tax for that dwelling (depending on its valuation band), and then make the following assumptions.
- The person will be liable for every day.
- The dwelling's valuation band will not change and it will remain a chargeable dwelling throughout the year.
- Any reduction under the disability reduction scheme has been properly calculated and applies throughout the year.
- The bill will be either eligible or not eligible for a discount throughout the year.
- Any council tax benefit (CTB) will apply throughout the year.[14]
- Liability for Scottish Water charges will apply throughout the year in Scotland.[15]

If more than one reduction applies to the council tax for the band, they must be applied in the following order:
- disability reduction scheme;
- discount;
- any discretionary reduction (see Chapter 4);
- CTB.

The local authority must ensure that if 100 per cent CTB is awarded, this is equal to your liability.

The bill can also take into account any credits from past periods, penalties due and repayment of any overpaid CTB.

Special rules apply if a bill is for a period earlier in the financial year, and if on the day it is issued you are no longer liable for council tax at that address. The bill will either:
- require payment of the amount due up to the last day of liability (calculated as described above but based on the actual, not estimated, circumstances); *or*

- if you are due a credit, require the amount payable (if any) after the credit has been offset against the chargeable amount.[16] This could apply, for example, following a delay in calculating CTB.

A bill that is issued after the end of the year to which it relates must require payment of the amount due for the year, calculated as described above, but based on the actual circumstances and after taking into account any credits carried over from earlier years.

4. **How bills are served**

Before you are required to pay council tax, a bill must be served. Bills may be served by:
- post; *or*
- being delivered to the liable person at her/his usual or last known address; *or*
- being delivered to some other person at the chargeable dwelling; *or*
- being fixed to some conspicuous part of the dwelling; *or*
- email.

In the case of a limited company, the bill should be addressed to the company's registered office and, in the case of a partnership, to the principal office of the partnership.

If a bill has been served in one of the above ways, the date of issue is the date the bill was posted or left at the address. In all other cases, it is the date of actual service of the notice. The bill should include the date of issue, which determines such matters as when payments become due.[17] Practice Note No. 5 (para 5.4) reminds local authorities to ensure that when a bill is sent by post, the first instalment due under it is payable at least 14 days after the day on which it is delivered to the Post Office. Paragraph 5.5 of the Practice Note suggests that local authorities should maintain records of the days on which bills are delivered to the Post Office so that they can present evidence of the date of issue for any particular bill. If the bill has not arrived at the appropriate address, the local authority needs to serve it again if it wishes to start enforcement proceedings (see also Chapter 11).

The Government has encouraged local authorities to establish arrangements for payment of council tax online, and electronic communication may also be used if you agree to this.

5. **Information the bill should contain**

The bill must contain certain prescribed information. This includes comparative information relating to areas that are subject to local government restructuring.[18]

There are minor variations between England, Wales and Scotland (see p43). It is for local authorities to decide the exact wording and how the information appears on the bill.

Information contained on council tax bills

– The name of the person to whom the bill is addressed; if not known, the bill may be addressed to 'The Council Tax Payer'.
– The day of issue.
– The period covered by the bill.
– The address of the chargeable dwelling.
– The dwelling's valuation band.
– The amount of council tax (and Scottish Water charges in Scotland) per chargeable dwelling for the relevant valuation band for each tier of local government (eg, district and county council) including, where applicable, a specified amount to cover parish or community council expenditure.
– How the amount of the council tax (and Scottish Water charges in Scotland) payable has been calculated, showing separate amounts of any disability reduction, discount or council tax benefit (CTB) and the period they cover.
– The reason for any discount, and a statement of the person's duty to inform the local authority of anything that affects entitlement to a discount and the fact that if s/he does not comply with this duty, without a reasonable excuse, the local authority may impose a financial penalty of £70 in England or £50 in Wales or Scotland.
– The amount (if any) to be credited against the amount of council tax which would otherwise be payable for the relevant year.
– The amount of any penalty, or any overpayment of CTB, being recovered under the bill.
– Council tax arrears from the preceding year(s), but only to the extent that they have not already been billed for.
– Annual percentage changes between the present and previous year.
– The amount of council tax payable and how it should be paid.
– The address, telephone number and email to which enquiries may be made.

Explanatory notes and accompanying information

The bill should be accompanied by a set of explanatory notes that provide key points of information on: valuation and banding, exempt dwellings, disability reductions, discounts, appeals and CTB. Additionally, in England and Wales the bill, if issued prior to the end of the financial year to which it relates, must also be accompanied by certain additional information explaining the local authority's income and expenditure.[19]

The Government has indicated that it wishes to increase the amount of information made available to council tax payers regarding spending in their local areas and the level of council tax. As a step towards this, local authorities are required to include information about the annual percentage changes in council tax between the previous year and the relevant year. If the valuation band of a dwelling has changed, the bill must show the percentage difference between the amounts calculated in the relevant year and the previous year.[20]

Invalid bills

A bill is invalid if it does not contain all the required information. Nevertheless, if the failure to comply with these requirements arose because of a mistake and the amount to be paid is otherwise correct, the bill will be treated as valid. The local authority must issue a correction as soon as practicable after the mistake has been found.[21]

6. Appeals against the amount of the bill

If you do not agree with the calculation of the amount you are liable to pay, you should write to the local authority. This includes both actual and estimated amounts.[22] You should explain in the letter which decision you believe to be incorrect and why – eg, because a disability reduction or discount has not been awarded.

For the special rules on appeals against a council tax benefit (CTB) decision, see Chapter 9. On all other matters, the local authority has two months in which to consider the representations made. If it fails to respond in writing within the two-month period, or if you are still dissatisfied with the response, an appeal can be made to the Valuation Tribunal for England (in England) or valuation tribunal (in Wales) and, via the local authority, to a valuation appeal committee in Scotland. This should normally be done within four months of the date the grievance was first raised with the local authority. An appeal cannot, however, be made on the basis that any assumption the local authority is required to make about the future may prove to be inaccurate.[23] The council tax bill must still be paid while the appeal is outstanding, subject to any agreement made with the local authority.

7. Payment arrangements

Most taxpayers have a right to pay by instalments. The 'normal' method of payment is by ten monthly instalments (see p153).[24] The local authority may, however, adopt a variety of different payment arrangements, including:

- in England and Wales, the council tenant instalment scheme (see p154). In Scotland the local authority may establish an agency arrangement with a housing body which then establishes its own payment arrangements;[25]
- special arrangements (see p156);

- discounted lump-sum payments (see p157);
- discounts for non-cash payments (see p157).

Instalments

In England and Wales, if the bill is issued:[26]
- up to 30 April in the relevant year, payments under the statutory scheme are made in 10 monthly instalments;
- from 1 May onwards, the monthly instalments must equal one less than the number of whole months remaining in the financial year (see below);
- between 1 January and 31 March in the relevant year, the total amount due is payable in a single instalment on the day specified on the bill.

The instalments must be payable one month after another, but the local authority may choose in which month to start and state this on the bill.[27]

In Scotland, a local authority cannot demand the first instalment payment to be made in the same month as the bill was issued. If the bill is issued:
- before 1 April in the relevant year, the local authority determines when the first of the 10 instalments is due – this can be either April or May;
- from 1 April onwards, the monthly instalments must equal one less than the number of whole months remaining in the financial year (see below);
- between 1 December and 31 March in the relevant year, the total amount due is payable in a single instalment on the day specified on the bill.

Number of instalments

Month in which demand notice is issued	Number of instalments
April (or before)	10
May	9
June	8
July	7
August	6
September	5
October	4
November	3
December	2
January	1
February	1
March	1

Amount of the instalment

The amount of the instalment is worked out by dividing the total amount of the bill by the number of instalments. If this gives an amount which is a multiple of a pound, the instalments will be of that amount.[28]

If the total amount due divided by the number of instalments does not give an amount which is a multiple of a pound, the amount payable should be divided by the number of instalments and rounded to the nearest pound. Amounts ending in 50p should be rounded up. This amount is the amount of the instalments other than the first. This first amount should be multiplied by the number of instalments less one, and the resulting amount should be subtracted from the total amount payable. The amount remaining is the amount of the first instalment.[29]

Example

The council tax is £500 and payments are to be by nine instalments.

The amount of all but the first instalment will be £56.

(ie, £500 ÷ 9 = £55.5555)

The first instalment will be £52.

(ie, £500 − (£56 x 8 instalments))

If someone has only a small amount of council tax to pay, the instalment method would be a very expensive way for the local authority to collect it. Consequently, local authorities have the power not to accept any instalment where the payment would be less than £5. If the calculation of instalments would produce an instalment of less than £5, the local authority may require that the second instalment be added to the first and that the number of instalments be reduced by one. If the total amount payable is less than £10, the local authority may request payment of that amount in a single instalment. If the total amount payable is £10 or more, the local authority may reduce the number of instalments to the greatest number that allows individual instalments of at least £5.[30]

Instalment scheme for council tenants

In Scotland the local authority may establish an agency arrangement with a housing body. It is then for that housing body to establish appropriate payment arrangements.[31]

In England and Wales a local authority may have an instalment scheme for its council tenants so that they can pay their council tax on the same day they pay their rent. This means that if you pay your rent weekly, for example, the local authority may also allow you to pay your council tax weekly.[32] The scheme may also be drawn up so that it continues to apply during any period in the year in which rent is not payable so long as such a period follows a period in which rent was payable.

The scheme must:
- apply to all council tenants;
- apply to all financial years following the introduction of the scheme unless varied or revoked;

- only be varied in its operation if this is agreed prior to the local authority first setting its council tax for the relevant year;
- not be revoked later than 31 December of the year immediately preceding the beginning of the financial year in which it will no longer apply;
- have at least ten instalments, but no more than 52;
- require the first instalment to be payable no earlier than 14 days after the day on which the bill was issued;
- require instalments to be payable on such day in each interval as is specified in the scheme;
- require the last instalment to be paid before the end of the relevant year;
- provide for how the amount of any instalment will be determined if the total amount, when divided by the number of instalments, does not give an amount which is a multiple of 10 pence.[33]

Instalments when liability ends

No further payments of instalments under either the statutory schemes or, in England and Wales, the council tenant's scheme are due once a person is no longer liable for the tax and, in Scotland, for Scottish Water charges. If more than one person is jointly liable, whether named on the original bill or not, this only applies if both or all of them are no longer liable. In England and Wales, if the only person or persons who are liable are people who were not named on the original bill, the local authority must issue a joint taxpayers' notice on them.[34]

If the original liable person or persons are no longer liable, the local authority must serve a notice on the former liable person or, where there was joint liability, at least one of the jointly liable persons. The notice should state the actual amount due up to the day liability ended. This should be done as soon as practicable after liability ends.[35]

If the amount due is less than the total amount paid, the liable person may require the local authority to repay the overpayment. If no request is made, the local authority may decide either to repay it or to credit it against a subsequent council tax debt on another property for which the same person is liable.[36] It cannot be used to meet any other debt recoverable by that local authority, such as overpayments of housing benefit.

If the amount due is greater than the total amount paid, the local authority will issue a bill requiring the liable person to pay the outstanding amount to the local authority. The local authority must allow at least 14 days from issuing the bill for this amount to be paid.[37]

If the former liable person becomes, once again, liable for the tax to the local authority in the same financial year, the matter is dealt with afresh. Any previous overpayment of tax by the liable person may, however, be credited against the subsequent liability.

Instalments when liability changes

The instalment schemes are based on the assumption that your circumstances will remain the same throughout the year. Liability may change, however, because:

- the council tax changes as a result of budgets being capped by central government; *or*
- the dwelling becomes exempt; *or*
- the dwelling's valuation band changes; *or*
- entitlement to a discount changes; *or*
- entitlement to a disability reduction changes; *or*
- entitlement to council tax benefit (CTB) changes; *or*
- liability to pay Scottish Water charges in Scotland changes.[38]

Following each of these circumstances, the local authority must adjust the remaining instalments (if any) as soon as practicable after the change, so that they accord with the new amounts due.[39] As many adjustments may be made as the circumstances require. The local authority must also serve a revised bill (an adjustment notice) each time an adjustment is made. This should state:

- the revised estimated liability for the relevant year assuming no further changes; *and*
- the amount of any instalments that remain 14 or more days after the issue of the notice.

In England and Wales, if instalments are payable under the statutory scheme and additional amounts are now due as a result of a change, the payments must be fixed in accordance with the rules for that scheme (see p153). In Scotland, the local authority has the discretion to set the amount of each remaining instalment. If no further instalments are due, the additional amount must be paid as a lump sum within a period set by the local authority. The local authority must give you at least 14 days from the date the bill was issued to pay the amount owing.

If the revised amount is less than the combined amounts of the instalments payable before the change, you should request that the overpayment is refunded. If you do not make such a request, the local authority may decide either to repay it or credit it against your subsequent liability.[40]

If a local authority revises its estimate of your council tax liability it must, when adjusting the remaining instalments, take into account any amounts paid before the day on which the adjustment takes effect, which were due to be paid after that day.[41]

Special payment arrangements

A local authority may agree with you that the council tax be paid in a particular manner.[42] These special payment arrangements may be entered into either before or after a bill has been issued, although in England and Wales if there is joint liability the arrangement can only be entered into with someone named on the bill. Special payment arrangements may prove useful if you are facing financial problems.

These special agreements may make provision for payments to be ended or adjusted. They may also allow for a fresh estimate to be made if the original estimate turns out to be wrong. If the special arrangement is entered into after the bill has been issued, it may make provision for dealing with any sums paid by instalments.

A bill issued under a special arrangement will (as the local authority determines) require payment of the amount concerned:

- within a set period of not less than 14 days after the day the bill is issued; *or*
- by instalments and payable at intervals and on days as specified on the bill.

The normal enforcement procedures (see Chapter 11) do not apply to special agreements. Practice Note No. 9 (para 1.11) advises local authorities to ensure that the agreement sets out the procedures to be followed in the event of non-payment.

Discounts for lump-sum payments

The local authority may decide to encourage payment of the council tax by lump sums as this improves its cash flow and reduces its collection costs. The benefits and costs of such an arrangement, not only to the local authority but to all taxpayers, need to be considered carefully. To encourage lump-sum payments the local authority can offer a discount.[43]

If the local authority has discount arrangements it must:

- decide to operate such a scheme and the amount to be discounted on or before the day it first sets its council tax for the year; *and*
- apply the scheme in the same way to people who pay the same number of instalments in the year. For example, if a 5 per cent reduction is to be offered to all who are liable to pay ten instalments, it must be offered to everyone who is liable.

Furthermore, for a lump sum to qualify for a discount:

- at least two instalments of council tax must be payable under the statutory instalment scheme or, in England and Wales, the council tenant instalment scheme; *and*
- the single lump-sum payment must be made on or before the day on which the first instalment would have been due.

Discounts for non-cash payments

Various methods are available to pay the council tax, but some are more cost-effective for local authorities than others. From the local authority's point of view, direct debit has the most advantages and direct debit mandate forms are often sent out with demand notices to encourage the use of this payment method. In addition, the local authority is able to offer a discount to taxpayers if they use such non-cash methods of payment.[44]

The local authority should consider the costs and benefits of such arrangements. The size of the discount and when non-cash payments are to be accepted must be decided by the local authority on or before the day it first sets the council tax for the year.

If an adjustment is needed to the amount paid and the amount has been paid by a discounted non-cash payment, the instalment or other payment on which the discounted amount was accepted must be treated as having been paid in full. Any sum to be repaid, or credited against any subsequent liability, however, is reduced by the same proportion as was allowed for the discount.

8. **Estimates based on incorrect assumptions**

If payments are made under the statutory instalment scheme or, in England and Wales, the council tenant instalment scheme, incorrect assumptions are dealt with as described on pp154 and 156. In other circumstances (eg, if a lump-sum payment has been made) it may become clear during the course of the year that an estimated amount has been based on an incorrect assumption. For example, your entitlement to a discount may change part-way through the year. In such circumstances, the local authority should calculate the appropriate amount that currently appears due for the year.[45]

Having made such a calculation, if:
- the new amount is **greater than** the estimated amount, the local authority should bill you and give you at least 14 days to make the interim payment;
- the new amount is **less than** the estimated amount, the local authority should notify you accordingly and make an interim repayment.

In England and Wales the one exception to the rule requiring repayment arises if an overpayment of council tax has occurred because you are no longer liable to make payments on one dwelling but become immediately liable to make payments to the same local authority on another dwelling. In these circumstances, the local authority may credit the overpayment against the new liability. This exception does not apply in relation to overpayments of lump-sum payments.[46]

9. **Incorrect payments**

The actual amount owed to the local authority will be known for certain only at the end of the financial year or when the taxpayer's liability ends. Consequently, another bill is required where a previous bill has been issued by the local authority for a financial year, or part of a financial year, and the payment or payments required to be made were in fact more than, or less than, the actual liability, and there has been no appropriate adjustment. The local authority should, as soon as practicable after the end of the year (or the part of a year), serve a new bill on the liable person. This should state the actual amount due and adjust the amounts required to be paid under the previous bill.[47]

If the amount stated in the new notice is greater than the amount previously required, you must pay the difference within a period specified by the local authority. This period must be at least 14 days following the issue of the new bill.[48]

If there has been an overpayment of council tax and you require a refund, this must be given. In any other case, the local authority may decide either to repay the amount in question to you or credit it against any future council tax liability.[49] The exception to this rule is where the overpayment of council tax has arisen because you are no longer liable to make payments on one dwelling but are immediately liable to make payments to the same local authority on another dwelling. In these particular circumstances, the local authority may require the amount of any overpayment, instead of being repaid, to be credited against the new liability.[50] This exception does not apply in the case of lump-sum payments.

In England and Wales, if the local authority is required to repay a sum but does not do so, you can take recovery action using the civil debt procedure in the county court.[51] The small claims procedure of the county court can be used for sums up to £5,000.

10. **Penalties**

In certain circumstances a civil penalty may be imposed by the local authority if you:
- fail to respond to a request for information to identify the liable person (see Chapter 6); *or*
- fail to notify the local authority that a dwelling is no longer entitled to an exemption (see Chapter 5); *or*
- fail to notify the local authority that you are no longer entitled to the same level of discount (see Chapter 8).

A penalty may be collected by the local authority by:
- including it on the council tax bill (see p151); *or*
- sending a separate bill.[52]

In the latter case, the local authority must allow at least 14 days for the bill to be paid. If the imposition of a penalty is subject to an appeal or, in England and Wales, arbitration:[53]

- no bill can be issued for the recovery of a penalty;
- no amount is payable in respect of the penalty.

In this case, the proportions of the instalments on the bill attributable to the penalty are not payable until the appeal or arbitration is finally disposed of, abandoned or fails for non-prosecution.[54]

If a penalty is paid and is later quashed either by the local authority or following an appeal, the local authority which imposed the penalty must repay it. This can be done by deducting an amount from any other penalty, council tax and, in Scotland, Scottish Water charges that is owed to the local authority and repaying any balance.[55]

Notes

1. Who has to pay the bill
1 **EW** Reg 22 CT(AE) Regs 1992
 S Reg 18 CT(AE)(S) Regs
2 **EW** Reg 2(3) CT(AE) Regs 1992
 S Reg 19(2) CT(AE)(S) Regs
3 **S** Reg 17 CT(AE)(S) Regs
4 **S** Reg 18 CT(AE)(S) Regs
5 **EW** Reg 28 CT(AE) Regs 1992

2. When bills should be issued
6 **EW** Reg 19 CT(AE) Regs 1992
7 **S** Reg 17 CT(AE)(S) Regs
8 **EW** Reg 18 CT(AE) Regs 1992
 S Reg 19 CT(AE)(S) Regs
9 **EW** Reg 18 CT(AE) Regs 1992
10 *Encon Insulation Ltd v Nottingham City Council* [1999] RA 382
11 *Regentford Ltd v Thanet District Council* [2004]
12 *Regentford Ltd v Thanet District Council* [2004] 246 (HC QBD)
13 *Hardy v Sefton* [2006] EWHC 1928

3. How the bill is calculated
14 **EW** Reg 20 CT(AE) Regs 1992
 S Reg 20 CT(AE)(S) Regs
15 **S** Reg 20 CT(AE)(S) Regs
16 **EW** Reg 20 CT(AE) Regs 1992
 S Reg 20 CT(AE)(S) Regs

4. How bills are served
17 **EW** Reg 17(4) CT(AE) Regs 1992

5. Information the bill should contain
18 **E** CTNDR(DN)(E) Regs; The Council Tax and Non-Domestic Rating (Demand Notices)(England)(Amendment) Regulations 2008 No.387
 W CT(DN)(W) Regs
 S Reg 28 and Sch 2 CT(AE)(S) Regs
19 **E** Sch 3 Part I CTNDR(DN)(E) Regs
 W Sch 2 Part II CT(DN)(W) Regs
20 Reg 6(1) CTNDR(DN)(E) Regs
21 **E** Reg 4 CTNDR(DN)(E) Regs
 W Reg 5 CT(DN)(W) Regs
 S Reg 29 CT(AE)(S) Regs

6. Appeals against the amount of the bill
22 **EW** s16 LGFA 1992
 S s81 LGFA 1992
23 **EW** Reg 30 CT(AE) Regs 1992

7. Payment arrangements
24 **EW** Reg 21 and Sch 1 Part I CT(AE) Regs 1992
 S Reg 21 and Sch 1 CT(AE)(S) Regs
25 **S** Sch 2 para 19 LGFA 1992
26 **EW** Sch 1 Part I CT(AE) Regs 1992
 S The Council Tax (Administration and Enforcement) (Scotland) Regulations 2000 No.261
27 **EW** Sch 1 Part I CT(AE) Regs 1992
 S Sch 1 CT(AE)(S) Regs
28 **EW** Sch 1 Part I CT(AE) Regs 1992
 S Sch 1 Part I CT(AE)(S) Regs

29 **EW** Sch 1 Part I CT(AE) Regs 1992
 S Sch 1 Part 1 CT(AE)(S) Regs
30 **EW** Sch 1 CT(AE) Regs 1992
31 **S** Sch 2 para 19 LGFA 1992
32 **EW** Sch 1 Part II LGFA 1992
33 **EW** Sch 1 Part II LGFA 1992
34 **EW** Reg 28 CT(AE) Regs 1992
35 **EW** Sch 1 Part III CT(AE) Regs 1992
 S Sch 1 Part II CT(AE)(S) Regs
36 **EW** Sch 1 Part III CT(AE) Regs 1992
 S Sch 1 Part II CT(AE)(S) Regs
37 **EW** Sch 1 Part III CT(AE) Regs 1992
 S Sch 1 Part II CT(AE)(S) Regs
38 **EW** Sch 1 Part III CT(AE) Regs 1992
 S Sch 1 Part II CT(AE)(S) Regs
39 **EW** Sch 1 Part III CT(AE) Regs 1992
 S Sch 1 Part II CT(AE)(S) Regs
40 **EW** Sch 1 Part III CT(AE) Regs 1992
 S Sch 1 Part II CT(AE)(S) Regs
41 **EW** Sch 1 CT(AE) Regs 1992
42 **EW** Reg 21 CT(AE) Regs 1992
 S Reg 21 CT(AE)(S) Regs
43 **EW** Reg 25 CT(AE) Regs 1992
 S Reg 24 CT(AE)(S) Regs
44 **EW** Reg 26 CT(AE) Regs 1992
 S Reg 25 CT(AE)(S) Regs

8. Estimates based on incorrect assumptions
45 **EW** Regs 24 and 25 CT(AE) Regs 1992
 S Regs 23 and 24 CT(AE)(S) Regs
46 **EW** Reg 24 CT(AE) Regs 1992

9. Incorrect payments
47 **EW** Regs 24, 25 and 31 CT(AE) Regs 1992
 S Regs 23, 24 and 27 CT(AE)(S) Regs
48 **EW** Regs 24, 25 and 31 CT(AE) Regs 1992
 S Regs 23, 24 and 27 CT(AE)(S) Regs
49 **EW** Regs 24, 25 and 31 CT(AE) Regs 1992
 S Regs 23, 24 and 27 CT(AE)(S) Regs
50 **EW** Reg 24 CT(AE) Regs 1992
 S Reg 23 CT(AE)(S) Regs
51 **EW** Reg 55 CT(AE) Regs 1992

10. Penalties
52 **EW** Reg 29 CT(AE) Regs 1992
 S Reg 26 CT(AE)(S) Regs
53 **EW** Reg 29 CT(AE) Regs 1992
 S Reg 26 CT(AE)(S) Regs
54 **EW** Reg 29 CT(AE) Regs 1992
 S Reg 26 CT(AE)(S) Regs
55 **EW** Reg 29 CT(AE) Regs 1992
 S Reg 26 CT(AE)(S) Regs

Chapter 11

· ·

Enforcement

This chapter explains:
1. Statutory enforcement in England and Wales (p163)
2. What happens when an instalment is not paid (England and Wales) (p164)
3. Liability orders (England and Wales) (p165)
4. Recovery methods (England and Wales) (p173)
5. Statutory enforcement in Scotland (p195)
6. Human rights and enforcement action (p201)

This chapter describes the statutory enforcement process. This is the way in which the local authority can recover unpaid amounts of council tax. The process in Scotland is different from the one in England and Wales. Some elements, however, such as the ability to make deductions from income support, pension credit, employment and support allowance or jobseeker's allowance, are common to both systems.

The local authority can agree a special payment arrangement with a taxpayer (see Chapter 10). The re-scheduling of payments under such an arrangement may often be the most appropriate response if you are in arrears. Non-payment of any amount due under a special payment arrangement is also covered by the statutory enforcement procedures.

At any point in the enforcement process, recovery action must stop if the outstanding amount (including costs) is paid.

1. Statutory enforcement in England and Wales

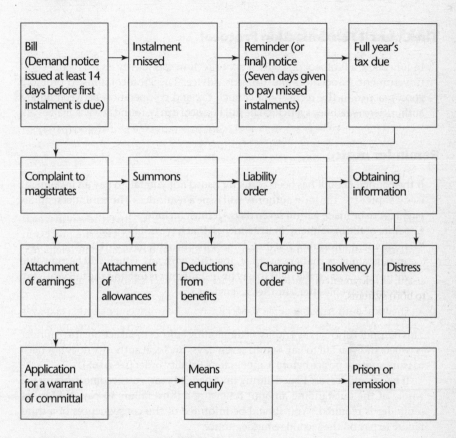

Bill (Demand notice issued at least 14 days before first instalment is due)	Instalment missed	Reminder (or final) notice (Seven days given to pay missed instalments)	Full year's tax due
Complaint to magistrates	Summons	Liability order	Obtaining information
Attachment of earnings	Attachment of allowances	Deductions from benefits	Charging order · Insolvency · Distress
Application for a warrant of committal	Means enquiry	Prison or remission	

Note: action stops if the amount due is paid.

2. What happens when an instalment is not paid (England and Wales)

The Council Tax Collection Protocol

In July 2009, a Protocol on council tax collection was jointly issued by the Local Government Association and Citizens Advice. The Protocol aims to promote good practice in the recovery of council tax and co-operation between billing authorities and advice agencies. The full Protocol can be found at www.lga.gov.uk

Reminder notice

If the council tax bill has been correctly issued but you fail to pay an instalment (see Chapter 10), the local authority will issue a reminder.[1] The reminder requires payment to be made within seven days.[2] It must include:
- a note of the instalment, or instalments, that have not been paid;
- a statement informing you that if no, or insufficient, payment is made to cover any instalments that are overdue, together with any which will become due within seven days, the right to pay by instalments is lost and the full year's tax becomes payable after a further seven days.

This reminder also acts as a notice of impending enforcement action. If a reminder is issued and you fail to pay within seven days, the local authority does not need to issue another notice before it applies for a liability order (see p165).

If two reminders are issued during the financial year, you become liable for the whole of the outstanding amount following a third failure to pay. No further reminder is required.[3] You should be informed of the consequences of a third failure to pay on the second reminder notice.[4]

Final notice

A final notice is required if a third failure to pay occurs, or where only one payment is due under the demand notice. It should state every amount that the local authority would seek on a liability order, unless that amount is the same as that on the second reminder.[5] In the case of joint taxpayers, a final notice may be addressed to all of them.[6] In all cases, once the outstanding amount has become payable following a reminder, or after seven days following the issuing of a final notice, the local authority may seek a liability order from the magistrates' court (see p165).[7]

Joint liability

If a bill has been issued in joint names, the local authority can seek to recover the unpaid amount from anyone who is jointly liable. If a joint bill has not been issued, the authority must send a notice to those who are jointly liable but who have not previously been issued with a bill before any recovery action can be taken against them. The jointly liable person must be given at least 14 days in which to pay the bill. If payment is not received, a reminder must be served on the jointly liable person. If payment is not received after seven days, an application may be made to a magistrates' court for a liability order (see below).

It is possible to apply for a liability order solely against the person to whom the bill was originally sent (even if a joint bill has not been sent), or against both that person and another person(s) who is (or are) jointly and severally liable with that person. It is not, however, possible for a summons to cover more than one person – separate summonses are necessary.

Write-offs

While local authorities normally pursue debts until they are recovered, in certain instances it may be appropriate for a local authority to consider writing off debts which are not cost effective to pursue or in cases of particular financial hardship.

Practice Note 9 (para 16.1) reminds authorities that they can write off small amounts. Para 16.3 advises, for example, that it may be appropriate to write off liability if a person dies soon after the start of the financial year and so only had a small liability.

3. **Liability orders (England and Wales)**

A liability order issued by a magistrates' court provides a local authority with a variety of options to recover the amount of council tax owed (see p173). A local authority must follow the rules on billing, as an order cannot be obtained if the local authority has not issued a reminder or final notice, as described on p164. Before seeking a liability order the local authority should, as a matter of good practice, carry out checks to see whether you:

- are entitled to council tax benefit (CTB) (see Chapter 9);
- have made a claim for benefit that has yet to be processed; *or*
- have appealed (see Chapter 12).

Some local authorities, however, fail to carry out sufficient checks. The problem is particularly acute in the cases of council tax payers who move in and out of low-paid jobs, relying on benefit during periods of unemployment. Delays in awarding benefits, supplying information to the local authority and delays in awarding CTB can result in many people whose liability for a particular domestic dwelling should be zero receiving summonses for non-payment. Because the enforcement process is effectively governed by a computer program, a failure to award benefit or an exemption – however caused – results in the automatic commencement of enforcement proceedings.

If any of the above circumstances apply, the local authority may suspend recovery action until benefit entitlement has been determined or an appeal decided. Considerable effort may be needed to persuade relevant officers of the local authority to suspend recovery proceedings. Where necessary, you should appeal to a valuation tribunal, although it can take time to obtain a hearing (see Chapter 12). The local authority may be willing to enter into an alternative payment arrangement with you in return for withdrawing proceedings. Many local authorities will wish to obtain a full liability order in spite of making a payment arrangement after a summons has been issued, as the liability order gives them the ability to enforce payment if the arrangements are broken.

Enforcement if council tax benefit has yet to be determined

The view of some local authorities is that a person is liable for the full amount of the council tax demanded by the local authority and a magistrates' court can order payment. In *R v Bristol Magistrates' Court, ex parte Willsman and Young*, it was decided, in a community charge case, that the magistrates' court could order payment, despite the fact that a claim for community charge benefit had been made and despite the fact that the local authority had failed to determine the claim within the statutory period.[8]

The decision to seek a liability order, however, is a discretionary one.[9] Consequently, the local authority must consider the relevant facts of the individual case and not act in an unreasonable manner.[10] In the above case, the applicants argued that the local authority's decision to apply for a liability order constituted an unreasonable exercise of its discretion. The evidence showed that it was, in fact, the local authority's practice not to apply for liability orders in cases where it knew that benefit applications were pending. In this case, the relevant liability orders had been sought in error.

If a local authority does seek a liability order, knowing that a benefit claim is pending, it is possible to argue that this constitutes an unreasonable exercise of the local authority's discretionary power. Furthermore, since the maximum 100 per cent CTB is, in theory, available for people in receipt of income support (IS) or on low incomes, arguably it was not the intention of Parliament to subject people who are entitled to full benefit to the stress and additional costs of court proceedings when the ultimate liability of the person would be zero.

To date, there has only been one (unsuccessful) challenge by a person in receipt of IS which was resolved before it went to court, so the High Court has yet to consider fully the issue or review the decision the *Willsman and Young* case.

In *Regentford Ltd v Thanet District Council* (see p147), the High Court considered that magistrates might refuse an order where excessive delays caused 'prejudice' to the taxpayer. However, the Court did not explore the scope of the meaning of what constituted 'prejudice'. It would, conceivably, apply to situations where original records were no longer available and a council tax payer had an argument that was difficult to defend.

In *Hardy v Sefton Metropolitan Council*, the High Court decided '. . . that the magistrates' court must enquire into questions as to whether the tax payer is entitled to set off monies owed by the billing authority, or is entitled to say in law that the billing authority is precluded from asserting any liability to pay.'

It may also be possible to use human rights law to object to a liability order where a sum has yet to be calculated. The European Court of Human Rights considers that there must be certainty in orders and judgments issued by courts and that this extends to the 'quantum' or size of a money judgment. If a liability order is made, but benefit entitlement is still to be determined in the year ahead, the amount ultimately due is uncertain, and may be revised. However, the matter has yet to be tested.

Time limits

An application for a liability order from the magistrates' court must be made within six years from the date the bill was issued.[11]

Obtaining a liability order

To obtain a liability order the local authority must apply to the magistrates' court for a summons to be issued to the debtor. In practice, this is issued by computer and endorsed with a facsimile signature of a justice of the peace. The decision to seek a summons must be in accordance with the regulations and be a reasonable one.[12]

While regulations state that a summons may be addressed to two or more joint taxpayers in joint names, natural justice would require that separate summonses should be issued against each defendant, in order to give each person notice of the hearing. If a single reminder is issued to two or more people who are jointly and severally liable, the local authority should produce separate summonses for each of the individuals against whom a liability order is to be sought.

The summons instructs the debtor to attend the court to show why s/he has not paid.[13] No warrant may be issued for the arrest of someone who does not appear and, in practice, most people who have been summoned do not attend. The 'hearing' takes place in their absence. You should have reasonable notice of the hearing as there must be at least 14 days between serving the summons and the hearing at which the liability order is made.[14]

The summons is not a prescribed form, but should set out the amount outstanding. It may also include the costs reasonably incurred. These represent the court's administration costs but also the costs associated with the local authority's action. While it is likely that local authorities will have discussed a level of costs with the clerk to the court, Practice Note No. 9 (para 12.1) points out that the court should be satisfied that the amount claimed in costs is no more than those reasonably incurred by the local authority.

It appears that many local authorities are using the issue of costs as a form of revenue raising, the legal basis of which appears to be uncertain. A Parliamentary answer obtained in February 2009 from Bridget Prentice, Minister for Justice, indicated the cost of issuing a liability order through the magistrates' court system was £3. You should therefore query other amounts included in the costs on a summons to establish why they have been incurred.

Serving the summons

A summons may be served on someone by:
- posting it to their usual or last known place of abode;
- delivering it to the person;
- leaving it at her/his usual or last known address;
- in the case of a company, leaving it at or posting it to its registered office;
- leaving it at, or posting it to, an address given by the person as an address at which service will be accepted.[15]

If you do not receive a summons for a liability order hearing and the magistrates' court makes the order in your absence, the order may be quashed by the High Court on judicial review.[16]

Payment of the outstanding amount

If the outstanding amount, plus costs, is paid, the local authority cannot continue with the application for a liability order.[17] If the amount outstanding has been paid but the costs have not, a liability order can still be made for the costs alone, although the local authority may be prepared to forego these.[18] The costs claimed by a local authority on a summons can sometimes be up to an additional £75 or £80.

Adjournments

You can apply to the court for an adjournment if, for instance, you have an arguable case that you should be exempt, if you are receiving CTB or if there is a matter that should go to a valuation tribunal (see Chapter 12). This is done by writing to the Justices' Chief Executive (formerly known as the Clerk to the Justices, but still often known as the Justices' Clerk).

In some courts the task of listing and adjourning proceedings is carried out by the local authority for reasons of administrative convenience. This raises questions of what is known as natural justice since there is no power in law to delegate the functions and duties of the court to a party to the case.

A sample letter for applying for an adjournment can be found in Appendix 3.

If you do not receive a reply from the magistrates' court, you should telephone the listing department of the court to enquire what is being done.

Attending court

If the matter cannot be adjourned by letter or by telephone, you will have to attend court. Before this, however, the local authority may try to reach an agreement or settlement with you. In some cases, the local authority will agree to withdraw the application, but it is much more common for it to insist on getting its liability order to rely on if the agreement is not kept. This also enables the local authority to obtain more in costs.

Any agreement that may be reached must be in writing. In some cases, the local authority will agree to withdraw the sum in costs.

The hearing

If it is not possible to reach a settlement or you wish to challenge the basis of the local authority's case, there must be a hearing where you must show why you have not paid the council tax.

You are entitled to be present and hear the case against you.

The procedure for the hearing follows rule 14 of the Magistrates' Courts Rules 1981 (order of speeches in a civil hearing).[19] You should be allowed an opportunity to examine all the evidence that the local authority produces in court and ask questions in cross-examination. The court normally must comprise two justices of the peace or a single magistrate, now known as a district judge (magistrates' court).[20] You may make a submission of 'no case to answer' if the local authority has failed to prove an essential part of its case. If the submission of 'no case to answer' succeeds, the local authority is not entitled to a liability order.

Representatives

You can represent yourself without a legal representative. In addition, you have the right to the assistance of a friend – eg, an adviser, who is not a lawyer.[21] Such a friend (who can be an adviser) can sit with you in court and help by taking notes, prompting and giving you advice on the conduct of the case. Such an adviser is known as a 'McKenzie friend'. It is sensible to mention to the court or the clerk that such an adviser is present.

A magistrates' court should ensure, as far as possible, that someone who is representing her/himself 'is not disadvantaged in any way and indeed the court will provide him with every reasonable means of assistance'.[22] Refusal of a 'McKenzie friend' without good cause would be grounds to have the proceedings quashed on appeal by way of judicial review to the High Court. The court may, however, exclude such a 'friend' from giving assistance if there is good reason to believe that s/he is interfering with the proper administration of justice. Some courts allow a McKenzie friend to speak, but this is at their discretion. The clerk is also able to provide assistance if this can be done without prejudicing her/his impartiality. You are also entitled to bring books, papers, pens, pencils and any other appropriate material.[23]

Grounds for granting a liability order

An order must be made if the magistrates are satisfied that:

- the sum is payable by the person concerned; *and*
- it has not been paid.[24]

The local authority must satisfy the court that:

- the council tax has been fixed by the local authority;
- the sums have been demanded in accordance with the regulations;
- full payment of the amount due has not been made by the required date;
- a reminder, second reminder or a final notice has been issued;
- the sum has not been paid within seven days of the reminder or final notice being issued and the full amount has become payable;
- the summons has been served for the amount outstanding at least seven days after the reminder or final notice; *and*
- the full sum claimed has not been paid.

The defences available to you include:

- the amount has not been demanded in accordance with the regulations (eg, the local authority failed to follow the correct time periods in serving bills and reminders);
- bills have been issued late (see Chapter 10);
- instalments have not been calculated in accordance with the regulations (see Chapter 10);
- the amount has been paid;
- you are not the person named on the summons;
- the level of charge is not in accordance with the sum set by the council.

Any matter concerning liability that could be the subject of an appeal to a valuation tribunal (see Chapter 12) cannot be raised in liability order proceedings – eg:[25]

- whether or not you are a liable person;
- whether or not the dwelling is a chargeable dwelling;
- entitlement to a disability reduction;
- entitlement to a discount or exemption.

Adjournments

Practices can vary greatly between courts, but if there is evidence of a serious objection to liability, many courts will adjourn the proceedings. The case for an adjournment may be strengthened if you have lodged an appeal with a valuation tribunal. Unless agreed in advance, an application for an adjournment must be made in the courtroom directly to the bench on the return day of the summons.

Evidence

Most of the evidence used by a local authority at a hearing will have been generated electronically. The local authority can use as evidence any statement contained in a document, including a computer-generated statement, which it believes would further its case at the hearing provided:

- the document forms part of a record compiled by the authority;
- direct oral evidence of any fact stated in it would have been admissible;
- if the document has been produced by a computer, it is accompanied by a certificate which:[26]
  - identifies the document and the computer from which it was produced;
  - includes a statement that the computer was operating properly, or if not, that the defect did not affect the production of the document or its accuracy;
  - explains the content of the document;
  - is signed by a person occupying a responsible position in relation to the operation of the computer.

The local authority officer presenting the case should be asked to produce the certificate for inspection. Failure to do so will make the computer evidence inadmissible and the local authority will be unable to prove its case in court.[27]

Your direct evidence, given on oath, is admissible, together with any other documents or statements.[28] Notice of any document used or any other hearsay statement[29] (ie, a statement made by any person not called as a witness in court) must be given to the clerk and the local authority. These rules are complicated and place a debtor at a disadvantage, as they require notice to be given to the clerk at least 21 days before a hearing, whereas a debtor may only receive 14 days' notice of a summons. However, one possible way around this problem is to serve copies of any documents on the local authority so that they become records held by the local authority (which are acceptable). Alternatively, in many cases the local authority will have had notice of the documentary evidence more than 21 days before a hearing – eg, where correspondence has been ongoing over a matter of benefit entitlement.

The liability order

The court may make a liability order for one person for one amount. It can also make one liability order for more than one person and more than one amount in the form of a schedule.[30] In either case, the liability order identifies the aggregate amount that can be recovered. If the full sum claimed has been reduced – eg, because CTB has been awarded, the liability order will be for a greater sum than the amount payable. In such cases, the order remains in force and the excess amount is treated as paid. If, following the issue of an order, you owe more than the amount specified, the local authority can only enforce up to the limit stated in the order. It must seek a new order to enforce the outstanding balance.

Appealing against a liability order

Sometimes a liability order may be wrongly issued by a magistrates' court, often in a debtor's absence. If this is the case, you can appeal to the High Court on a point of law within 21 days of a decision or apply for judicial review within three months. Professional legal advice should be sought. Public funding is available for appeals to the High Court for people on low incomes.

Since 2002, it has also been possible for a liability order to be 'set aside'. A local authority can apply to a magistrates' court to have a liability order quashed, on the basis that it should not have been made.[31] If the court decides that it would have granted an order for a lesser sum, it may make a liability order for a lesser sum together with the costs reasonably incurred in obtaining the order. The local authority must issue a summons for a new amount within six years.

One potential drawback for the council taxpayer is that the right to quash the order is wholly reliant on the local authority being willing to make the application. Unreasonable refusals to quash liability orders could be challenged by judicial review. A complaint of maladministration may also be made (see Chapter 13). In the meantime, you remain subject to the order.

Caselaw has also established that magistrates can set aside liability orders if there has been a mistake.[32] For example, in *R (on the application of Tull) v Camberwell Green Magistrates' Court and another*, the High Court ruled that magistrates were wrong not to have quashed three liability orders made between 1996 and 1998 against an applicant who was unaware of the proceedings until January 2004.[33]

Guidance on setting aside liability orders is contained in *R (on the application of Newham London Borough Council) v Stratford Magistrates' Court*, in which the High Court ruled that the following apply when deciding to set aside a liability order.

- There must be a genuine and arguable dispute about the liability to pay.
- There must have been substantial procedural error, defect or mishap for the liability order to have been made.
- The application to set aside was made promptly after the defendant had notice of its existence.[34]

There is no prescribed form for making an application to set aside a liability order. A letter should be sent to the court's clerk or justices' adviser identifying the liability order and requesting a hearing to consider setting it aside. This is crucial if a local authority is seeking to enforce a liability order through bankruptcy proceedings (see p186). It may also be necessary in order to lodge an appeal with the valuation tribunal (see Chapter 12).

4. **Recovery methods (England and Wales)**

The liability order gives the local authority the power to:
- obtain information about the financial circumstances of the debtor and thus assess the best course of recovery action (see below);
- make an attachment of earnings order (see p174);
- make an attachment order on an elected member's allowances (see p177);
- apply to the Department for Work and Pensions (DWP) for deductions to be made from the debtor's income support (IS), pension credit (PC), jobseeker's allowance (JSA) or employment and support allowance (ESA) (see p177);
- use bailiffs to seize the debtor's goods (known as 'distress') (see p179);
- apply for a charging order against the dwelling in respect of which the debtor's liability arose (see p186);
- apply to bankrupt the debtor (if s/he is an individual) or to wind up the company (if the debtor is a corporate body) (see p186).

The local authority may decide which recovery method it wishes to use in each case and may use it more than once, but it may not pursue more than one method at any one time.[35] In the case of joint liability, it may pursue only one person at a time.[36] So, if one of the joint taxpayers is the subject of an attachment of earnings order, the local authority cannot seize the goods of the other.

Information from the debtor

Once the liability order has been made and, for as long as the amount in question remains unpaid,[37] the local authority may request you to provide the following information:
- the name and address of your employer;
- your earnings or expected earnings;
- statutory deductions from pay (these must be disregarded when calculating the amount to be deducted under an attachment of earnings order);
- your work or identity number used by your employer;
- details of existing attachment of earnings orders;
- details of other sources of income – eg, occupational pension, benefits, councillor's allowances;
- whether there is anyone jointly liable for the whole, or any part, of the amount for which the order was made.[38]

You do not have to supply the information if the request is not made in writing, or if the information is not in your possession or control.[39] Otherwise, you must provide the information within 14 days of the request being made.[40] You do not, however, have to advise the local authority of a change of circumstances unless the local authority makes a fresh request for the relevant information. If a liability order has been granted against people who are jointly liable, the local authority can require this information from any, or all, of them. If you fail, without a reasonable excuse, to supply the requested information, you are guilty of a criminal offence and may be fined by the magistrates' court up to a maximum of level 2.[41] If you 'knowingly or recklessly' supply false information, you could be found guilty of a criminal offence and fined up to a maximum of level 3.[42]

Attachment of earnings order

A local authority which has obtained a liability order against a person who is employed may arrange to have standard deductions made from her/his earnings.[43] This is known as an 'attachment of earnings order'. Practice Note No. 9 (para 5.2) advises that attachment of earnings orders are a practical and, in many cases, preferable alternative to distress (see p179). The decision to use this method of recovery, however, is a discretionary one and the local authority must consider all the relevant factors before deciding to adopt this method. Certain costs arising from unsuccessful enforcement activity may also be recovered by an attachment of earnings order.

In practice, however, relatively few attachment of earnings orders are made. As many people who have liability orders against them are not in regular or stable employment, this method of enforcement is impracticable. Also, the local authority often does not know where debtors are employed.

A local authority cannot have more than two council tax attachment of earnings orders against a person at one time.[44]

The order

The form of the attachment of earnings order is specified in the regulations.[45] A Welsh language version has also been prescribed.[46] The order should be addressed to, and may be served upon, 'any person who appears to the authority to have the debtor in his employment; any person on whom it is so served, who has the debtor in his employment, shall comply with it'. It does not have to be addressed to a person by name. A copy should also be sent to you. The order must specify:

- the fact that a liability order has been obtained against you and the outstanding sum;
- the rate at which deductions are to be made from net earnings (see p175);
- the period within which each deduction made is to be paid to the local authority – ie, within 19 days of the end of the month in which the deduction is made.

The order must be signed by the proper officer at the local authority. Practice Note No. 9 (para 5.6) advises that a facsimile signature is acceptable.

How long does the order last?

Once an attachment of earnings order has been made, it remains in force until:

- the whole amount to which it relates has been paid; *or*
- it is cancelled by the issuing authority.[47]

The local authority may cancel the order on its own initiative or following an application by you or your employer.[48]

The debtor's duties

While an attachment of earnings order is in force, you must notify the local authority in writing if you:[49]

- leave a job; *or*
- become employed or re-employed.

The notification must include:[50]

- the name and address of your employer;
- your work or identity number in the employment; *and*
- a statement of earnings or expected earnings from the job, and the deductions or expected deductions for income tax, Class 1 national insurance (NI) contributions and contributions to an occupational pension scheme.

This notification must be given within 14 days of the day on which you leave, start or recommence the employment, or (if later) the day on which you are informed by the local authority that the order has been made.[51] If you do not comply, without a reasonable excuse, you commit an offence[52] and may be fined.[53] If you make a statement which you know to be false, you may also be found guilty of an offence.[54]

Employers must also tell the local authority within 14 days of the date a debtor enters their employment and they become aware that an attachment of earnings order is in force or on the day on which they become aware that an attachment of earnings order exists.[55] An employer is guilty of an offence and liable to a fine if s/he fails to provide the required notification without reasonable excuse, or if s/he makes a false statement.[56]

In addition to each amount deducted under the attachment of earnings order, the employer is able to deduct a further £1 towards administration costs each time a deduction is made.

The deductions to be made

The deductions under an attachment of earnings order are made from your net earnings (see p176).[57] The amount deducted depends on the payment period. If you are not paid weekly or monthly or are paid on an irregular basis, a daily rate is used. Special rules cover more unusual payment arrangements. The debtor, local authority and employer can agree to a lower deduction than the statutory amount. The employer should alter the deductions if your earnings change.

'**Earnings**' include any fees, bonus, commission, overtime pay or other emoluments payable in addition to wages or salary or payable under a contract of service. They also include statutory sick pay.[58] The following are not treated as earnings:[59]

- sums payable by any public department of the Government of Northern Ireland or of a territory outside the UK;
- pay or allowances payable to a member of the armed forces;
- social security benefits;
- tax credits;
- allowances payable in respect of disablement or disability;
- wages paid to a seaman, other than of a fishing boat.

'**Net earnings**' are defined as the gross earnings minus:[60]

- income tax;
- Class 1 NI contributions;
- amounts deducted towards a superannuation scheme; *and*
- tax credits.

Deductions from weekly net earnings[61]	Deduction rate %
Below £75	0
£75.01 to £135	3
£135.01 to £185	5
£185.01 to £225	7
£225.01 to £355	12
£355.01 to £505	17
£505.01 and over	17 for the first £370 and 50 for the remainder

Deductions from monthly net earnings	Deduction rate %
Below £300	0
£300.01 to £550	3
£550.01 to £740	5
£740.01 to £900	7
£900.01 to £1,420	12
£1,420.01 to £2,020	17
£2,020 and over	17 for the first £2,020 and 50 for the remainder

Deductions from daily net earnings	Deduction rate %
Below £11	0
£11.01 to £20	3
£20.01 to £27	5
£27.01 to £33	7
£33.01 to £52	12

| £52.01 to £72 | 17 |
| £72.01 and over | 17 for the first £72 and 50 for the remainder |

Priority of attachment of earnings orders

There is a priority for attachment of earning orders if more than one has been made against the same individual.[62] Council tax attachment orders should be dealt with one at a time and in the order in which they are made. If an order is already in force – eg, for child support arrears, a council tax order will be applied to the balance of pay remaining after the other deductions have been made. If an order in respect of council tax is in effect when another order is made, the council tax order should continue to be met and the balance considered attachable for the other order.[63]

Elected members' allowances

If you are a local authority councillor (but not a member of the Common Council of the City of London or the Receiver for the Metropolitan Police District), the local authority can make an order to deduct 40 per cent from your member's allowances – eg, for attending conferences and meetings and for special responsibilities. The decision to use this method of recovery is a discretionary one. The local authority must consider all the relevant factors before deciding to adopt this method.

Once an order has been made it remains in force until:
- the whole amount to which it relates has been paid; *or*
- it is cancelled by the issuing authority.[64]

The local authority may cancel the order on its own initiative or following an application by the debtor.

Restrictions on voting

If an elected member fails to pay an amount of council tax within two months of the due date, s/he cannot vote on any matter which influences the setting of the local authority's council tax.[65] You must disclose this fact at any meeting where this rule applies. If you fail to comply with this rule you are, on summary conviction, liable to a fine not exceeding level 3 on the standard scale unless you prove that you did not know that it applied to you at the time of the meeting or the matter in question was the subject of consideration at the meeting. In England and Wales, prosecutions may only start with the permission of the Director of Public Prosecutions.[66]

Deductions from benefits

If a liability order has been obtained, the local authority may apply for deductions to be made from your IS, JSA, income-related ESA or PC.[67] The decision to use this method of recovery is a discretionary one. The local authority must consider all the relevant factors before deciding to adopt this method.

Although many council tax payers on IS, income-based JSA, income-related ESA or PC receive 100 per cent council tax benefit (CTB), this is not the case where:

- they are jointly liable with someone other than a married or unmarried partner; *or*
- there is a non-dependant in the household.

Deductions from IS/JSA/ESA/PC may also be pursued by the local authority if you were liable to pay council tax prior to being entitled to one of these benefits.

The maximum weekly amount that can be deducted is the equivalent of 5 per cent of the personal allowance for a single claimant aged 25 or over. If there is more than one type of deduction being made – eg, for rent and fuel arrears, the maximum weekly deduction is an amount equal to three times 5 per cent of the personal allowance for a single claimant aged 25 years or over.[68]

Deductions are not possible:

- if there is insufficient benefit in payment to allow a deduction;
- the amount payable after deductions have been made is 10 pence a week; *or*
- if there are higher priority deductions for other debts, such as rent, fuel or water.

The maximum weekly amount that can be deducted from contributory JSA is one-third of the weekly amount of JSA for a person of your age, rounded down to the nearest penny, being £15.61 for those under 25 and £19.71 for those 25 and over for the year to 31 March. If you are in receipt of contribution-based JSA, but would have been entitled to income-based JSA, the lower 5 per cent deduction is made.

The application

To obtain the deduction, the local authority must supply the following information to the local Jobcentre Plus office:

- the name and address of the debtor;
- the name and address of the local authority making the application;
- the name and place of the court which made the liability order;
- the date on which the liability order was made;
- the amount specified in the liability order;
- the total sum which the local authority wishes to have deducted.[69]

Deductions from IS/JSA/ESA/PC can only be made in respect of one application from the local authority at any given time. If a second application is made before the sum specified in the first application has been fully recovered, the second has to wait until the first has been cleared.[70]

As far as is practicable, you and the local authority should be notified of the decision in writing within 14 days. You should also be notified of your right to appeal against the decision. The local Jobcentre Plus office should make the deductions provided:
- you are entitled to IS/JSA/ESA/PC throughout any benefit week; *and*
- no deductions are being made for council tax arrears under any other application.[71]

Payment of deductions to the local authority

Payments deducted from IS/JSA/ESA/PC should be made to the local authority concerned, as far as is practicable, at intervals not exceeding 13 weeks.[72]
Deductions should end if:
- there is no longer sufficient entitlement to IS/JSA/ESA/PC to enable a deduction to be made; *or*
- the local authority withdraws its application for deductions to be made; *or*
- the debt is discharged.[73]

If the whole of the amount to which the deductions relate has been paid, the local authority must notify the local Jobcentre Plus office within 21 days, or as soon as practicable after that.[74]

Providing information to the debtor

The local Jobcentre Plus office must notify you in writing of the total amount deducted under any application if:
- you request this information in writing; *or*
- the deductions end.[75]

Distress

'**Distress**' is a remedy that enables a local authority to use bailiffs to seize a debtor's possessions anywhere in England or Wales and sell them, usually by auction, to pay off the debt.

Future changes
Currently, plans to reform the law of distress under the Tribunals, Courts and Enforcement Act 2007 are being reviewed. There are unlikely to be major changes until after the next general election.

Distress can be prevented if all amounts due have been paid.[76] Once distress has been levied, a sale can be prevented by paying the full amount due.[77] Practice Note No. 9 (para 4.3) advises that, while distress can be an effective recovery method, local authorities should consider other methods (such as attachment of earnings or deductions from benefit) in preference to distress as an initial enforcement option. If some other method of recovery is in force, the local authority has no power to levy distress.[78]

Distress cannot be attempted by a local authority unless the debtor has been sent a written notice[79] at least 14 days before any first visit to her/his home. The written notice must mention the following specified matters:

- the fact that a liability order has been made;
- the amount for which the liability order was made and the amount which remains outstanding, if this is different;
- a warning that unless the amount specified is paid within 14 days distress may be used;
- a warning that further costs may be incurred;
- a copy of the fees payable;
- the local authority's address and telephone number.

Goods that cannot be seized

The local authority cannot seize goods which do not belong to you. The council tax rules make it clear it is only the goods of the debtor that can be taken.[80] The local authority cannot seize:

- goods on lease or hire purchase;
- goods belonging to a landlord or other members of the household.

The following goods are also exempt:[81]

- tools, books, vehicles and other items of equipment that you need for your employment, business or vocation; *and*
- clothing, bedding, furniture, household equipment and provisions necessary for your and your family's basic needs.

General powers of bailiffs

Distress must be carried out by a certificated bailiff who has the written authorisation of the local authority. In practice, most local authorities use private bailiffs. The written authorisation of the local authority must be shown if a person asks to see it.[82]

Can bailiffs enter the premises?

At common law, bailiffs have no power to force initial entry or break open an outer door which is locked or bolted.[83] This is a rule known popularly as 'An Englishman's home is his castle', dating back to 1604. However, under the Tribunals, Courts and Enforcement Act 2007, regulations might be made to allow forced entry in limited circumstances where an enforcement agent can obtain a court order. At present, it is unclear how this power would operate and the Government indicated in March 2009 that it would not introduce a power to force entry. A spokesman for the Conservatives has stated the same.

To be a lawful entry, the bailiff must enter a property peacefully through an unlocked door or through an open window. S/he may not open a closed window (even if it is not locked). Bailiffs cannot obtain a court order to gain entry to any property, nor can an occupier be sent to prison merely for refusing to allow bailiffs to enter. A householder is entitled to refuse entry to bailiffs without a warrant and also to use reasonable force in resisting bailiffs who try unlawfully to push their way in.[84]

Can force be used against you?

At common law, bailiffs cannot use force against a person. However, the Tribunals, Courts and Enforcement Act allows regulations to be made which could allow for the use of force against people within the premises. However, on 17 March 2009 the Ministry of Justice announced that it would not be making regulations allowing force against the person and that there would be a public consultation on the issue of bailiffs' powers before any changes were made to the law. Draft regulations are likely to be issued in autumn 2009 and the process opened up to consultation.

What happens once the bailiffs gain entry?

If a bailiff is able to gain peaceful entry to the building, s/he is then entitled to enter and search any room for a debtor's goods and seize them. S/he is entitled to force any inner door which is locked. This applies even to those rooms which the debtor does not occupy. It also applies to any building in which her/his goods are located and not just the one s/he occupies as a main residence. Once the bailiff has gained peaceful entry, with or without the consent of the occupier, withdrawing consent or refusing permission to enter other parts of the property are of no effect. This applies even if the occupier was misled into believing that the bailiff only wanted to discuss the situation and not levy distress on that occasion.

There are a number of different ways of possessing goods.[85]

- **'Walking possession'** is where the debtor signs an agreement which enables the goods to stay on the premises without physical supervision by the bailiff until payment is made or the goods are eventually removed for sale.
- **'Close possession'** is the same, except that the bailiff stays on the premises for at least the greater part of the day to supervise the goods.
- **'Removal'** is where the bailiff takes the goods away with a view to selling them.

The most common form of possession in council tax arrears cases is walking possession. Having taken walking possession of a debtor's goods, the bailiff cannot be refused entry if s/he has to return to remove those goods at a later date. The bailiff is entitled to force entry under these circumstances, but reasonable notice should be given to the householder before any forcible entry to recover distrained goods is made.[86]

The bailiffs must leave:
- a copy of Regulation 45 and of Schedule 5 (charges connected with distress) Council Tax (Administration and Enforcement) Regulations 1992 (as amended); *and*
- a memorandum setting out the appropriate costs (see below).

Additionally, a copy of any close or walking possession agreement entered into must be handed to the debtor.[87]

Many bailiffs who have been unable to gain entry to a debtor's home have attempted to carry out what was referred to as 'constructive distress'. This involved posting a 'notice of distress' through the letterbox claiming that (usually unspecified) goods on the premises had been seized. In *Evans v South Ribble District Council*, it was held that it is not possible to carry out constructive distress in this way.[88] For a seizure of goods to be lawful, the bailiff must enter the property (except in the exceptional circumstances where the goods s/he is attempting to seize are on the point of removal and those doing the removing are directly confronted).

Charges connected with distress from 1 April 2007[89]

Matter	Charge
Visiting premises with a view to levying distress (where no levy is made):	
– the first or only visit	£22.50
– the second visit	£16.50
Levying distress	The lesser of:
	– the costs and fees reasonably incurred; *and*
	– where the sum due at the time of the levy does not exceed £100, £22.50; *or*
	– where the sum due at the time of the levy exceeds £100, 24.5% on the first £100 of the sum due, 4% on the next £400, 2.5% on the next £1,500, 1% on the next £8,000 and 0.25% on any additional sum
Attending once with a vehicle to remove the goods (where goods are not removed)	Reasonable costs and fees incurred
Removing and storing goods for sale	Reasonable costs and fees incurred
Possession of goods:	
– close possession (the person in possession to provide her/his own board)	£15 a day
– walking possession	£12

Appraising an item distrained, at the written request of the debtor	Reasonable fees and expenses of a broker (no charge is payable unless the debtor has been first advised of the charge and how it was calculated)
Other expenses of a sale by auction: – held on the auctioneer's premises	The auctioneer's commission fee, out-of-pocket expenses (but not exceeding in aggregate 15% of the sum realised), together with reasonable advertising costs and fees
– held on the debtor's premises	The auctioneer's commission fee (but not exceeding 7.5% of the sum realised), together with the auctioneer's out-of-pocket expenses and reasonable advertising costs and fees
Where no sale takes place by reason of payment or tender Where goods have been seized but not sold	Either: – £24.50; *or* – the actual costs incurred, to a maximum of 5% of the amount in respect of which the liability order was made, whichever is the greater

Bailiffs can only impose those charges which appear in the above schedule, plus the outstanding amount remaining due under the liability order. There is no power for the bailiff or the local authority to impose any charges for writing letters, making arrangements to pay or for any costs associated with bounced cheques.

It is also not unknown for bailiffs to seek to make a charge for attending with a van at the same time as conducting the levy. Although the higher courts have not ruled on this issue, it is clear from the table of charges that the so-called 'van call' is intended to take place on a different occasion from that on which the levy has been made.

Some bailiffs may also impose a charge when entering into a walking possession and making an arrangement to pay. They do this on the basis that the goods are seized when distress is levied, on the assumption that the debtor will make the payments agreed under the walking possession agreement, and that the goods will be freed from the levy and seizure at that time. This is clearly wrong in that each event listed to the schedule of charges is intended to involve some action on the part of the bailiff. If no action takes place (ie, the bailiff no longer pursues the debtor for payment because the debt is then cleared), there can be no lawful imposition of a further charge.

In a case where a bailiff conducts a visit to enforce more than one liability order at a time but does not seize goods, the bailiff is only entitled to one visit fee, not one for each liability order.

A charge is due if goods have been removed by the bailiff and are later released as a result of payment, or (in very rare circumstances) where the auction sale is to take place on the debtor's premises, but if it is later cancelled as a result of payment.

Any spurious charges should be challenged, first with the bailiffs concerned and, if that fails, with the local authority, if necessary using the local authority's formal complaints procedure. If neither succeeds, an application should be made to a county court judge to examine the charges – a process known as 'taxation'.

National enforcement standards indicate that care should be taken with vulnerable households. See Appendix 2.

Sale of goods

Practice Note No. 9 (para 4.12) advises local authorities to ensure that they obtain the best price for the goods seized. Goods are usually sold by auction. The sale should not normally take place until at least five days after the removal of the goods. You or an adviser should try to prevent the sale of goods wherever possible, since it is not a cost-effective way of clearing the debt from a debtor's point of view. The proceeds from the sale usually only represent a fraction of the goods' replacement value. If a sale does take place and raises more money than was owed, the balance, minus the costs associated with the sale, should be returned.

Delays in levying distress

It is not unknown for debtors to receive letters from bailiffs relating to periods of liability going back several years. If a local authority has delayed unreasonably in using bailiffs to recover an old debt, a complaint of maladministration may be made (see Chapter 13).[90]

Codes of practice

The local authority is responsible for ensuring that the activities of its bailiffs comply with the law. Local authorities must ensure their bailiffs have a certificate from a county court. Bailiffs who apply for a certificate must undergo a standard security check, regardless of whether they are applying for a first certificate or a renewal. National enforcement standards issued by the former Lord Chancellor's Department (now the Ministry of Justice) recognise that, in particular, vulnerable groups should be protected.[91] See Appendix 2. If a local authority fails to observe its code of practice – eg, it decides to use bailiffs and a member of a household has a disability, or if it has failed to calculate council liability correctly – this may amount to maladministration and be grounds for a complaint to the Local Government Ombudsman (see Chapter 13).[92]

Return of council tax debt to the local authority

Some local authority finance departments claim that, once a bailiff is instructed, it is not possible to return the debt to the local authority. This is wrong in law as the bailiffs are the servants of the local authority and subject to its direction, since the liability order grants a range of options to be pursued. The Local Government Ombudsman has indicated that local authorities must act appropriately and in a proportionate way when enforcing debts (see Chapter 13). Any blanket refusal to consider taking back a particular debt from the bailiffs may be challenged by way of judicial review. It may also be a matter for investigation by the District Auditor.

Complaints against bailiffs

If a bailiff behaves wrongly a complaint may be made to the firm concerned and to the professional body of bailiffs and enforcement agents, the Enforcement Services Association. The procedure on complaints can be found at www.ESA. A complaint should normally be made first to the bailiff company concerned. If the response is unsatisfactory or there is no response at all, a complaint may then be made to the Enforcement Services Association. Failure to answer the initial complaint will be taken into consideration.

Complaints may also be made to the local authority using its complaints procedure for any wrongful action by its bailiffs or bailiffs which it employs. If the bailiff holds a certificate for the collection of rent, a complaint can be made to the county court which issued the certificate. Such a complaint should normally only be made in extreme cases, but the certificate which the bailiff needs to practice may be cancelled or declared void.

Appealing against distress

If you are unhappy about the use of distress, you can appeal to a magistrates' court.[93] However, distress is not considered unlawful simply because of a defect in the liability order.[94] The most common ground of appeal is when bailiffs have seized goods belonging to a non-liable person.[95]

If the court is satisfied that a levy was irregular it may:
- order any goods taken to be returned if they are still in the local authority's possession; *and*
- award the aggrieved person an amount of money for any goods seized and sold.

The award is equal to the amount which, in the opinion of the court, would be awarded as damages for the goods if proceedings were brought in connection with trespass.[96] If the court is satisfied that the levy was irregular, it may also make an order requiring the local authority to desist from levying in such a manner.[97]

Legal advice is essential before commencing an appeal, not least because of the risk of costs if the appeal fails. In more complex cases the county court or the High

Court may also be used to bring an action against the local authority or the bailiffs concerned.

Charging orders

This method of recovery is available if the debtor is the owner or part-owner of the dwelling. It cannot be used if s/he is a tenant or licensee. If the local authority has obtained one or more liability orders and the total debt outstanding is at least £1,000, it can apply to the county court for a charging order against the dwelling, provided it is the one that gave rise to the council tax arrears.[98] The decision to use this method of recovery is a discretionary one. In practice, local authorities may use a charging order if a person has £5,000 or more in council tax arrears. The local authority must consider all the relevant factors before deciding to adopt this method and a local authority is likely to attract criticism if it seeks to obtain a charging order for a relatively small amount.

In deciding whether to grant a charging order, the county court must consider all the circumstances of the case including:[99]

- the personal circumstances of the debtor; *and*
- whether any other person would be 'unduly prejudiced' if an order were granted.

A charging order effectively 'mortgages' the property with the debt. If the debt remains unpaid, the local authority may apply to the court for the property to be sold to pay the debt. In practice, the court rarely orders the property to be sold. Obtaining a charging order does mean, however, that if the property is sold or remortgaged, the local authority is potentially entitled to receive the outstanding amount from the proceeds of the sale. This is only the case, however, if there are sufficient funds remaining after any charge with a higher priority, such as a mortgage, has been met. If you are a householder who has negative equity with an existing mortgage lender, the use of a charging order will not result in any recovery.

Bankruptcy proceedings

If a liability order has been obtained, the (outstanding) amount on it is a debt for the purposes of bankruptcy (if the debtor is an individual) or winding-up proceedings (if the debtor is a registered or unregistered company).[100]

This means that the local authority can apply to bankrupt an individual or wind up a company, but only if s/he owes at least £750 (the local authority can combine all the debts owed to it – eg, rent and council tax). The court may make an order following a hearing or series of hearings if there is an appeal or any challenges to the procedure. In the event of bankruptcy or winding-up proceedings, no other recovery action can be taken. This does not affect the bankrupt individual's ongoing council tax liability.

If you are facing bankruptcy proceedings, you should obtain professional advice as quickly as possible. The implications for homeowners are serious because bankruptcy can result in loss of the home. A useful and free plain English guide to bankruptcy is produced by the Insolvency Service of the Department of Trade and Industry.[101] It is available at www.insolvency.gov.uk.

Procedure

Bankruptcy proceedings are complex, and specialist advice is needed. Only a basic outline of the procedures is set out here. An adjournment might be obtained if there is a realistic prospect of settling the debt.

Bankruptcy proceedings are started by serving a document known as a 'statutory demand' on the debtor. This has to comply with the Insolvency Rules.[102]

The demand must:
- be dated and signed by the proper officer of the local authority;
- state the amount of the debt and how it has arisen;
- specify whether it is a debt payable immediately or not;
- give details of the liability order and when it was granted by a magistrates' court;
- state details of any other charge or costs.

The demand must also give details about the rights of the debtor, and ways of complying with the demand. It must include an explanation of why bankruptcy proceedings must be started if the demand is not complied with, details of how the demand may be complied with and details of how to contact the local authority. The demand must inform you that you have a right to apply to the county court or High Court to have the demand set aside. This must be done within 18 days of service.[103] If the local authority fails to comply with the rules – eg, it starts proceedings on the wrong form, this will not automatically invalidate the demand.[104] For this to happen, 'prejudice' has to be caused to the council tax debtor.[105]

Response by the council tax debtor

On receipt of the demand, you may pay the debt, provide a security against it, or settle or adjust the debt to the satisfaction of the local authority. If you reduce the amount owed to below £750, a bankruptcy petition cannot be presented. Alternatively, you can seek to 'set aside' (see below) the demand through the High Court (in London) or the county court (elsewhere)

Setting aside

An application to set aside a statutory demand may be made by a debtor on Form 6(4), which is available from the county court. The application to set aside must be supported by a copy of the demand, and an affidavit or statement of truth. A letter to the local authority requesting that a demand is set aside is not sufficient to comply with the rules.[106] The statement should specify the date of the service of the demand and the grounds on which it is to be set aside. You must make the application within strict time limits.

When a court can set aside a statutory demand

The application to set aside the statutory demand may be granted if:[107]

- you appear to have a counterclaim, set-off or cross-demand, which equals or exceeds the amount of the statutory demand; *or*
- the debt is disputed on grounds which appear to the court to be substantial; *or*
- it appears that the local authority holds some security in respect of the debt and the court is satisfied that the value of this equals or exceeds the full amount of the debt; *or*
- the court is satisfied on other grounds that the demand ought to be set aside.

You may be able to make a case if the local authority has failed to award council tax benefit, has miscalculated the year's council tax liability, has failed to award a discount or grant an exemption, or has failed to repay money owed from an earlier year. In such cases it may be best for you to rely on grounds 'which appear to be substantial'.[108]

To succeed, it may be necessary to show that the disputed part of the debt would reduce the overall level of council tax debt to below £750.

Triable issue

Both the previous and current Practice Directions for insolvency proceedings issued by the courts indicate that the statutory demand may be set aside if a 'triable' issue can be shown. This means there is a possible defence to the debt claim which needs to be examined by the court. However, equally, the court may refuse to set aside a liability order if it is founded on a judgment or order.[109]

This may cause particular difficulties if you have a *bona fide* case which should go before a valuation tribunal, because the court may not appreciate that this is where disputes between debtor and the local authority are to be settled. Similarly, the court may not realise that the council tax regulations themselves seek to prevent these arguments being raised in the magistrates' courts at the liability order hearing where the order is made.

Other grounds

Under the Insolvency Rules, the court has a broad discretion to set aside a statutory demand if satisfied that it ought to do so.[110] The courts consider the list of potential grounds to be an open one, and may include maladministration or harassment by the creditor. This may bring into play wider principles of justice, where the court might consider it unjust for the debtor's inability to pay to be established for the purpose of allowing a bankruptcy petition to be presented.

Possible grounds on which a demand might be challenged include where the local authority has failed to award a discount, benefit or other reduction to which the debtor is entitled.

It is possible that human rights principles could be used if bankruptcy is disproportionate to the size of the debt. In *Griffin v Wakefield MBC*,[111] the Court of Appeal held that bankruptcy was not a more severe enforcement method than imprisonment. However, it is arguably much more severe than deductions from benefit or attachment of earnings orders, which may be available to the local authority. Furthermore, the court might consider the human rights of those living with a debtor, such as dependent people or people with disabilities. These issues have yet to be fully tested.

Suspension of the time limit

Once documents are filed, the court will review their content. The effect of filing is to suspend the time limit for compliance, giving you time to negotiate or otherwise settle the debt. In other cases, you may apply to set aside the liability order in the magistrates' court (see p172).

If the application to set aside the statutory demand is dismissed at this stage, the three-week period for compliance with the demand begins to run again.[112] If, on reviewing the document, the court is satisfied that the application to set aside should be heard, a hearing date will be set with at least seven days' notice to the debtor and the local authority.

Proving the bankruptcy debt

It is always essential that the local authority be put to strict proof over the existence of a liability order. The local authority should be required to produce a copy of the liability order or prove that the order exists.

The High Court has indicated that it will be prepared to look at whether the debt can be proved and this may be the only option for the debtor in many cases.

Often the computerised bulk summonsing procedures used by local authorities may not actually result in a hard copy of an individual order against a debtor being signed or endorsed by a court.

If you have had no notice of liability order proceedings, you should request that the local authority produces the liability order.[113] If no liability order can be produced which is endorsed by a signature of a justice of the peace or other court stamp, the application may fail on the grounds that the order was not properly obtained from the magistrates' court.

In the case of *London Borough of Lambeth v Simon*,[114] the local authority alleged non-payment of council tax debts and sought to present a bankruptcy petition against the debtor in the High Court. The local authority had obtained three liability orders for council tax amounting to £2,258 for 1997/98, 1998/99 and 2004/05. A statutory demand had been served, but the debtor had made no attempt to set aside either the demand or the liability orders. The debtor contested the petition on the basis that a previous bankruptcy order which post-dated the three liability orders had been annulled in May 2005 on the basis that all his debts had been paid. At the hearing of the petition the debtor presented a letter from the local authority which tended to confirm his claim that the liability orders had been paid in full. The petition was dismissed as the local authority had made errors and the Court was not satisfied that the statements in the petition were true. The Bankruptcy Registrar expressed the view that petitions by local authorities should comply with Rule 6.8 of the Insolvency Rules, requiring that, 'There shall be stated in the petition, with reference to every debt in respect of which it is presented (a) the amount of the debt, the consideration for it... (b) when the debt was incurred or became due.'

The Court also referred to the fact that, in other cases, liability orders were shown not to exist or they could not be proved by the production of a sealed order or a statement from the clerk to the magistrates that an order has been made. In some cases, no credit for payments was shown. Thus, the integrity of the debt on which bankruptcy petitions were based was in question. The Court stated that, in future, petitions by local authorities relying on liability orders should set out a full history of the account at both the statutory demand and the petition stages, properly showing all debts and credits. If a liability order is being relied on, the local authority must be able to prove its existence to the satisfaction of the court.

Paying the debt

The council tax debtor may avoid bankruptcy by paying the debt at the stage of the final bankruptcy order and the court may adjourn proceedings if there is a realistic chance of the debtor raising the money. However, repeated adjournments are unlikely, and the debtor may still be liable for the costs of the bankruptcy proceedings even if the council tax is paid.

The bankruptcy petition

If a debtor fails to set aside a statutory demand, the local authority may then present a bankruptcy petition against the debtor. Normally, the High Court or county court will accept the liability order as validly issued and may refuse to examine the grounds on which it was granted. By the time the bankruptcy petition reaches court, it will usually be too late for the debtor to challenge the liability order by applying to the magistrates' court or the High Court. However, in *Mohammed v Southwark Borough Council*,[115] the Court indicated that there were circumstances in which it would look at issues regarding liability for the tax or the amount of tax. In particular, the Court considered itself entitled to deal with the argument intended to be the subject of a valuation tribunal appeal. The debtor could also try to raise reasonable arguments previously put forward at a hearing to set aside a statutory demand.

Effectively, the bankruptcy court action provides a last chance to dispute council tax liability or local authority calculations.

The only advantage to a bankruptcy order being made against a debtor is that no other enforcement measure can be used thereafter, including imprisonment. However, unless the debtor is living in rented accommodation, bankruptcy is likely to result in loss of home and severe financial hardship.

Imprisonment

England and Wales are the only countries in Europe in which a person can be sent to prison for not paying a local tax. There is no imprisonment for failure to pay council tax in Scotland.

As the law currently stands, English or Welsh local authorities may, in certain circumstances, apply to the magistrates' court for a warrant committing the debtor to prison.[116] This is a coercive measure designed to extract payment from someone who has the means to pay the debt. It is not a punishment for failure to pay.[117]

A taxpayer who is unable to pay and is threatened with committal should contact the local authority immediately in writing, setting out the financial problems which they are experiencing.

A request should be made for the local authority to consider using its power under section 13A of the Local Government Finance Act 1992 to reduce or remit the debt.

The overall figures for committal to prison for council tax debt have shown a marked decline in the last decade. In a Parliamentary answer given on 2 November 2005, Fiona McTaggart, Undersecretary of State at the Home Office, provided figures for the number of people committed to prison since 1997 as follows: 1997 – 357; 1998 – 194; 1999 – 101; 2000 – 41; 2001 – 29; 2002 – 21; 2003 – 30; 2004 – 26.

However, what these figures do not reveal is the extent of how the threat of imprisonment is used to coerce payment. Similarly, it is not clear if these figures include instances where a warrant is issued and the debtor taken into custody in the court, but payment is made before s/he is taken to prison.

If either before or after a warrant is issued the amount in question is paid or offered to the local authority, it must accept the amount concerned and no further action should be taken.[118]

If someone pays the amount due after the local authority has applied for a warrant but before it is issued or a term of imprisonment fixed and the issue of a warrant is postponed, a local authority may recover reasonable costs in connection with the committal proceedings.

Maximum costs connected with committal

Application for a warrant to be issued	£85
Application for an arrest warrant with bail	£85
Application for an arrest warrant without bail	£105

An application for a warrant can only be made if:[120]
- the debtor is aged 18 or over; *and*
- the local authority has sought to levy distress; *and*
- the bailiff attempting to levy has reported to the local authority that s/he was unable (for whatever reason) to find any or sufficient goods.[119] This includes cases where a bailiff has been unable to obtain entry. If a liability order has been made against joint taxpayers, a warrant may not be applied for, unless the local authority has sought to levy distress against all of them and the bailiff has been unable to find any or sufficient goods belonging to all of them.

Practice Note No. 9 (para 14.1) advises that a local authority which has not attempted any remedy other than distress should satisfy itself, by looking again at any information it holds on the debtor, that none of the other available remedies would prove more effective. Magistrates and their legal advisers are expected to be familiar with the principles governing committal to prison, set out in *Stones' Justices' Manual,* the basic rule book on which courts rely on a day-to-day basis for guidance. Magistrates are required to consider alternative enforcement methods before issuing a committal warrant as part of the process.[121]

Means inquiry

The court must examine the debtor's means before issuing a warrant (a 'means inquiry'). This involves questioning the debtor in court about her/his circumstances, income, outgoings, debts and savings to discover the reason for her/his failure to pay and her/his means. To enable such an inquiry to take place, the debtor may be summoned to appear before a magistrates' court.[122]

A warrant to commit someone to prison is only issued if the court is satisfied that failure to pay is due to the debtor's:
- wilful refusal; *or*
- culpable neglect;[123] *and*
- the debtor has the means on the day to pay the debt.[124]

If magistrates do not conduct a proper means inquiry, the proceedings will be unlawful and any committal order may be quashed on appeal to the High Court. Magistrates are expected to assess properly the debtor's means and not to make irrational assumptions. A typical error of many means inquiries is to fail to ask the debtor if s/he has any savings or capital. A lack of accessible savings or capital is likely to mean that the debtor lacks the ability to pay the sum immediately.

Only a failure by the debtor to pay council tax which is 'blameworthy' is considered to be wilful refusal or culpable neglect. If you are unable to pay council tax because you are too poor, or the failure arose through illness, job loss, a domestic disaster such as a fire or flood, unexpected pregnancy, being forced from a property as a result of domestic violence, or a failure to pay benefit, you should not be at risk of imprisonment. In such cases, an application should be made by the court to remit the debt (see p194).

Where wilful refusal or culpable neglect is found, the decision to issue a warrant of commitment must still be a reasonable one. A debtor will often be asked to make an offer of payment. If a viable offer has been made, magistrates should accept it and not issue the warrant.[125]

The maximum period of imprisonment is three months,[126] but the maximum period should be reserved for only the most extreme cases, such as deliberate non-payment.[127]

Mothers with young children

The provisions of the Human Rights Act 1998 now apply to committal for debts recoverable in magistrates' courts. In *R (Stokes) v Gwent Magistrates' Court*, the High Court held that the decision to jail a young mother for 12 days for owing £455 was an infringement of Article 8 of the European Convention on Human Rights (right to family life).[128] Magistrates' courts, therefore, have to consider whether the proposed interference with the rights of the children is proportional to the amount of debt involved.

Committal proceedings for default on local taxes have often involved mothers with young children and the disproportionate nature of committal has been expressed in other cases. Arguably, in every case where someone could be imprisoned the effect on family life must be considered. In some cases, for instance, there could be a loss of accommodation if a person is committed to prison for a long term.

There would seem to be very few cases where a commitment warrant would be justified or proportional, particularly with the availability of deductions from benefit and attachment of earnings orders. The courts have also indicated that committal is inappropriate where the amounts concerned are small.[129]

Immediate committal

Immediate committal should be a rare situation and will be harder for a court to justify. A magistrates' court may, and normally does, postpone the issue of a warrant for such time and on such conditions as it decides.[130] These conditions normally include the debtor being ordered to pay the amount outstanding by reasonably achievable instalments. The conditions imposed must be reasonable ones.[131]

In *R v Faversham and Sittingbourne Justices, ex parte Ursell*, it was held that the court, which had fixed a term of imprisonment for wilful refusal to pay the community charge but postponed the issue of a warrant on condition of future payment in instalments, must hold a further hearing before issuing a warrant of commitment to prison following breach of the condition.[132] The magistrates' court must be satisfied that the debtor has been served with proceedings and knows about the hearing.[133] You must be given notice of the date and time of that further hearing and an opportunity to attend. You may wish to require the local authority to prove non-payment and are entitled to draw the court's attention to any change in circumstances since the decision to fix a term of imprisonment was made, which renders it inexpedient for the warrant of commitment to be issued. In *R v Mid-Hertfordshire ex parte Cox*, it was held that magistrates must examine events which have happened since the previous court fixed a term of imprisonment and postponed the issue of the warrant.[134] When the debtor goes back to court the magistrates must consider all the circumstances that have happened and decide whether to issue the warrant of commitment, postpone it again or make some other order.[135]

The case of *R v Northampton Magistrates' Court, ex parte Newell* confirmed that a warrant could be issued committing a defaulter to prison for breach of the conditions when s/he is not present in court, providing that s/he had been given notice of the hearing.[136]

Special care should be taken if a debtor is illiterate.[137]

If a person has been committed to prison and:[138]

- the whole of the amount outstanding is paid, s/he should be released;
- part of the amount outstanding is paid, her/his sentence should be reduced on a proportionate basis.

The liability, including that of someone who is jointly liable,[139] must be written off after a warrant of commitment has been issued, as no further recovery action can be taken in relation to the relevant amount.[140]

Challenging a decision to imprison

A decision to imprison someone can be challenged by appealing (within 21 days) or by judicial review (within three months). In practice, if the warrant of commitment has been issued and the debtor is already in prison, judicial review is the preferred route of appeal as the High Court can grant immediate bail to an imprisoned debtor, pending the full appeal hearing. The debtor will need to have a solicitor who can arrange an application to the High Court via a barrister. The application for leave and bail can be made directly to a High Court judge outside normal court hours in emergency cases.

If imprisonment is quashed on judicial review the magistrates or the local authority may be liable to pay costs if the commitment was flagrantly wrong.

Remission of the debt

If the magistrates' court does not fix a period of imprisonment and the debtor is unable to pay or the debts are very old, it can remit the debt. Remission may be in part or in full.[141] The council tax debt is extinguished for the financial year in question, but liability remains for subsequent years.

Magistrates should remit part of the debt where an order to pay instalments would result in an unreasonably long repayment period.[142] Any period in excess of three years is considered unreasonable.[143] However, the court may choose to postpone the warrant to a specific date (where the payment level appears not to achieve payment within three years) and conduct a review at that time to see if repayment ought to be increased or reduced.

Once the magistrates have set a term of imprisonment there is no power to remit. So if your circumstances deteriorate and you can no longer pay the amounts ordered, you should tell the court, which can simply postpone the issue of the warrant indefinitely, without any payments being ordered.

Use of handcuffs

In two cases involving the committal to prison of people over pension age in 2008, it was reported that both had handcuffs applied. Normally, there should be no question of handcuffing a civil prisoner unless there is a risk of violence or escape. The Divisional Court has ruled that the unnecessary use of handcuffing on prisoners who were either in- or out-patients was capable of infringing Article 3 of the European Convention on Human Rights (against inhuman and degrading treatment).[144]

Recovery of costs after unsuccessful enforcement action

A local authority can use an attachment of earnings order to recover costs incurred in attempting to levy distress or in an abortive application for a warrant of commitment.[145] However, no further steps can be taken once a person has been committed to prison and has served her/his term of imprisonment.

---

5. Statutory enforcement in Scotland

Reminders and losing the right to pay by instalments

If an instalment under the statutory instalment scheme or any special agreement has not been paid by the due date, the local authority must serve a reminder notice on the liable person. The reminder notice requires payment to be made within seven days.[146] It must include:
- a note of the instalment(s) required to be paid and the remainder to be paid for the year;
- a statement informing the taxpayer that if no, or insufficient, payment is made to cover any instalments that are, or will become, due within seven days of the issue of the reminder, the right to pay by instalments is lost and the remaining balance for the year becomes payable after a further seven days.

If two reminders have been issued during the financial year, even if a person pays what s/he owes, s/he becomes liable for the whole of the outstanding amount following a third failure to pay, without the need for another reminder.[147] On the second reminder notice, you should be informed of the consequences of a third failure to pay.[148]

The local authority may take recovery action where any sum, including the 10 per cent statutory surcharge and civil penalties, which has become payable to the local authority has not been paid.[149] Additionally, if an elected member of a local authority is in at least two months' arrears, there are restrictions on her/his ability to vote on specific matters (see p177).[150]

Summary warrant or decree

If council tax, Scottish Water charges or a civil penalty is owed, the local authority can apply to the sheriff's court for a 'summary warrant' or seek a 'decree' granted in an action of payment. The summary warrant allows for a special accelerated enforcement procedure. The sheriff must grant a summary warrant if the local authority provides a certificate.[151] The certificate must contain the following statements:

- that the person specified in the application has not paid the sums due;
- that the local authority has served a reminder notice on the person requiring her/him to pay the amount due within 14 days from the day on which the notice was served;
- that this period has expired without full payment;
- that in respect of each person on the application, either:
  - a period of 14 days has passed without her/him initiating an appeal (see Chapter 12) because s/he disagrees with the local authority's decision that the dwelling is a chargeable dwelling, or that s/he is liable to pay the tax, or with the calculation of the amount which must be paid, including her/his entitlement to a disability reduction or a discount; *or*
  - the local authority has notified the person in question that it believes the grievance is not well-founded, or steps have been taken to deal with the grievance, or two months have passed since the service of the aggrieved person's notice;
- the amount unpaid by each person.[152]

Where two or more people are jointly liable, the local authority may seek a warrant which shows them as jointly or individually liable for the outstanding sum.[153]

Information from the debtor

If a summary warrant or decree for payment has been granted, you must provide specified information required by the local authority.[154] The obligation lasts for as long as any part of the relevant amount remains unpaid. The information required is:

- the name of your employer;

- the address of the employer's premises where you work;
- if there are no such premises in Scotland, the address of any one place of the employer's business in Scotland;
- your national insurance number;
- details of your bank account;
- the name and address of any other person(s) who is jointly liable to pay the whole or any part of the amount in respect of which the warrant or decree was granted.

The information must be supplied in writing within 14 days of the day on which the request is made by the local authority.[155] Failure to comply could result in a civil penalty being imposed.

Deductions from benefits

If a local authority has obtained a summary warrant or a decree against a debtor and s/he is entitled to income support (IS), pension credit (PC), employment and support allowance (ESA) or jobseeker's allowance (JSA), it may also apply to the Department for Work and Pensions for deductions to be made from the debtor's benefit, as described on p177.

Other recovery methods

The summary warrant authorises the local authority to recover the unpaid council tax, Scottish Water charges and civil penalties and a surcharge of 10 per cent of the amount owing by either:
- an earnings arrestment (see below); *or*
- an arrestment and action of furthcoming and sale (see p200);[156]
- attachment and exceptional attachment orders.

Enforcement of the summary warrant is by sheriff's officers or messengers at arms. Their fees and expenses in connection with execution of the warrant are charged to the debtor.[157] Special permission is now needed from the sheriff for a special attachment to seize goods.

Sheriffs cannot demand entry to a person's home unless a court order known as an 'exceptional attachment order' has been obtained. Forced entry cannot take place unless there is a person present who is at least 16 and is not, because of her/his age, knowledge of English, mental illness, mental or physical disability or otherwise, unable to understand the consequence of the procedure being carried out.

Earnings arrestment

A sheriff's officer serves an 'earnings arrestment' schedule on your employer. This requires the employer to deduct a prescribed amount from your net earnings on every pay day. The arrestment remains in effect until either the debt has been paid in full or you stop working for the employer.

Deductions made under earnings arrestment

Net weekly earnings	Deduction
Below £63	Nil
£63.01 to £75	£2
£75.01 to £80	£4
£80.01 to £85	£5
£85.01 to £95	£6
£95.01 to £105	£8
£105.01 to £115	£10
£115.01 to £125	£12
£125.01 to £135	£14
£135.01 to £145	£16
£145.01 to £155	£18
£155.01 to £165	£20
£165.01 to £175	£22
£175.01 to £185	£24
£185.01 to £195	£27
£195.01 to £210	£30
£210.01 to £230	£34
£230.01 to £250	£38
£250.01 to £270	£42
£270.01 to £290	£47
£290.01 to £310	£52
£310.01 to £330	£57
£330.01 to £350	£62
£350.01 to £370	£68
£370.01 to £400	£82
£400.01 to £430	£97
£430.01 to £460	£113
£460.01 to £500	£131
£500.01 to £540	£149
£540.01 and over	£149 in respect of the first £540 plus 50 per cent of the remainder

Net monthly earnings	Deduction
Below £273	Nil
£273.01 to £310	£9
£310.01 to £330	£14
£330.01 to £350	£19

£350.01 to £380	£26
£380.01 to £420	£33
£420.01 to £460	£40
£460.01 to £500	£47
£500.01 to £540	£54
£540.01 to £580	£61
£580.01 to £620	£68
£620.01 to £660	£75
£660.01 to £700	£82
£700.01 to £740	£90
£740.01 to £800	£104
£800.01 to £860	£118
£860.01 to £930	£132
£930.01 to £1,000	£147
£1,000.01 to £1,070	£162
£1,070.01 to £1,140	£177
£1,140.01 to £1,220	£196
£1,220.01 to £1,300	£217
£1,300.01 to £1,400	£239
£1,400.01 to £1,500	£261
£1,500.01 to £1,600	£324
£1,600.01 to £1,800	£396
£1,800.01 to £2,000	£472
£2,000.01 to £2,200	£562
£2,200.01 to £2,400	£652
£2,400.01 and over	£652 in respect of the first £2,400 plus 50 per cent of the remainder

Net daily earnings	*Deduction*
Below £9	Nil
£9.01 to £11	£0.25
£11.01 to £12	£0.50
£12.01 to £14	£0.80
£14.01 to £16	£1.10
£16.01 to £18	£1.80
£18.01 to £20	£2.15
£20.01 to £22	£2.50
£22.01 to £24	£2.85
£24.01 to £26	£3.20
£26.01 to £28	£3.60
£28.01 to £31	£4.20
£31.01 to £34	£4.90
£34.01 to £37	£5.80

£37.01 to £41	£6.70
£41.01 to £45	£7.70
£45.01 to £49	£9.00
£49.01 to £54	£10.80
£54.01 to £59	£12.60
£59.01 to £64	£15.30
£64.01 to £70	£18.00
£70.01 to £75	£20.70
£75.01 and over	£20.70 in respect of the first £75 plus 50 per cent of the remainder

An arrestment and action of furthcoming or sale

'**Arrestment**' is the process by which money or goods held by a third party for a debtor may be frozen. It could be applied, for example, to money held in a debtor's bank account. If a debtor's bank account details are unknown, usually bank arrestments are initiated by serving letters on the main banks. When money is identified as being held by a third party – eg, a letting agency, an arrestment is served by an officer of the court in the presence of one witness and it freezes the funds. They cannot be withdrawn until the debt has been settled. Usually, the debtor is asked to sign a mandate authorising the release of funds equal to the arrears and costs to the local authority. Any money that remains in the account is released. If a mandate is not signed, the local authority must raise an action of '**furthcoming**' to allow arrested funds to be transferred. You cannot defend the action by disputing the debt, but you can defend it by showing that the arrestment was invalid, procedurally irregular or gained nothing.

Time to pay orders

From April 2008 you can apply to a sheriff's court for a '**time to pay order**'. If granted, the local authority cannot seek to enforce a council tax debt while the order is in force.

The court must grant the order if it is satisfied that it is reasonable in all the circumstances to do so. It must have regard to:
• the nature of and reasons for the debt;
• any action taken by the creditor to assist the debtor in paying the debt;
• the financial circumstances of the debtor;
• the reasonableness of the debtor's proposal to pay the debt;
• the reasonableness of any refusal by the creditor or any objection to any proposal to pay the debt.

Enforcement costs

The amount added to the debt is 10 per cent of the outstanding balance. The sheriff's officer's fees set by the court, together with costs necessarily incurred in connection with the execution of a summary warrant, can also be charged to a debtor once formal recovery proceedings begin through a summary warrant

Future changes

As with England and Wales, there are proposals to reform the civil enforcement system in Scotland. The Scottish Government published a report and consultation, *Enforcement of Civil Obligations in Scotland*, which is available at www.scotland.gov.uk/consultations/justice/civOb-01.asp and entered into a consultation process. Many of the responses were incorporated into the Bankruptcy and Due Diligence etc (Scotland) Act 2007.

6. **Human rights and enforcement action**

Human rights law is likely to have a growing effect on local authority actions, particular when the provisions of the Tribunals Courts and Enforcement Act come into force. These and the use of other measures may be affected by the Strasbourg principle of 'proportionality'.

Cases involving the seizure of goods to pay taxes have been before the European Court of Human Rights, notably in *K v Sweden*[158] and *Camenzind v Switzerland*.[159] In the UK, cases of fine enforcement have been considered subject to proportionality where mothers with young children are affected, such as *R (Stokes) v Gwent Magistrates' Court*.[160] In this case, the High Court held that enforcement activity could be contrary to Article 8 of the European Convention on Human Rights (protecting privacy, rights to the home and family life).

Following this principle, it would appear open to a court to decline to execute a warrant if a debt is relatively small and the hardship caused to a vulnerable household would be severe. Determining whether a person is vulnerable requires a public authority such as a local authority, a court or even an enforcement agent to exercise discretion.

Liability under the Human Rights Act

Under the Human Rights Act 1998, proceedings are directed not at the UK Government but against the public authority responsible for the act or omission which constitutes a breach of human rights.

Section 6(1) of the Act states: 'It is unlawful for a public authority to act in a way which is incompatible with a Convention right.' If it is claimed that a public authority has acted, or is proposing to act, in a manner which is unlawful under this section, someone who is or would be a victim of the unlawful act may either bring legal proceedings against the authority in an appropriate court or tribunal or rely on the Convention right in any legal proceedings.

There is no definition of public authority in the Act, but it states that it includes 'any person certain of whose functions are functions of a public nature'.[161] Within 'public authority' are bodies that may exercise a mix of public or private actions. Arguably, those carrying out the seizure of goods may fall into the category of a public authority, potentially including private firms of bailiffs or individuals with authority to collect a range of debts. This has yet to be tested by the courts, but may mean that private firms of bailiffs who become enforcement agents will be amenable to judicial review as public authorities.

Notes

2. What happens when an instalment is not paid (England and Wales)
1 Reg 23 CT(AE) Regs 1992
2 Reg 23 CT(AE) Regs 1992
3 Reg 23 CT(AE) Regs 1992
4 Reg 23 CT(AE) Regs 1992
5 Reg 33 CT(AE) Regs 1992
6 Reg 54 CT(AE) Regs 1992
7 Reg 34 CT(AE) Regs 1992

3. Liability orders (England and Wales)
8 *R v Bristol Magistrates' Court ex parte Willsman and Young* [1991] RA
9 Reg 34 CT(AE) Regs 1992
10 *Associated Provincial Picture Houses Ltd v Wednesbury Corporation* [1948] 1 KB 223
11 CT(AE) Regs 1992; *Regentford Ltd v Thanet District Council* [2004] 246, 18 February 2004 (HC)
12 *Ratford and Haywards (Receivers and Managers) v Northavon District Council* [1986] RA 137
13 *Ratford and Haywards (Receivers and Managers) v Northavon District Council* [1986] RA 137
14 Reg 35(2A) CT(AE) Regs 1992
15 Reg 35 CT(AE) Regs 1992
16 In *R (on the application of Clark-Darby) v Highbury Magistrates Court* [2002] the High Court quashed a liability order where the person had not received the notice of the hearing as it was unjust to allow the order to stand.

17 Reg 34 CT(AE) Regs 1992
18 Reg 34 CT(AE) Regs 1992
19 r14 Magistrates' Court Rules 1981
20 Reg 2 CCCTNR(E)(MC) Regs
21 *R v Leicester City Justices, ex parte Barrow and another* [1991] 25 July 1991 (CA)
22 *R v Burnley Justices ex parte Ashworth* [1992] 32 RVR 27
23 *R v Leicester City Justices ex parte Barrow and another* [1990] 25 July 1991 (CA)
24 Reg 34 CT(AE) Regs 1992
25 Reg 57 CT(AE) Regs 1992
26 Reg 53(4) CT(AE) Regs 1992
27 *Sutton v Islington London Borough Council* [1997] CO/1784/94, 17 October 1997, unreported
28 Magistrates' Courts (Hearsay Evidence in Civil Proceedings) Rules 1999
29 rr3-6 Magistrates' Courts (Hearsay Evidence in Civil Proceedings) Rules 1999
30 Regs 35 and 48 and Sch 2 Forms A and B CT(AE) Regs 1992
31 s82 LGA 2003; reg 5 CT(AE) Regs 2004
32 *Liverpool City Council v Pleroma Distribution Ltd* [2002] All ER (D) 302
33 *R (on the application of Tull) v Camberwell Green Magistrates' Court and another* [2005] RA 30
34 *R (on the application of Newham London Borough Council) v Stratford Magistrates' Court* [2008] All ER (D) 17 January 2008

4. Recovery methods (England and Wales)

35 Reg 52 CT(AE) Regs 1992
36 Reg 54 CT(AE) Regs 1992
37 Reg 36 CT(AE) Regs 1992
38 Reg 36 CT(AE) Regs 1992
39 Reg 36 CT(AE) Regs 1992
40 Reg 36 CT(AE) Regs 1992
41 Reg 56 CT(AE) Regs 1992
42 Reg 56 CT(AE) Regs 1992
43 Reg 37 CT(AE) Regs 1992
44 Reg 37(4) CT(AE) Regs 1992
45 Sch 3 CT(AE) Regs 1992
46 CT(AE)(AEO)(W) Regs
47 Reg 37a(2) CT(AE) Regs 1992
48 Reg 41 CT(AE) Regs 1992
49 Reg 40 CT(AE) Regs 1992
50 Reg 40 CT(AE) Regs 1992
51 Reg 40 CT(AE) Regs 1992
52 Reg 56 CT(AE) Regs 1992
53 Reg 56 CT(AE) Regs 1992
54 Reg 56 CT(AE) Regs 1992
55 Reg 39(6) and (7) CT(AE) Regs 1992
56 Reg 56 CT(AE) Regs 1992
57 Reg 38 and Sch 4 CT(AE) Regs 1992
58 Reg 32 CT(AE) Regs 1992
59 Reg 32 CT(AE) Regs 1992
60 Reg 32(1) CT(AE) Regs 1992; CT(AE)(A)(E) Regs
61 New figures inserted into Schedule 4 by The Council Tax and Non-Domestic Rating (Amendment)(England) Regulations 2006 No.3395; The Council Tax and Non-Domestic Rating (Amendment)(England) Regulations 2007; and CT(AE)(A)(W) Regs
62 Reg 42 CT(AE) Regs 1992
63 Reg 42 CT(AE) Regs 1992
64 Reg 42 CT(AE) Regs 1992
65 s106 LGFA 1992
66 s106 LGFA 1992
67 CT(DIS) Regs as amended by The Employment and Support Allowance (Consequential Provisions)(No.2) Regulations 2008 No.1554
68 Reg 5 CT(DIS) Regs
69 Reg 4 CT(DIS) Regs
70 Reg 8(4) CT(DIS) Regs
71 Reg 8 CT(DIS) Regs
72 Reg 8(5) CT(DIS) Regs
73 Reg 8(3) CT(DIS) Regs
74 Reg 8(6) CT(DIS) Regs
75 Reg 8(7) CT(DIS) Regs
76 Reg 45 CT(AE) Regs 1992
77 Reg 45 CT(AE) Regs 1992
78 Reg 52 CT(AE) Regs 1992
79 Reg 45a(1) and (2) CT(AE) Regs 1992
80 Reg 45 CT(AE) Regs 1992
81 Reg 45(1a) CT(AE) Regs 1992
82 Reg 45 CT(AE) Regs 1992
83 *Semayne's Case* [1603] 5 CO Rep 91(a); *Southam v Smout* [1963] 3 All ER 104
84 *Vaughan v McKenzie* [1969] 1 QB 557
85 Sch 5 para 2(2) CT(AE) Regs 1992
86 *Khazanaci v Faircharm Investments Ltd* and *McLeod v Butterwick* [1998] 17 March 1998 (CA)
87 Reg 45(5) CT(AE) Regs 1992
88 *Evans v South Ribble District Council* [1991] 12 July 1991 (QBD)
89 Change in the table put into place by The Council Tax and Non-Domestic Rating (Amendment)(England) Regulations 2007 No.501
90 Complaint against Tameside Metropolitan Borough Council 98/C/4810 reported at [1999] RVR 283
91 A consultative document issued by the Public Law Project, 14 Bloomsbury Square, London WC1A 2LP
92 Local Government Ombudsman Report 96/A/3626
93 Reg 46(1) CT(AE) Regs 1992
94 Reg 45(7) CT(AE) Regs 1992
95 Reg 46(1) CT(AE) Regs 1992
96 Reg 46(3) CT(AE) Regs 1992
97 Reg 46(4) CT(AE) Regs 1992
98 Reg 50(1)-(3) CT(AE) Regs 1992
99 Reg 51(1) CT(AE) Regs 1992
100 Reg 49 CT(AE) Regs 1992
101 The Insolvency Service, 21 Bloomsbury Street, London WC1B 3FF (Tel: 020 7637 1110)
102 r6.1 Insolvency Rules 1986, as amended by The Insolvency Rules (Amendment) Rules 1987 No.1919
103 r6.2(1)(d) Insolvency Rules 1986 No.1925
104 *Cartwright v Staffordshire and Moorlands DC* [1998] BPIR 328
105 *Re a Debtor (no 1 of 1987)* [1989] 1 WLR 271 (CA)
106 *Ariyo v Sovereign Leasing plc* [1998] BPIR 177
107 r6.5(4) Insolvency Rules 1986 No.1925
108 r6.5(4)(b) Insolvency Rules 1986 No.1925
109 *Morley v IRC (re a Debtor)* (No 657-SD-1991) [1996] BPIR 452
110 r6.5(4)(d) Insolvency Rules 1986 No.1925
111 *Griffin v Wakefield MBC* [2000] (CA)
112 r6.5(1) Insolvency Rules 1986 No.1925

113 *Smolen v Tower Hamlets* LBC [2006] RVR 296

114 *London Borough of Lambeth v Simon* [2007] BIPR 1629 June 6 2007

115 *Mohammed v Southwark Borough Council* [2006] RVR 124

116 Reg 47(1) CT(AE) Regs 1992

117 *Stevenson v Southwark Borough Council* [1993] RA 113

118 Reg 47(6) CT(AE) Regs 1992

119 Reg 47(1) CT(AE) Regs 1992

120 Reg 54 CT(AE) Regs 1992

121 *R v Birmingham Magistrates' Court ex parte Mansell* [1988] RVR 112; *R v Alfreton Justices ex parte Gratton* [1993], *The Times,* 8 December 1993

122 Reg 48(5) CT(AE) Regs 1992

123 Reg 47(2) CT(AE) Regs 1992

124 *R v Poole Justices ex parte Benham* [1992] 156 JP 157

125 *R v Alfreton Justices ex parte Gratton* [1993], *The Times,* 8 December 1993

126 Reg 47(7) CT(AE) Regs 1992

127 *R v Highbury Corner Magistrates Court ex parte Uchendu* [1994] RA

128 *R (Stokes) v Gwent Magistrates' Court* [2001]

129 *R v Worthing Justices ex p Waller* [1988] COD 69

130 Reg 47(3)(b) CT(AE) Regs 1992

131 *R v Alfreton Magistrates ex parte Gratton* [1993], *The Times,* 8 December 1993; *R v Leicester Justices ex parte Wilson* [1993], 16 December 1993, unreported

132 *R v Faversham and Sittingbourne Justices ex parte Ursell* [1992], *The Times,* 18 March 1992

133 *R v Newcastle-Upon-Tyne Justices ex parte Devine* [1998] RA 97

134 *R v Mid-Hertfordshire ex parte Cox* [1995] ALR 205

135 *R v Mid-Hertfordshire Justices ex parte Cox* [1995] ALR 205

136 *R v Northampton Magistrates' Court ex parte Newell* [1992] RA 283

137 *R v Barnet Justices ex parte Ribbans* [1997] CO/2757-96, 18 June 1997, unreported

138 Reg 47(6)-(8) CT(AE) Regs 1992

139 Reg 54 CT(AE) Regs 1992

140 Reg 52(1) CT(AE) Regs 1992

141 Reg 48(2) CT(AE) Regs 1992

142 *R v Newcastle-Upon-Tyne Justices ex parte Devine* [1998] RA 97

143 *R v Newcastle-Upon-Tyne Justices ex parte Devine* [1998] RA 97

144 *R(on the application of Graham) v Secretary of State for Justice; R v (on the application of Allen v Secretary of State for Justice* [2007] All ER (D) 383, 23 November 2007

145 s80 LGA 2003; reg 6 CT(AE) Regs 1992

5. **Statutory enforcement in Scotland**

146 Reg 22 CT(AE)(S) Regs

147 Reg 22 CT(AE)(S) Regs

148 Reg 22 CT(AE)(S) Regs

149 s97 and Sch 8 para 1 LGFA 1992

150 s112 LGFA 1992

151 Sch 8 para 2 LGFA 1992

152 Reg 30 CT(AE)(S) Regs

153 Reg 30 CT(AE)(S) Regs

154 Reg 31 CT(AE)(S) Regs

155 Reg 31 CT(AE)(S) Regs

156 Sch 8 para 2 LGFA 1992

157 Sch 8 para 4 LGFA 1992

6. **Human Rights and enforcement action**

158 *K v Sweden* [1991] 71 DR 94

159 *Camenzind v Switzerland* [1999] 28 EHRR 458

160 *R (Stokes) v Gwent Magistrates' Court* [2001] JPN 766

161 s6(3)(b) Human Rights Act 1998

Chapter 12

••

Appeals

This chapter covers:
1. Valuation tribunals and valuation appeal committees (below)
2. Matters that can be appealed (p206)
3. How appeals are dealt with (p213)
4. Appeal hearings (p214)
5. Reviews of tribunal decisions (p222)

---

1. Valuation tribunals and valuation appeal committees

In England and Wales, appeals are dealt with by valuation tribunals. In Scotland, these appeals are heard by valuation appeal committees.

Valuation tribunals and valuation appeal committees determine:
- disputes over the banding of a property;
- disputes between the council taxpayer and the local authority over liability and the amount of council tax;
- disputes over exemptions and discounts.

Both tribunals and appeal committees should conduct themselves in a more informal and less intimidating way than a court of law and, prior to 2007, typically dealt with around 27,000 appeals a year (although not all proceeded to a full hearing).

Valuation tribunals

Valuation tribunals are designed to provide a free mechanism to review and correct any erroneous decisions which affect taxpayers either concerning the valuation band given to a property or decisions on liability, exemptions, discounts and calculations. Valuation tribunals are designed to be independent of both the local authority and the Valuation Office Agency (VOA).

Often a local authority will negotiate to settle a dispute if a council tax payer is prepared to appeal.

Valuation tribunals have undergone major changes in 2009. The Tribunals, Court and Enforcement Act 2007 established two new tribunals, the First-tier Tribunal and the Upper Tribunal, with powers to transfer to them the functions of the large number of existing tribunals. The jurisdiction of the Lands Tribunal which heard certain rating appeals was transferred to the Upper Tribunal on 1 June 2009.

From 1 November 2007 the valuation tribunals in England and Wales are supervised and regulated by the Administrative Justice and Tribunals Council. The Council comprises the Parliamentary Commissioner for Administration, and 10–15 members chosen by the Lord Chancellor and Scottish and Welsh Ministers. The Administrative Justice and Tribunals Council has a Scottish and Welsh Committee.

The Valuation Tribunal for England

From 1 October 2009, a central valuation tribunal was established for England. This replaced the previous 56 valuation tribunals, which had their jurisdiction transferred to the Valuation Tribunal for England on this date.

The Lord Chancellor appoints the President and Vice President of the Valuation Tribunal for England, who will have responsibility for the new system. The aim of the Government is to put the valuation tribunal system under the direction of a single President to streamline and standardise procedures throughout England and Wales, so that decisions will be of a consistent quality.

Members and chairs of the Tribunal will also be selected by the Lord Chancellor. Members are likely to remain local people serving in a voluntary capacity.[1] Members do not necessarily have any particular professional qualifications.

The Tribunal is advised on matters of law and procedure by its clerk, who is a salaried employee of the Tribunal. The clerk is also the taxpayer's point of contact. The clerk should be able to respond to requests for advice on procedures in advance of the hearing. S/he cannot, however, advise on the substance or merits of the appeal.

Valuation appeal committees

In Scotland, appeals are dealt with by valuation appeal committees.[2] The committee is made up of local people appointed by the appropriate sheriff principal. A committee consists of a chairperson and three to six ordinary members. Members are unpaid and independent of the assessor and the local authority. The committee is assisted by a paid secretary who is usually a lawyer.

2. Matters that can be appealed

Appeals can be made to a tribunal in England and Wales or a committee in Scotland on:

- valuations (see p208);
- liability (see p209);
- discounts;
- exemption;
- completion notices (see p211);
- calculations on the amount of tax (other than council tax benefit (CTB) decisions);
- penalties (see p212).

A number of matters are excluded from appeals to a valuation tribunal (or committee). These include matters for which there is some other route of appeal – eg, to the First-tier Tribunal, the magistrates' court or the High Court. For instance, disagreements over entitlement to CTB do not go to a tribunal/committee, but to the First-tier Tribunal, as described in Chapter 9. **Note:** if a local authority does not backdate your CTB in respect of earlier financial years, however, you may be able to challenge this at a valuation tribunal or committee. This can be done on the basis that there is an error in the calculation of a bill.

Any decision about the civil rights and obligations of a citizen normally has a further right of appeal. It is arguable that because section 16 of the Local Government Finance Act 1992 allows a taxpayer to challenge 'any calculation', this may allow you to challenge sums from previous years when you were prevented by the backdating rules from applying for CTB. However, this matter has yet to be ruled on by the courts.

Also, in England and Wales, the following matters can only be dealt with by the High Court:

- the classes of dwellings that are exempt;
- a determination by the local authority to prescribe a class of dwellings where the owner, rather than the resident, is liable;
- any determination made by a Welsh local authority to give a smaller or no discount on certain furnished property that is no one's sole or main residence;
- the setting of the council tax.

Council tax payments if there is an outstanding appeal

A person who has been served a bill must make the payments required by the bill or by any subsequent special agreement reached with the local authority. The fact that an appeal has been made does not affect this obligation, though some local authorities are willing to suspend recovery action until an appeal has been dealt with. If an appeal is upheld, any overpayment of tax should be refunded or credited against future liability.

One exception to this is if an appeal has been made against a penalty imposed by the local authority. In such cases, the penalty does not have to be paid until the appeal has been decided. If a sum in council tax relates to a previous year, it could also be argued that the matter should wait for a determination by a tribunal.

If the local authority seeks a liability order through the magistrates' court, the magistrates' court may also agree to an adjournment if an appeal to a valuation tribunal/committee about liability has started. An adjournment should always be granted if there is the prospect of a successful appeal in a case where a local authority is seeking a committal order against a debtor.

Valuations

Appeals in England[3]

Chapter 3 describes the way in which you may make a proposal to the listing officer or assessor to alter the valuation list. Standard forms for making proposals are available from the valuation office or the assessor. From 1 October 2009, new rules were introduced for England on the alteration of lists. Although these largely re-enact the previous law, the Valuation Tribunal for England may become more formal in its practice and procedure.

Since the introduction of the Appeals Direct system in England in 2007, you are now expected to play a greater part in taking a banding appeal to a valuation tribunal. The listing officer is no longer obliged to refer the appeal to a tribunal automatically. Not every person who makes a proposal to alter their property banding wants to become involved in a full tribunal hearing, and the system gives you the choice of whether or not to proceed. It is hoped that this system will reduce the number of appeals reaching tribunals and enable resources to be applied where a dispute cannot otherwise be settled by negotiation.

Under Appeals Direct, the valuation office has four months to decide whether or not to alter the list and to issue you with a decision notice. During this four-month period, you can try to negotiate and reach an amicable solution with the valuation office on the banding. It is envisaged that the listing officer will discuss the proposal with you and any interested parties before issuing a decision notice. The notice will state that the listing officer either agrees to alter the valuation list or that s/he rejects the proposal and no alteration will be made. A letter will be sent with the notice explaining that you and any interested party have a right of appeal. This must be done within two months of the date of the decision letter.

The Valuation Tribunal for England should aim to list the appeal within six months of receiving the appeal notice and give you not less than four weeks' notice of the hearing.

If you decide to appeal, the listing officer will prepare a presentation pack. This typically includes background information relating to the case, accompanied by evidence of comparable property values. You can also present your valuation evidence and it is likely that similar cases will be heard on the same day.

If a listing officer believes that a proposal has not been validly made and serves an invalidity notice on you, you can appeal against the invalidity notice (within four weeks) directly to the Valuation Tribunal for England.

You must serve a notice of appeal to the clerk of the Tribunal with a copy of the notice. The notice must also include a written statement of the following if they are not included on the invalidity notice:[4]

- the address of the dwelling;
- the reasons for the appeal against the invalidity notice;
- the names and addresses of the proposer and the listing officer.

If the listing officer reconsiders the matter and withdraws an invalidity notice after an appeal has been started s/he must inform the Tribunal.[5]

If the listing officer agrees the proposal or decides to alter the list, whether or not an agreement has been reached, the list will be altered within six weeks.[6]

Appeals in Wales and Scotland

In Wales and Scotland the appeal system still requires the listing officer or the regional assessor to refer appeals to the tribunal or appeals committee.

The closing date for appeals in Wales against new valuations was 31 December 2005; thereafter, only limited rights of appeal are possible until the next revaluation.

Deciding which valuation applies

When determining a council tax banding, the tribunal/committee will apply the same valuation assumptions that were applied in the original valuation (see Chapter 3). You must show that, on applying the new valuation assumptions to your dwelling, a different sale price to that which the valuation office reached would be obtained. An appeal is only likely to succeed, therefore, if you can show that a mistake was made in the way the assumptions were originally applied to the individual dwelling, indicating that a different value should have been reached and the difference in value is sufficient to justify moving the dwelling into another valuation band.

The mistake may include, for instance, an error about the number of rooms in a property, or the size of its garden or the existence of something in the locality which would have a material effect on the valuation of a property – eg, it is next door to an industrial or commercial building, the nature of which is likely to bring down the value of a neighbouring property.

The valuation tribunal/committee is bound to follow the valuation assumptions and cannot consider whether the valuation assumptions are wrong in law or that the regulations themselves are defective.

Liability

You can appeal if you disagree with the local authority's decision:

- that a dwelling is not exempt (Chapter 5);
- that someone is, or is not, a liable person (Chapter 6);
- that a disability reduction should not be granted (Chapter 7);

- that a discount should not be granted (Chapter 8);
- that the amount payable is correct.

There are two stages to appeals on liability and calculation issues. The first stage involves writing to the local authority.[7] The letter should state the decision that is in dispute and the reason(s) for the disagreement. The local authority has two months in which to consider these matters and may ask for additional information. A further appeal may be made to a tribunal/committee if the local authority:[8]

- rejects the appeal;
- makes some changes, but fails to satisfy you; or
- fails to make a decision within the two-month period.

Tactically, it is advantageous to mention the right of appeal to the valuation tribunal or committee in the early stages of correspondence. In the case of a dispute over liability, a calculation or an exemption, a letter can, for example, include the following line: 'In the event that you do not accept my submission, please treat this letter as notice of appeal to the valuation tribunal established under section 16 of the Local Government Finance Act 1992.'

As a precaution against the loss of relevant correspondence by the local authority, it may also be advisable to send a copy to the relevant tribunal, with an accompanying letter stating that you wish an appeal to be listed in the event that a negotiated settlement cannot be reached with the local authority. Such a copy should be marked 'for information' and dated clearly. In the event that the local authority loses the appeal, this will provide a record to establish it was made within the time limits.

Appeals in England and Wales[9]

An appeal to the Valuation Tribunal for England or to a valuation tribunal in Wales must normally be made:[10]

- within two months of the date the local authority notified you of its decision; or
- within four months of the date when the initial representation was made if the local authority has not responded.

The tribunal President has the power to allow an out-of-time appeal if you have failed to meet the appropriate time limit because of reasons beyond your control.[11]

You, or someone on your behalf, must write directly to the clerk of the relevant tribunal. The appeal letter should state:[12]

- the reasons for the appeal;
- the date on which the first letter regarding the matter was served on the local authority;
- the date, if any, when you were notified by the local authority of its decision.

Appeal forms on which the required information is requested are available from the relevant tribunal's office. The clerk should notify you within two weeks that the appeal request has been received. The clerk should also send a copy of the appeal letter or form to the local authority.[13]

If you are considered to be resident in more than one local authority area and therefore liable for the tax, you may appeal against the decisions and may choose one of the relevant valuation tribunals to hear the appeal.[14] You should write to the clerks of the relevant tribunals informing them of your decision.

Appeals in Scotland

In Scotland, an appeal to a committee must be made by writing to the local authority within four months of the date on which the grievance was first raised with it in writing.[15] There is no power to consider out-of-time appeals. The letter should state:[16]
- the reasons for the appeal; *and*
- the date on which the first letter disputing the matters was served on the local authority.

The local authority must pass the appeal to the secretary of the relevant valuation appeal committee.[17]

Completion notices

In England and Wales, the local authority and, in Scotland, the assessor, may issue a completion notice that states the date on which a newly erected or structurally altered property is considered to be a dwelling. While the matter can be discussed with the local authority or the assessor, an appeal can be made to a tribunal or committee.

Appeals in England and Wales[18]

An appeal to the Valuation Tribunal for England or to a valuation tribunal in Wales must normally be made within four weeks of the notice having been sent.[19] The President of the tribunal may, however, allow an out-of-time appeal if you have failed to meet this time limit for reasons beyond your control.[20]

You, or someone on your behalf, should write directly to the clerk of the relevant tribunal.[21] The letter should:
- state the reasons for the appeal; *and*
- be accompanied by a copy of the completion notice.

Appeal forms on which the information is requested are available from the relevant tribunal office. The clerk should notify you within two weeks that the appeal request has been received. The clerk should also send a copy of the appeal letter or form to the local authority.[22]

Appeals in Scotland

In Scotland, an appeal to the valuation assessment committee must be made in writing to the assessor within 21 days of receiving the completion notice.[23] There is no power to consider out-of-time appeals. The letter should state the reasons for the appeal and be accompanied by a copy of the completion notice.[24] The assessor must pass the appeal to the secretary of the relevant valuation appeal committee.[25]

Penalties

The local authority has power to impose a penalty in certain instances where someone is required to provide information but fails to provide it, or provides information which s/he knows to be false. While the matter may be discussed with the local authority and it has the power to withdraw the penalty, an appeal can be made to a tribunal or a committee. For more on penalties, see p159. Grounds on which a penalty may be quashed include if:

- the local authority already has the information;
- you have valid reasons for withholding the information – eg, on grounds of confidentiality;
- the amount of information being sought is excessive or the demand is impossible to comply with;
- the information is irrelevant or it is not within the remit of the local authority to seek.

Appeals in England and Wales[26]

An appeal to the Valuation Tribunal for England or a valuation tribunal in Wales must normally be made within two months of the penalty being imposed.[27] The President of the tribunal has the discretion to allow an out-of-time appeal if you have failed to meet the time limit for reasons beyond your control.[28] The appeal is made by the aggrieved person, or someone acting on her/his behalf, by writing directly to the clerk of the relevant tribunal. The letter should state:[29]

- the reasons for the appeal; *and*
- the date, if any, s/he was notified by the local authority of the penalty.

Appeal forms on which the required information is requested are available from the relevant tribunal office. The clerk should notify you within two weeks that the appeal request has been received. The clerk should also send a copy of the appeal letter or form to the local authority.[30]

Appeals in Scotland

In Scotland, an appeal to the committee must be made by writing to the local authority within two months of the penalty being imposed.[31] There is no power to consider out-of-time appeals. The letter should state:

- the reasons for the appeal; *and*

- the date, if any, you were notified by the local authority of the penalty.[32]

The local authority must pass the appeal to the secretary of the relevant valuation appeal commitee.[33]

---

3. **How appeals are dealt with**

While there are many similarities in the way in which the Scottish valuation assessment committee and the English and Welsh valuation tribunals deal with appeals, different rules apply in Scotland from those which apply in England and Wales.[34] Additionally, in England and Wales there are a number of differences in the way in which tribunals deal with appeals on valuation matters and the way in which they deal with appeals on other council tax issues. From 1 October 2009, the Valuation Tribunal for England (see p206) has wide powers to manage cases, give directions and strike out proceedings for failure to follow directions.

An appeal is normally dealt with by an oral hearing but, if all the parties agree, it can be dealt with by written representation (see below).[35] In most cases, it is advisable to request an oral hearing.

Withdrawing an appeal

In England and Wales, if an appeal was made before the Appeals Direct system came into force and the listing officer decides after the appeal has been initiated that it is well-founded, s/he may withdraw the appeal by writing to the clerk of the relevant tribunal. You may also withdraw an appeal on a valuation matter by writing to the valuation tribunal.[36] Appeals can also be withdrawn on application on the day of the hearing.

In Scotland, an appeal may be withdrawn by writing to the secretary of the committee, or at the hearing by asking the permission of the committee. If the assessor decides, after the appeal has been initiated, to agree to the original proposal or the local authority decides not to contest the appeal, it is considered to be withdrawn.[37]

Post-appeal agreement

In England, from 1 October 2009 an agreement may be reached between all the parties before the hearing or consideration of written representations (see below). The agreement details the alteration and the listing officer must serve a copy on the Valuation Tribunal for England and all the parties to the agreement. The alteration to the list must take place within six weeks.[38]

Written representations

Prior to the Appeals Direct system coming in force, Practice Note No. 6 (para 7.1) described the ability to deal with disputes by written representations as a relatively quick and effective procedure for resolving straightforward appeals. For an appeal to be dealt with in this way, all the parties (normally you, the listing officer/assessor and the local authority) must give their written agreement.[39]

There is no maximum time limit in which the tribunal or committee must determine the appeal on the basis of written representations. Once it is agreed that the appeal is to be dealt with in this way, the clerk must serve notice on the parties accordingly, and all parties have four weeks in which to send in their written representations. Copies of these are sent to the other parties. There is then a further four-week period in which comments may be made. At the end of this last period, the clerk or secretary sends the available material to the tribunal or committee within four weeks. On receiving the referral, the tribunal or committee may:[40]

- require any party to provide additional material;
- order that the appeal be dealt with by a hearing; *or*
- go on to reach a decision.

Where additional information is required, copies of that material must be provided to all the other parties. Each party may, within four weeks of receiving the additional material, supply a further statement in response.[41]

In Scotland, permission to deal with the appeal by written representation may be withdrawn by any of the parties at any time before a decision is reached. This might happen, for example, if the other party's arguments are not as expected. Where permission has been withdrawn, the appeal must be dealt with by an oral hearing.[42]

Pre-hearing reviews

In the case of an English or Welsh appeal on valuation matters, the tribunal chair may order a pre-hearing review to clarify the issues to be dealt with at the hearing as part of its case management powers. The chair may direct that a pre-hearing review is held to consider any matter, such as the procedure to be followed, evidence and time limits.[43] This may be done either at the request of the appellant, any other party, or on the chairperson's own initiative. At least four weeks' notice must be given of a pre-hearing.

4. **Appeal hearings**

Notice

In England, from 1 October 2009 the Valuation Tribunal for England must give each party 'reasonable notice'. This normally means 14 days, unless parties consent or there are urgent or exceptional circumstances. In Wales, if the appeal is to be dealt with at a hearing, the clerk to the tribunal must give at least four weeks' written notice of the date, time and place of the hearing.[44] In Scotland, the secretary to the committee must give not less than 35 days' written notice.[45] There is no maximum time limit in which the tribunal or committee must hear the appeal.

In Wales, the clerk must advertise the date, time and place of the hearing:[46]
- at the tribunal's office; *and*
- outside an office earmarked by the local authority for this purpose; *or*
- in another place within the local authority's area.

In Scotland, the secretary must advertise the details at a local authority office and the place at which the hearing will be, if different.[47]

In all cases the advert must name a place where a list of the appeals to be heard may be inspected by members of the public.[48]

People disqualified from participating in the hearing

Natural justice refers to the rules and procedures to be followed by any body, including a tribunal or committee, which has the duty of adjudicating disputes. One of the principles of natural justice is the rule against bias. This requires that someone should not take part in a hearing if a reasonable person would think that her/his participation is likely to lead to bias. In England and Wales, the following people may be excluded from participation as a member, clerk or officer of a tribunal in relation to a particular appeal:[49]
- an elected member of the local authority in which the dwelling is situated; *or*
- the appellant's spouse; *or*
- someone who supports the appellant financially.

Someone is not disqualified, however, simply because s/he is a member of a local authority (eg, a county council), which derives its revenue directly or indirectly from council tax payments that may be affected by exercising her/his functions.[50] If the appellant is a current or former employee or member of the relevant tribunal, her/his appeal is dealt with by another tribunal.[51] If a President of the tribunal considers that a conflict of interest would make it inappropriate for a tribunal to hear an appeal, another tribunal will be appointed.[52]

It is not wrong for a clerk to retire with the tribunal during its deliberations,[53] but no other person should be present without the consent of all parties when the tribunal retires to consider its decision.

Representatives

On the day of the hearing any party may:[54]
- represent themselves; *or*

- be represented by a lawyer; *or*
- be represented by anyone else.

In England and Wales, someone who is representing her/himself may have the assistance of someone else – eg, a friend, a relative or an adviser.[55] Members of the tribunal or the panel from which the valuation committee is drawn are not permitted to represent parties at its hearings.[56] Additionally, in England and Wales, employees of the tribunal are also barred from acting in that capacity. In Scotland the committee may, if it is satisfied that there are good and sufficient reasons for doing so, refuse to permit a particular person to represent a party at a hearing.[57]

How the hearing is conducted

In England and Wales, the appeal is heard by three members of the tribunal, one of whom must be the chair and who must preside. Where all parties who attend the hearing agree, the appeal may be decided by two members of a tribunal and in the absence of a chair.[58] In Scotland the minimum number of people who can constitute a valid committee is three.

Public hearing

The hearing normally takes place in public. In England and Wales, the tribunal can decide to hold the hearing in private if any of the parties request it and the tribunal considers that the interests of that party would be prejudicially affected if the hearing were held in public.[59] Someone who might disrupt a hearing or who is likely to prevent another person giving evidence may be excluded. In Scotland, the committee may, if it has reasonable cause, hold the hearing in private.[60]

Failure to appear

In England and Wales, if you (in Scotland, you or your representative) fail to appear at the hearing, the appeal may be dismissed. In England and Wales, an appeal on a valuation matter may also be dismissed if any party other than the listing officer fails to attend. In England, the Valuation Tribunal for England may also strike out an appeal for failure to follow a direction.[61]

In England and Wales, if a party can show reasonable cause for not appearing s/he may request the tribunal to review its decision (see p222). The request must be made within four weeks of the notice of the decision being given.[62]

In Scotland, if you have a reasonable excuse for your absence, the committee may set a new date, time and place for the hearing.[63] It must give all parties at least seven days' notice. For a hearing to be recalled in this manner you must write to the committee (normally within 14 days of being notified that the original appeal was dismissed) requesting a new hearing date and setting out the reason for the original absence. If the committee considers that there are special circumstances, it may allow an out-of-time request.

If any party does not appear at the hearing, the tribunal or committee may hear and determine the appeal in her/his absence.[64]

Order of the hearing

The tribunal or committee may determine the order of the hearing – ie, which party puts its case first. Usually, the local authority will put its case first and you will then be given an opportunity to put questions. Parties at the hearing may examine and cross-examine any witness and call witnesses. The tribunal or committee may require any witness to give evidence by oath or affirmation.[65] At the end of the hearing, the tribunal will normally retire to consider its verdict or the parties to the appeal will be asked to leave the room. The clerk to the tribunal can advise the tribunal, but no other person should be present while the tribunal is engaged in deliberations. If any other person is present, the decision may be challengeable on grounds of breach of natural justice.

Adjournment and dismissal

A hearing may be adjourned for such time, to such a place and on such terms (if any) as the tribunal or committee thinks fit. Reasonable notice of the time and place to which the hearing has been adjourned must be given to every party.[66]

In some cases, a tribunal may dismiss an appeal brought by the valuation office if the valuation officer fails to show that the council tax payer has been properly served with notices and documents.

Witnesses

The Valuation Tribunal for England may summons a person to attend as a witness and order her/him to produce any documents or answer any questions relating to the proceedings.[67] A summons must normally be given to a person with 14 days' notice (or a shorter period if the Tribunal directs). A summons or order must state that a person may apply to vary or set aside the summons or order if s/he has not had the opportunity to object to it and must state the consequences of non-compliance. There is currently no equivalent rule in Wales or Scotland.

Evidence

Where facts, such as the value of a dwelling, are in dispute each party to the hearing should provide evidence that supports her/his view of the facts. The rules relating to evidence are different in Scotland from those that apply in England and Wales.

England and Wales

Tribunals are not bound by any rules relating to the admissibility of evidence before courts of law; rather, they are concerned with the weight of any evidence.[68] For example, what someone else has been heard to say (hearsay) would be admissible at a hearing, but given less weight than the direct evidence of a witness.

Evidence can be given orally or in written form, such as valuation reports. You should make sure that you have multiple copies of any documents wherever possible. Where the valuation of a dwelling is in question, evidence could include photographs or even a video. Occasionally physical evidence may even be produced. In *Morgan v Dew*, damaged pillowcases and sheets were produced to prove local pollution existed which the appellants contended had an adverse effect on house valuation.[69]

However, since the appeal in *Tilly v Listing Officer of Tower Hamlets LBC*, it seems that the High Court expects a stricter approach to valuation evidence.[70] In this case, the appellant sought a judicial review of the dismissal of a second valuation tribunal appeal. She alleged the value of her property had been adversely affected by chemical pollution arising from developments in London's Docklands. She was successful at her first hearing and later lodged a second appeal to secure a further reduction in banding from D to C. She produced a report from the South East Institute of Public Health on chemical pollution and argued such pollution affected the value of her home. The tribunal dismissed her appeal on the basis that pollution was already known at the time of the first alteration.

On appeal to the High Court it was held that, although the tribunal had erred in concentrating on the date the pollution was first discovered, it refused to interfere with the decision. No substantial wrong or miscarriage of justice had been caused. The High Court considered that the evidence produced was wholly inadequate for the tribunal to form an opinion, as the applicant had not produced evidence of the value of her flat and how its value had been affected. In its judgment the court stated:

> It is not enough to say this or that change of circumstances has occurred in the locality and leave it to the tribunal to translate it into an impact on property values.[71]

It appears the High Court considered it was impossible for the tribunal to translate statistics in the report into an effect on house prices that would require a change in valuation band.

This has important implications, as it seems that the High Court now expects appellants to be put to stricter proof on their grounds for an alteration in valuation, even though property valuation has always been considered more of an art than a science. In future cases it may be that the best form of evidence is a valuation report from an independent valuer demonstrating a link between the blighting and the price a dwelling would have fetched in a theoretical sale on 1 April 1991 (see Chapter 3). It leaves less scope for inference by the tribunal.

A further important decision is the Court of Appeal judgment in *Chilton Merryweather (LO) v Hunt and Others* in which the Court ruled that the word 'physical' in relation to physical changes in the environment did not include changes in traffic and pollution and noise caused by greater car use on a motorway.[72]

You should expect to be asked questions by members of the valuation tribunal and by the valuation officer or local authority representative. For example, if you allege that your property value is affected by blighting or a nuisance of some kind, you may be asked what steps you have taken to remedy the problem. If you have taken no such steps, the conclusion might be drawn that the problem is not sufficiently serious as to make an impact on the property value.

In appeals that do not relate to valuation matters the local authority must give the other parties two weeks' notice if it wishes to produce evidence of information supplied in connection with a disability reduction or information in relation to liability. This information may be inspected and copies taken if at least 24 hours' notice is given to the local authority.[73] In a valuation appeal, the listing officer must give at least two weeks' notice of information s/he proposes to use at the hearing. Again, you and any other party to the appeal may, having given 24 hours' notice, inspect the documents and make a copy of all the documents or an extract if you wish.[74] The listing officer may inform you that s/he wishes to use evidence based on the HM Revenue and Customs' confidential records of sale prices of similar houses. If this is the case, you have the right to inspect the relevant documents and to request information relating to a maximum of four comparable dwellings or, if the listing officer specifies more, the same number as is specified by the officer. The listing officer has a duty to produce both sets of documents at the hearing.[75]

Historic values

The Government has indicated that it is prepared to allow the valuation office greater freedom in the future to release information to taxpayers concerning property values obtained before 2000. This information could be of use, particularly with appeals in England where a taxpayer may be able to show a trend in rising house prices for properties with a particular banding and argue that her/his property is similar. Currently, such information is shared only once an appeal proceeds to a valuation tribunal, but the Government proposed to make pre-2000 sales information available at an earlier stage.

Scotland

In Scotland, the committee may require a party to provide the other parties by a set date with:[76]
- a written statement outlining the evidence to be given at the hearing; *and*
- copies of all documents which are to be produced for the hearing.

If a committee has made such a requirement, no other material may be produced unless the committee allows it.[77]

If there is to be a hearing, the committee has the power to grant to any of the parties the same rights of access to documents as could be granted, or provided, by the Court of Session.[78] The committee may require:[79]

- someone's attendance at the hearing as a witness; *or*
- the production of any document relating to the appeal.

If someone fails to comply with such a written requirement, s/he is liable on summary conviction to a fine not exceeding level 1 on the standard scale.[80] No one need produce any material or answer any questions which s/he would not need to answer in a court of law – eg, professional confidences.[81] Additionally, if someone is required to appear as a witness at the hearing and it takes place more than 10 miles from her/his home, s/he does not have to appear unless her/his necessary expenses are paid.[82]

Appeals about liability, exemptions, discounts and calculations

These may be brought under section 16 (section 81 in Scotland) of the Local Government Finance Act 1992. The valuation tribunal can examine and reverse decisions by the local authority in cases of dispute concerning liability, status and calculations regarding tax. The local authority prepares a bundle of papers, including correspondence, outlining its position. In response, you may submit papers and evidence. These should be sent at least one week before the tribunal or committee hearing or within the time limit specified in any direction in England. There will be an opportunity to ask questions and for the taxpayer to present her/his case and give evidence and call witnesses.

Decisions and orders

Following a hearing, the tribunal or committee has the discretion to give an oral decision to the parties concerned. Whether or not an oral decision is given, a written decision, together with a statement of reasons, must be supplied to the parties. In England and Wales this should be done as soon as is reasonably practicable after the decision has been made.[83] Sometimes a handwritten copy is given to the parties on the day, with a more formal typed copy supplied afterwards. In Scotland it must be done within seven days of the decision.[84] After the tribunal or committee has made a decision, it has the power to make orders to give effect to its decision.[85]

Although local authorities and valuation officers have tended to treat previous tribunal decisions involving points of law as binding, it should not be assumed that the tribunal will automatically find against the appellant. Because a tribunal has decided one appeal in a particular way, it does not necessarily follow that the same approach will be taken with a different appeal. Tribunals are not precedent-making bodies. In *West Midlands Baptist (Trust) Association (Incorporated) v Birmingham City Council*, Lord Salmon stated: [86]

> No doubt previous decisions of a tribunal on points of law should be treated by the tribunal with great respect and considered as persuasive local authority, even when made by a layman. But they should never be treated as binding.
> This is particularly so with valuation decisions, where there is room for legitimate disagreement or where better and more accurate evidence may be produced than at an earlier hearing regarding another property.

Information on valuation matters and appeals can be found at the Valuation Office Agency website (www.voa.gov.uk) and the Valuation Tribunal website (www.valuation-tribunals.gov.uk). The latter is regularly updated, with summaries given in recent valuation tribunal decisions.

Records of decisions

In Scotland, each party has the right to make a recording of the hearing at her/his own expense. The committee should be informed of the intention to make a recording before the hearing begins. [87]

In England and Wales, the clerk has a duty to make arrangements for the tribunal's decisions to be recorded. The record may be kept in any form, whether documentary or otherwise. The record must contain the following information in appeals about proposals: [88]

- the appellant's name and address;
- the matter appealed against;
- the date of the hearing or determination;
- the names of the parties who appeared (if any);
- the decision of the tribunal and its date;
- the reasons for the decision;
- any order made in consequence of the decision;
- the date of any such order;
- any certificate setting aside the decision;
- any revocation.

In other appeals the record must also contain: [89]

- the date of the appeal; *and*
- the name of the billing authority whose decision was appealed against.

A copy, in documentary form, of the relevant entry in the record must, as soon as is reasonably practicable after the entry has been made, be sent to each party to the appeal. Each record must be retained for six years. [90]

Anyone may, at a reasonable time given by the tribunal, inspect the records free of charge. If, without a reasonable excuse, a person having custody of records intentionally obstructs someone from inspecting the records, s/he is liable on summary conviction to a fine not exceeding level 1 on the standard scale.[91]

The member who presided at the hearing or determination of an appeal may authorise that any clerical errors be corrected in the record. A copy of the corrected entry must be sent to the people to whom a copy of the original entry was sent.[92]

5. Reviews of tribunal decisions

There are limited circumstances in which a tribunal's decision can be reviewed.

In England and Wales, except where a decision has been the subject of an appeal to the High Court, a tribunal may review its decision or set it aside.[93] This may only be done following a written application from any of the parties on the grounds that:

- a document relating to the proceedings was not sent to, or was not received at an appropriate time by, a party (or party's representative);
- a document was not sent to the Valuation Tribunal for England;
- a party did not appear and can show reasonable cause for their non-appearance; or
- the decision is affected by a decision of, or on appeal from, the High Court or the Upper Tribunal; or
- there has been procedural irregularity; or
- in relation to a decision on a completion notice, new evidence has become available (unless it could have been established by reasonably diligent inquiry or foreseen previously).

An application for a review (or 'set aside') must be made within 28 days of the day on which written notice of the tribunal's decision was sent. The application must be considered by the tribunal President.[94] If a tribunal sets aside a decision, the matter may be reheard or reconsidered by either the same tribunal or a differently constituted one or, in England, treated as an appeal.[95]

As soon as is reasonably practicable after the outcome of the request for a review is known, the clerk to the tribunal must write to the applicant and every other party to the appeal informing her/him of the outcome. Additionally, where an appeal to the High Court remains undetermined, the clerk must also notify the High Court as soon as reasonably practicable after the decision has been made.[96]

Further appeals

After the tribunal or committee there is no further appeal except on a point of law – ie, where the law has been interpreted incorrectly. In England and Wales this is made to the High Court; in Scotland, to the Lands Valuation Appeals Court. The appellant, listing officer, assessor and local authority all have an equal right of appeal. In England and Wales, the High Court has made it clear that it will not normally interfere with findings of fact made by a tribunal, unless it can be shown that the tribunal has acted perversely – eg, the errors of fact are so severe that they amount to errors of law, and thus come within the jurisdiction of the High Court.[97]

You are strongly advised to seek legal advice before embarking upon this course of action, as costs are likely to be in excess of £1,500 and could be much higher depending on the complexity of the case and whether the appeal is contested. Legal aid may be available if you are on a low income. The High Court has the discretion whether or not to award costs against an appellant, but the normal rule is that the loser will pay the costs of the other side. However, the Court's decision will depend very much on the facts and the conduct of the parties, whether they choose to appear and whether the matter could have been settled otherwise.

If the listing officer or the local authority brings the appeal, different rules apply. Costs cannot be awarded if the listing officer has brought the appeal or where the council tax payer does not contest the appeal or attend the hearing. In cases where the local authority appeals to the High Court against a valuation tribunal decision, the liability for costs will fall against the tribunal and not the council tax payer.

In England and Wales, an appeal on a point of law to the High Court must be made within four weeks of:
- the date on which notice is given of the decision or order; *or*
- the date of a decision following review; *or*
- a determination by a tribunal that it will not review its decision where the application for review was made within four weeks of the original decision.

The High Court does have a residual discretion to hear appeals which are out of time (by judicial review) but this should not be relied on, as the right is purely discretionary.[98]

If the tribunal or committee has acted in breach of natural justice (ie, there has not been a fair hearing or there has been some bias in the proceedings), an application for judicial review may also be made. Strict compliance with the rules on appeals and judicial review is expected.[99]

In Scotland any appeal from a committee decision must be made within 14 days. The appeal is started by writing to the secretary of the committee to state a case for the Lands Valuation Appeal Court. See www.saa.gov.uk/resources/193706/gw_appeal_procedures.pdf for more information. Legal advice should be obtained before starting an appeal.

Matters excluded from High Court appeals
In reviewing the decision of a valuation tribunal, the High Court will only consider matters which are relevant to the particular decision of the valuation

tribunal; it cannot consider complaints about the misconduct of individual valuation officers or local authority staff involved.

The High Court cannot look at the validity of an Act of Parliament.[100] Claims that the Secretary of State should have created different bands or made other regulations, applying different valuation assumptions to those in force will not be successful, since the Secretary of State has made regulations in accordance with the wide powers granted under legislation. The High Court will not substitute different meanings or words to those used and will not consider challenges against the validity of regulations, unless it can be shown that the Secretary of State has made regulations which are *ultra vires* – ie, outside the scope of powers granted to her/him by Parliament under the main legislation.

Notes

1. **Valuation tribunals and valuation appeal committees**
   1 **EW** Regs 3 and 4 VT(Amdt)(E) Regs
   2 **S** s81 LGFA 1992

2. **Matters that can be appealed**
   3 Procedural rules for the Valuation Tribunal for England are contained in the VTE(CTRA)(P) Regs, which came into force on 1 October 2009.
   4 **E** Reg 7(6) CT(ALA) Regs, as amended by reg 5 CT(VALA)(E) Regs
   W Reg 8(6) CT(ALA) Regs, as amended by reg CT(VALA)(E) Regs
   5 **E** Reg 7(7) CT(ALA)(E) Regs
   W Reg 8(7) CT(ALA) Regs, as amended
   6 **E** Reg 9(3) CT(ALA)(E) Regs
   W Reg 10(3)CT(ALA) Regs, as amended
   7 **EW** s16 LGFA 1992
   S s81 LGFA 1992
   8 **S** s81 LGFA 1992
   9 Procedural rules for the Valuation Tribunal for England are contained in the VTE(CTRA)(P) Regs, which came into force on 1 October 2009.
   10 **EW** Reg 36 VCCT(Amdt) Regs
   11 **E** Reg 21(6) VTE(CTRA)(P) Regs
   W Reg 36 VCCT(Amdt) Regs
   12 **EW** Reg 37 VCCT(Amdt) Regs
   13 **EW** Reg 37 VCCT(Amdt) Regs
   14 **EW** Reg 35 VCCT(Amdt) Regs
   15 **S** Reg 22 CT(ALA)(S) Regs
   16 **S** Reg 22 CT(ALA)(S) Regs
   17 **S** Reg 22 CT(ALA)(S) Regs
   18 Procedural rules for the Valuation Tribunal for England are contained in the VTE(CTRA)(P) Regs, which came into force on 1 October 2009.
   19 Reg 36 VCCT(Amdt) Regs
   E Reg 21(5) VTE(CTRA)(P) Regs
   20 Reg 36 VCCT(Amdt) Regs
   E Reg 10 VTE(CTRA)(P) Regs
   21 Reg 37 VCCT(Amdt) Regs
   E Reg 10 VTE(CTRA)(P) Regs
   22 **EW** Reg 37 VCCT(Amdt) Regs
   E Reg 25 VTE(CTRA) (P) Regs
   23 **S** Reg 24 CT(ALA)(S) Regs
   24 **S** Reg 24 CT(ALA)(S) Regs
   25 **S** Reg 24 CT(ALA)(S) Regs
   26 Procedural rules for the Valuation Tribunal for England are contained in the VTE(CTRA)(P) Regs, which came into force on 1 October 2009.
   27 **EW** Reg 36 VCCT(Amdt) Regs
   E Reg 21(4) VTE(CTRA)(P) Regs
   28 **EW** Reg 36 VCCT(Amdt) Regs
   29 **EW** Reg 37 VCCT(Amdt) Regs
   30 **EW** Reg 37 VCCT(Amdt) Regs
   31 **S** Reg 23 CT(ALA)(S) Regs
   32 **S** Reg 23 CT(ALA)(S) Regs
   33 **S** Reg 23 CT(ALA)(S) Regs

3. **How appeals are dealt with**
   34 **E** VTE (CTRA)(P) Regs
   W CT(ALA) Regs and VCCT(Amdt) Regs
   S CT(ALA)(S) Regs

35 **EW** Reg 20 CT(ALA) Regs; reg 40 VCCT(Amdt) Regs
   E Reg 29 VTE(CTRA)(P) Regs
   S Reg 27 CT(ALA)(S) Regs
36 **EW** Reg 19 CT(ALA) Regs; reg 39 VCCT(Amdt) Regs
   E Reg 19 VTE(CTRA)(P) Regs
37 **S** Reg 26 CT(ALA)(S) Regs
38 Reg 13 CT(ALA)(E) Regs
39 **EW** Reg 20 CT(ALA) Regs; reg 40 VCCT(Amdt) Regs
   E Reg 29(1) VTE(CTRA)(P) Regs
   S Reg 27 CT(ALA)(S) Regs
40 **S** Reg 27 CT(ALA)(S) Regs
41 **S** Reg 27 CT(ALA)(S) Regs
42 **S** Reg 27 CT(ALA)(S) Regs
43 **E** Reg 6 VTE(CTRA)(P) Regs
   W Reg 21 CT(ALA) Regs

4. Appeal hearings

44 **EW** Reg 22 CT(ALA) Regs; reg 41 VCCT(Amdt) Regs
   E Reg 30 VTE(CTRA)(P) Regs
45 **S** Reg 28 CT(ALA)(S) Regs
46 **EW** Reg 22 CT(ALA) Regs; reg 41 VCCT(Amdt) Regs
47 **S** Reg 28 CT(ALA)(S) Regs
48 **EW** Reg 22 CT(ALA) Regs; reg 41 VCCT(Amdt) Regs
   S Reg 28 CT(ALA)(S) Regs
49 **EW** Reg 23 CT(ALA) Regs; reg 42 VCCT(Amdt) Regs
50 **EW** Reg 23 CT(ALA) Regs; reg 42 VCCT(Amdt) Regs
51 **EW** Reg 17 CT(ALA) Regs; reg 35 VCCT(Amdt) Regs
52 **EW** Reg 35 VCCT Regs; reg 17 CT(ALA) Regs
53 *Boyd v Community Charges Registration Officer for South Staffordshire DC and Staffordshire and Shropshire Valuation and Community Charge Tribunal* [1992] RA 235
54 **EW** Reg 24 CT(ALA) Regs; reg 43 VCCT(Amdt) Regs
   E Reg 13 VTE(CTRA)(P) Regs
   S Reg 34 CT(ALA)(S) Regs
55 **EW** Reg 24 CT(ALA) Regs; reg 43 VCCT(Amdt) Regs
   E Reg 13 VTE(CTRA)(P) Regs
56 **EW** Reg 24 CT(ALA) Regs; reg 43 VCCT(Amdt) Regs
   E Reg 13 VTE(CTRA)(P) Regs
   S Reg 34 CT(ALA)(S) Regs
57 **S** Reg 34 CT(ALA)(S) Regs
58 **EW** Reg 25 CT(ALA) Regs; reg 44 VCCT(Amdt) Regs
   E Reg 32 VTE(CTRA)(P) Regs

59 **EW** Reg 25 CT(ALA) Regs; reg 44 VCCT(Amdt) Regs
   E Reg 31 VTE(CTRA)(P) Regs
60 **S** Reg 32 CT(ALA)(S) Regs
61 **EW** Reg 25 CT(ALA) Regs; reg 44 VCCT(Amdt) Regs
   E Reg 10 VTE(CTRA)(P) Regs
   S Reg 31 CT(ALA)(S) Regs
62 **EW** Reg 30 CT(ALA) Regs; reg 49 VCCT(Amdt) Regs
   E Reg 40 VTE(CTRA)(P) Regs
63 **S** Reg 31 CT(ALA)(S) Regs
64 **EW** Reg 25(5) CT(ALA) Regs; reg 44(4) VCCT(Amdt) Regs
   E Reg 32 VTE(CTRA)(P) Regs
65 **EW** Reg 25 CT(ALA) Regs; reg 44 VCCT(Amdt) Regs
   S Reg 33 CT(ALA)(S) Regs
66 **EW** Reg 25 CT(ALA) Regs; reg 44 VCCT(Amdt) Regs
   E Reg 30 VTE(CTRA)(P) Regs
67 Reg 18 VTE(CTRA)(P) Regs
68 **EW** Reg 25 CT(ALA) Regs; reg 44 VCCT(Amdt) Regs
   E Reg 17 VTE(CTRA)(P) Regs; *Garton v Hunter (Valuation Officer)* [1969] 2 QB 37
69 *Morgan v Dew* [1964] RA 294
70 *Tilly v Listing Officer of Tower Hamlets LBC* [2001] RVR 250
71 LJ Jowitt, *Tilly v Listing Officer of Tower Hamlets LBC* [2001] RVR 250
72 *Chilton-Merryweather v Hunt and Others* [2008] RA357
73 **E** Reg 17 VTE (CTRA)(P) Regs
   W Reg 45 VCCT(Amdt) Regs
74 **E** Reg 17 VTE(CTRA)(P) Regs
   W Reg 26 CT(ALA) Regs
75 **E** Reg 17 VTE(CTRA)(P) Regs
   W Reg 26 CT(ALA) Regs
76 **S** Reg 29 CT(ALA)(S) Regs
77 **S** Reg 29 CT(ALA)(S) Regs
78 **S** Reg 30 CT(ALA)(S) Regs
79 **S** Reg 30 CT(ALA)(S) Regs
80 **S** Reg 30 CT(ALA)(S) Regs
81 **S** Reg 30 CT(ALA)(S) Regs
82 **S** Reg 30 CT(ALA)(S) Regs
83 **EW** Reg 28 CT(ALA) Regs; reg 47 VCCT(Amdt) Regs
   E Reg 37 VTE(CTRA)(P) Regs
84 **S** Reg 36 CT(ALA)(S) Regs
85 **EW** Reg 29 CT(ALA) Regs; reg 48 VCCT(Amdt) Regs
   E Reg 38 VTE(CTRA)(P) Regs
86 *West Midlands Baptist (Trust) Association (Incorporated) v Birmingham City Council* [1967] RVR 780 (CA)
87 **S** Reg 35 CT(ALA)(S) Regs

88 **E** Reg 41 VTE(CTRA)(P) Regs
   W Reg 31 and Sch 4 CT(ALA) Regs
89 **EW** Reg 50 and Sch 4 VCCT(Amdt) Regs
   E Reg 41 VTE(CTRA)(P) Regs
90 **EW** Reg 31 CT(ALA) Regs; reg 50
   VCCT(Amdt) Regs
   E Reg 41 VTE(CTRA)(P) Regs
91 **EW** Reg 31 CT(ALA) Regs; reg 50
   VCCT(Amdt) Regs
   E Reg 41 VTE(CTRA)(P) Regs
92 **EW** Reg 30 CT(ALA) Regs; reg 49
   VCCT(Amdt) Regs
   E Reg 39 VTE(CTRA)(P) Regs

5. **Reviews of tribunal decisions**

93 **EW** Reg 30 CT(ALA) Regs; reg 49
   VCCT(Amdt) Regs
   E Reg 40 VTE(CTRA)(P) Regs
94 **EW** Reg 30(2) CT(ALA) Regs; reg 49(3)
   VCCT(Amdt) Regs
   E Reg 40 VTE(CTRA)(P) Regs
95 **EW** Reg 30(5) CT(ALA) Regs; reg 49(7)
   VCCT(Amdt) Regs
   E Reg 40(7) VTE(CTRA)(P) Regs
96 **EW** Reg 30(6) and (7) CT(ALA) Regs; reg
   49(8) and (9) VCCT(Amdt) Regs
   E Reg 41(10) VTE(CTRA)(P) Regs
97 *Hayes v Humberside Valuation Tribunal
   and Kingston Upon Hull City Council*
   [1998] RA 37
98 *R v London South Eastern Valuation
   Tribunal and Neale (LO), ex parte Moore*
   [2001] RVR 94
99 *R v London South West Valuation Tribunal
   ex parte de Melo* [2000] RVR 73
100 *British Railways Board v Pickin* [1974] 765
   (CA)

Chapter 13

Complaints to the Ombudsman

This chapter covers:
1. The work of the Ombudsman (below)
2. What is maladministration (p228)
3. Making a complaint (p230)
4. Examples of complaints and settlements (p233)

Many decisions made by the local authority in calculating, administering and enforcing the council tax can be appealed. Some errors, however, generate no right of appeal, but can still result in serious injustice to the person who is affected by the mistake concerned.

If bureaucratic wrong-doing of some kind has occurred, a complaint can be made to the local authority. If you are dissatisfied with the response, you can then make a complaint to the Local Government Ombudsman. The Ombudsman works to obtain redress for people affected by bureaucratic error – known as 'maladministration'. Local taxation matters are just one area covered by the Ombudsman, who also has jurisdiction to investigate complaints about housing, planning, social services and education. A separate Ombudsman, the Commissioner for Parliamentary Administration, looks into complaints about central government administration.

If maladministration is established, the Ombudsman may recommend that financial compensation be paid to you or, in some cases, members of your family.

1. The work of the Ombudsman

The post of Local Government Ombudsman was originally established in 1974. Parliament created the Commission for Local Administration (known as the Ombudsman) to investigate complaints against local authorities on behalf of the public. The Commission continues to deal with complaints against local authorities in England and a separate Ombudsman has now been established for Wales and Scotland.[1]

The remit of the Ombudsman is to examine and investigate complaints from members of the public who claim to have experienced injustice as a result of bureaucratic error or wrong-doing. Such mistakes and errors fall under the umbrella term of 'maladministration'. The Ombudsman has the power to look into many different types of error which do not generate a right to take court action, but nonetheless give grounds for complaint.

The Ombudsman may investigate maladministration by any district, borough, city or county council and, therefore, can deal with mistakes by billing authorities in administering council tax in their areas. The Local Government Ombudsman does not cover town or parish councils or improper behaviour by individual elected councillors, except if it involves wider wrong-doing in the administration of the council as a whole.

During 2005/06, the Commission for Local Administration in England received a total of 18,626 complaints from the public about local government. Of these, 996 (5 per cent) related to local taxation matters.[2]

2. **What is maladministration**

'**Maladministration**' is an open-ended term covering a wide range of bureaucratic mistakes and abuses. It is not defined in statute and when the term was first introduced into Parliament it was considered to include 'bias, neglect, delay, incompetence and inaptitude, arbitrariness and so on' on the part of public authorities.[3]

Maladministration can thus cover many forms of bureaucratic wrong-doing which may not be serious enough to justify court proceedings, but which nonetheless can cause injustice – eg, delays in answering letters or losing records. It can include many forms of improper behaviour by local government staff, whether through lack of care or deliberate wrong-doing. Other examples of maladministration include:[4]

- rudeness;
- bias;
- knowingly giving misleading advice;
- unwillingness to recognise the rights of the taxpayer;
- failing to mitigate the effects of rigid adherence to the law where this results in inequitable treatment;
- not acting in a timely way;
- sending documents to the wrong address;
- allocating payments to the wrong account;
- failing to notify a person of her/his loss of appeal rights;
- ignoring valid advice;
- taking disproportionate redress;
- operating faulty procedures.

Injustice

The Ombudsman intervenes in cases which have resulted in injustice, caused by a local authority but which it has failed to redress adequately or at all. As with maladministration, the concept of **'injustice'** is a wide one and open to different interpretations. Arguably, it should mean more than a trivial problem or minor inconvenience, although much will depend on the actual effect of the error on the individual taxpayer concerned. Maladministration causing nuisance, embarrassment, financial loss or serious inconvenience and distress to a taxpayer certainly falls within the remit of injustice.

However, a complaint to the Ombudsman should not be used simply as a way of 'getting back' at a local authority or simply to get particular officials into trouble. Neither should a complaint be brought simply because you believe a decision to be wrong. Similarly, if a local authority has taken steps to correct an injustice and you are satisfied, the Ombudsman cannot be expected to take the matter any further.

Maladministration and council tax

In the most recent report for 2008 the Local Government Ombudsman states:

> The Ombudsman receives many complaints about the way councils take recovery action over failure to pay council tax. Sometimes people receive summonses when they should not have done, and the consequences of that action can lead to councils granting liability orders that enable them to refer alleged debts to bailiffs. Where unjustified recovery action has been taken, the Ombudsman would expect an appropriate remedy to be provided.

Because of its complexity, the administration of council tax can frequently generate errors which, if uncorrected, may result in inconvenience, stress and embarrassment to taxpayers. Even when a mistake is discovered, the local authority may not act properly or quickly enough to remedy the problem.

For example, a local authority may fail to record entitlement to a discount, repeatedly list the wrong person on a bill or fail to award payment to the correct account. This may result in sending reminder notices to and summonses against a person who has actually paid the tax or who is exempt. Problems may also be caused by sending demands in the names of people who have died after the local authority has been informed of the death, or failing to record that someone is severely mentally impaired.

Inadequate liaison between accounts and benefits sections in a local authority may generate problems. For example, although court action may be suspended, computerised enforcement systems may continue to issue warning letters even when the local authority has assured a person the mistake has been remedied. A local authority is not entitled to hide behind an excuse of 'computer error' to cover up inefficiency in such cases.

Another form of maladministration is an unreasonable delay in processing a council tax benefit (CTB) claim or delay in referring an appeal to a tribunal. Although a claimant may ultimately receive CTB after a long delay, s/he may face considerable inconvenience, stress and financial difficulty and embarrassment in the meantime. Significantly, the Ombudsman does not consider automatically issuing a summons against a person who is waiting for her/his CTB to be calculated to be 'fair or reasonable' and that a local authority 'should take into account the circumstances of the individual before taking such action.[5]

Other examples might include seeking a liability order against a person after an undertaking has been given not to obtain one, obtaining an order against a person who has offered to pay the sum in full, concealing the existence of a liability order or commencing enforcement action where an undertaking has been given by the local authority not to do so. Grounds may also exist for complaint if a local authority acts unreasonably by refusing to quash or cancel a liability order which has been obtained in error (see Chapter 11).

Matters which the Ombudsman cannot examine

There are a number of matters which the Ombudsman cannot investigate. These include:
- the amount of tax set by the local authority;
- decisions of courts or valuation tribunals;
- whether a person is liable for council tax;
- decisions about banding;
- the conduct of court proceedings.

These matters can only be challenged through the High Court or a valuation tribunal.

3. Making a complaint

The Ombudsman investigates complaints by:
- individuals;
- family members of individuals;
- advice agencies acting on behalf of individuals.

There is rarely public funding (formally legal aid) available to bring a complaint to the Ombudsman, but a complaint can be pursued via a solicitor who may be acting for a client in a benefits case on a funded basis.

No alternative remedy

In order to bring a complaint, there must be no other remedy available to you. In some cases, this may be because there is no right of appeal to a court or a tribunal

– eg, because the grounds of complaint fall outside one of the issues which can be considered by a valuation tribunal. Alternatively, the wrongful conduct may not provide a basis to start court action – eg, failing to reply to letters concerning council tax – but nonetheless can cause serious difficulties to an individual. In such cases the Ombudsman can investigate.

Normally, if a legal remedy exists, you are expected to pursue it, as opposed to making a complaint to the Ombudsman. Thus, in a dispute over benefit entitlement, you are expected to appeal to the First-tier Tribunal. But there is also a limited provision which allows the Ombudsman to investigate if it would be unreasonable to expect you to pursue a legal remedy or appeal. A complaint to the Ombudsman would be appropriate, for example, if judicial review by the High Court is unavailable or impractical to pursue (for example, if you would find it difficult to obtain evidence), or if you are unlikely to have the means to pursue a legal remedy.[6]

How to make a complaint

If you have experienced maladministration you should begin by making a complaint to the local authority concerned. Local authorities each have their own particular complaints procedure. Every local authority should be prepared to provide details of its complaints system, and normally details of the procedure can be obtained either by writing to the local authority or from its website.

The complaint should set out the specific details of what has taken place and the effect it has had on you. It is best that such complaints are written in clear and polite language and without using emotive or abusive language. (Extremes of language or unsubstantiated allegations are only likely to result in a complaint being viewed in a less favourable light on any impartial review.) You should not threaten legal action against the local authority as an alternative to investigation by the Ombudsman, as the Ombudsman's jurisdiction only arises where there is no practical alternative.

Local authorities often have more than one stage in their complaints procedure and you will usually have to complete all stages before the Ombudsman will consider the complaint. If you remain unhappy with the final outcome, or the council is taking too long to look into the matter (12 weeks is considered reasonable) you can complain to Ombudsman. Complaints should normally be brought within 12 months of the events.

If the response from the local authority is not satisfactory, the complaint may be referred to the Ombudsman.

The Ombudsman issues guidance on bringing a complaint. This is available at www.lgo.org.uk.

The Ombudsman has an advice team that can be contacted on 0300 061 0614 or 0845 602 1983 (8.30am to 5.00pm, Monday to Friday). Text messages can also be sent to 0762 480 4323.

Complaint forms can normally be downloaded or completed online.

When bringing a complaint it is usually a good idea to include a short chronology of events and correspondence, to provide a summary of key dates and the history of the matter, particularly where the case is complex. In the chronology you should list the date as accurately as possible and the event which occurred – eg, what the local authority did or did not do.

Action the Ombudsman can take

The remit of the Ombudsman is to obtain redress for the citizen. This may involve an investigation and publishing a report summarising the investigation and its findings (the complainant is normally given a pseudonym). The Ombudsman may issue directions to the local authority – eg, requiring it to make an apology or take appropriate action to remedy the maladministration and pay compensation to the person adversely affected. The Ombudsman also encourages local settlements (25.9 per cent of complaints were resolved locally in 2005/06).

There is no system to enforce an award of compensation but, in practice, local authorities usually accept the findings made by the Ombudsman. Directions may also be issued to local authorities to change their procedures to prevent the problem reoccurring.

Contacts

Adviceline: 0845 602 1983
Email: enquiries@lgo.org.uk
www.lgo.org.uk

England

The Commission for Local Administration in England
10th Floor
Millbank Tower
Millbank
London SW1P 4QP
Tel: 020 7217 4620
Fax: 020 7217 4621

Copies of the Annual Report and reports of investigations into complaints can also be obtained from this address or from www.lgo.org.uk

Wales

The Public Services Ombudsman for Wales
1 Ffordd Yr Hen Gae
Pencoed CF35 5LJ
Tel: 01656 641150
Fax: 01656 641199

Enquiries may also be sent to enquiries@ombudsman-wales.org.uk and further information is obtainable at www.ombudsman-wales.org.

Scotland

Scottish Public Services Ombudsman
4 Melville Street
Edinburgh EH3 7NS
Tel: 0870 011 5378
Fax: 0870 011 5379

Enquiries may also be sent to enquiries@scottishombudsman.org.uk and further information is obtainable at www.scottishombudsman.org.uk.

---

4. **Examples of complaints and settlements**

The following cases are examples of complaints of maladministration involving council tax which have been upheld. Cases often depend on their individual facts, but the settlement figures give an indication of the size of any award.

Suicide of taxpayer

Southwark Borough Council (00/A/19293 RVR [2002] 289)

The complaint was brought by relatives of a taxpayer who had committed suicide after receiving a summons for non-payment of council tax. The taxpayer was a single man with learning difficulties receiving benefits. In October 2000 his council tax benefit was cancelled and he was sent a fresh form to complete. Four days later he was sent a demand for £235.10 payable in instalments. The taxpayer visited the local authority's office and submitted a claim form, but the local authority continued recovery action. The taxpayer applied again for council tax benefit and provided information on his entitlement to jobseeker's allowance. Nonetheless, a summons was issued again in respect of £235.10. The summons was accompanied by an additional sheet warning that bailiffs or imprisonment could follow the granting of liability order. The taxpayer hanged himself in his flat and police called to the scene found the opened summons and a suicide note referring to his debt problems. Relatives of the deceased complained to the council but did not receive a satisfactory response.

On investigation, it was considered that the three-and-a-half-month delay in processing benefit amounted to maladministration. Further maladministration was found in sending out a summons whilst the relevant benefit claim had yet to be determined. The Ombudsman said that the summons had contributed to the distress and anxiety suffered by the deceased. The way in which the local authority had responded to relatives was also criticised.

Outcome: A settlement of £3,200 to the family of the deceased and £1,000 payment to a charity of their choice was approved.

Unnecessary recovery action

Hackney Borough Council (03/A/09613) 7 October 2004

The complainant, Ms Murray (pseudonym), set up a standing order to pay council tax in April 1998. In July 1998, the Council realised that because there was no council tax reference number on the standing order form, payments received were not being allocated to Ms Murray's account. Despite assurances from the Council on several occasions that it would rectify the problem, this was not achieved until January 2004. Arrears for 1998/99 were wrongly carried forward each year and the council began unnecessary recovery actions including summonses, liability orders and letters from bailiffs.

Outcome: The Ombudsman found maladministration and recommended the Council pay Ms Murray £1,800 compensation and undertake changes to its accounting systems.

Wrongful attribution of liability

Oxford City Council and Southwark Borough Council (02/B/09186 and 02/B/16542) 8 October 2003

A complaint was brought by Mr D Parry (pseudonym) that Oxford City Council was making deductions from his benefit for arrears of council tax. Mr Parry had been a student in Oxford over 30 years earlier but had not lived there since. The Ombudsman found that the Council had believed that its debtor, another Mr D Parry, had moved from Oxford to London NW2 but when they could not find him there, they found the complainant living in SE15. This alone convinced them it was the same debtor and they contacted Southwark LBC. Although Mr Parry had been a council tenant with Southwark for many years, Southwark LBC released information to enable deductions from the complainant's benefit and further compounded the error with delays in refunding his benefit. The Ombudsman found maladministration in the 'bizarre treatment' of the complainant and considered that depriving him of money on a very low income must have resulted in difficulty.

Outcome: It was recommended that Oxford City Council pay £750 and Southwark pay £250 to the complainant.

Delay in housing and council tax benefit

Lambeth Borough Council (01/B/17580) 14 February 2003

The Ombudsman found maladministration in delays by the Council in assessing the council tax benefit and housing benefit claims of a married couple and in the delay in responding to a review of the decision. Whilst considering the benefit claims the Council began legal proceedings to take possession and obtained a liability order for non-payment of council tax. The delay in assessing benefits was ten-and-a-half months and nine months to respond to the appeal. The decision to commence proceedings was also maladministration.

Outcome: The Council agreed to an apology and to ensure that benefits were being paid correctly and to make an *ex gratia* payment of £1,000 to the complainants in recognition of their distress, inconvenience, time and trouble.

Delay in housing and council tax benefit

Allerdale District Council (03/C/07422) 12 January 2005

The Council failed to assess and determine housing benefit and council tax benefit for the period September 2002 to March 2003. It also failed to respond to the complainants' letter of appeal regarding their claim and cancelled their benefit claim from 3 March 2003 without giving reasons. The circumstances of the complainants were complicated by the fact that they ran a small business at the time in question and they had failed to respond promptly to a request for information from the local authority.

Outcome: The Ombudsman found maladministration and recommended the Council pay £500 for stress and court costs incurred and directed the Council to review its procedures.

Rating list errors and failures

Torbay Council (00/B/10806 1 August 2001 reported at [2001] RVR 194)

The Ombudsman held that the Council should have taken reasonable steps to ensure that all the information about properties was accurate and that failure to do so was maladministration, the complainants having suffered considerable aggravation, uncertainty, time and trouble in pursuing the matter.

Outcome: The Ombudsman recommended an *ex-gratia* payment of £1,000 in compensation.

Delays in processing overpayment appeal

Liverpool City Council (01/C/07860)

An advice agency complained on behalf of a claimant about unreasonable delays in passing appeals against decisions to recover council tax benefit and housing benefit to the Appeals Service. The Ombudsman found a delay of nine months unreasonable.

Outcome: The Ombudsman considered an offer to pay £375 compensation a reasonable settlement to the complaint.

Delay in processing appeal

Liverpool City Council (01/C/15191)

An advice agency complained on behalf of a claimant that the council had delayed in passing an appeal against a decision to recover an overpayment of housing benefit and council tax benefit. The appeal had been brought in August 2001, but the papers were not passed to the Appeals service until June 2002.

The Ombudsman found the delay of ten months unreasonable and criticised the commencement of court proceedings after the appeal had been made.

Outcome: The Council agreed to pay £300, which included £50 to reflect the distress caused by the summons.

Unnecessary enforcement and attendance at court

Sandwell Metropolitan Council (No 03/B/12862)

The Council issued a summons when a council tax benefit claim was pending, the complainant having provided all the necessary information. It proceeded with court action even after the benefit claim had been assessed and the complainant did not owe the money that was being sought. As a result, the complainant overpaid his council tax by £400. A further incorrect bill was issued requiring the complainant to pay another £196. The taxpayer complained to the Council and the sums were later credited and repaid to him, but not for several months. The taxpayer was forced to attend an unnecessary court hearing and the local authority delayed in answering correspondence.

Outcome: Although the local authority had refunded money to the taxpayer, the Ombudsman found maladministration causing injustice. There had been inadequate liaison between the accounts and benefits sections of the revenues department and the taxpayer had experienced stress, inconvenience and an unnecessary attendance at court. The Council had also delayed in replying to the taxpayer's complaints. The Ombudsman recommended £400 compensation be paid and that the Council review its procedures.

Delayed appeal and bailiff action

Waltham Forest Borough Council (03/A/01900) 28 October 2003

Mr Gower (pseudonym) complained that the Council had unreasonably delayed assessing claims for housing benefit and council tax benefit, did not provide reasons on appeal and unreasonably took recovery action before his appeal had been determined. The Ombudsman considered that a delay of three months in assessing his claim was unreasonable and amounted to maladministration. The Ombudsman found that Mr Gower was caused prolonged anxiety by the slow progress of his claims and the growth in his rent and council tax arrears. Recovery action caused further stress, which was compounded when, after being told that the Council would suspend bailiff action, he was nonetheless served with a bailiff notice threatening distress and removal of goods.

Outcome: The Ombudsman considered that an offer of £225 in settlement by the Council was too low and recommended £500, together with a review of the way in which it communicated with its bailiffs.

Housing benefit/discretionary housing payment delay

Lambeth Borough Council (04/B/1233) 22 November 2004

The claimant sought housing benefit and a discretionary housing payment. The Council delayed in referring the matter to a rent officer until five months after a request by solicitors to do so and intervention by the Ombudsman. The Council then took a further five months from the rent officer's decision to decide her claim for a discretionary housing payment. During this period the landlord of the property changed and payment was made to the previous landlord. High levels of rent arrears led to the claimant being evicted in May 2004.

Outcome: The Ombudsman found maladministration and directed the Council to pay £2,500 compensation and court costs incurred at the eviction hearing, apologise in writing for all errors, re-house the claimant permanently and undertake a review of procedures.

Delay in processing benefit and failure to respond to complaint
Waltham Forest Borough Council (04/A/10401)
Mr and Mrs Mohammed (pseudonym) applied for council tax benefit and housing benefit after their circumstances changed. There was a delay in processing their claim and a reminder notice was issued for council tax arrears. Mr and Mrs Mohammed contacted the Council and recovery action was stopped. However, proceedings recommenced and a summons was issued. A complaint was made by an advice service but not passed to the Council's complaints team. A second complaint was made, by which time a liability order had been obtained and a bailiff's letter issued.
Outcome: The Ombudsman found maladministration in the delay in assessing benefit, failure to halt recovery action and the failure to identify the advice service letter as a complaint. The Ombudsman approved a £500 compensation offer made by the Council, which also wrote off costs and paid the credit balance.

Mistake in determining discount leading to hardship
London Borough of Brent (05/A/17099) February 26 2007
The Council wrongly awarded a 50 per cent empty property discount to the taxpayer in 2002. Having discovered the error in April 2004, the Council issued a retrospective bill for £4,649.96 and asked him to pay in the next 13 months. The taxpayer was a pensioner in poor health and unable to meet the bill in time. The Council failed to act in accordance with its anti-poverty strategy and to consider the means of the taxpayer. After the year expired, the local authority obtained a liability order.
Outcome: The Ombudsman identified several faults in the approach by the council. He approved a reduction of £1,479.34 granted by the Council to the taxpayer as a suitable settlement. A report examining the Council's anti-poverty strategy and its approach to debt collection was published in the public interest.

Bankruptcy as a disproportionate method of enforcement
Wolverhampton City Council (06B16600) 31 March 2008
The local authority issued bankruptcy proceedings against a debtor owing council tax on a disputed debt of less than £2,000. This increased the debt to £38,000.
Outcome: The Ombudsman recommended that the Council meet the costs of annulling the bankruptcy order. In his report, the Ombudsman said that a charging order should have been considered by the Council. The Ombudsman stated: 'The Council cannot, it seems to me, turn a blind eye to the consequences to the debtor of any recovery option it pursues. Some courses will no doubt be administratively more convenient and less costly than others. But in selecting those options the impact on the debtor should be weighed in

the balance. The dire and punitive consequences of bankruptcy, involving a multiplication of the original debt many times over and frequently incurring the loss of the debtor's home, must be a factor to be taken into account in deciding that the 'last resort' is indeed appropriate. I have seen no evidence that this relevant consideration was taken into account. And that too was maladministration.'

Maladministration causing injustice

London Borough of Camden (07A12661) July 2008

The Council's revenue team commenced bankruptcy proceedings for council tax arrears against a woman who, because of mental health difficulties, was unable to conduct her own affairs. Before doing so, the Council did not adequately record what checks it had made and did not check with the social care department, which would have shown that bankruptcy was not an appropriate recovery method.

Outcome: The Ombudsman found part of the Council knew of the woman's problems, but the revenue department did not find this out because it failed to make effective internal enquiries. Had it done so, the Council would most likely have taken different steps, with less serious consequences.

The Ombudsman ruled: 'I do not think it unreasonable for revenue officers to look beyond their own departmental information and consider a council's records as a whole.' This was in line with data protection guidance issued by the Information Commissioner. The Ombudsman ruled that the failure to make checks led to unwarranted action and found maladministration causing injustice. The Council agreed to apply to court to annul the bankruptcy. On annulment, the Ombudsman recommended that the Council should contact credit rating agencies to advise them of the position and that the Council should change its procedures to make stringent checks for potential vulnerability before taking action leading to bankruptcy, a charging order or committal.

Wrongful pursuit of council tax debt after liability ceased

(Case reference confidential)

The taxpayer 'Mr J' was involved in a long-running dispute with the Council about liability for council tax on a property. He received a summons for two years worth of arrears. Shortly before the hearing, the Council issued a letter accepting he did not have sole or main residence and that liability was with a 'Mrs K'. The Council requested details of when Mrs K vacated the property and a forwarding address. Nonetheless, the Council pursued a liability order against Mr J and he was threatened with bailiffs. Mr J made a complaint, but received no reply for three months. The Council still served four demand notices covering the previous three years.

Outcome: On investigation the Ombudsman learned from the Council that it had continued to pursue Mr J because he failed to provide the information on Mrs K. The Ombudsman found that this approach was incorrect. While not criticising the Council for asking Mr J for that information, liability for the tax was not determined by the supply of information. The Council had no legal basis on which to pursue Mr J for arrears arising after the date from which it had decided he was no longer the liable person. The Council should not have proceeded with the court action.

The Council agreed to settle the complaint by apologising to Mr J for its errors and paying him £350 compensation.

Notes

1. The work of the Ombudsman
1 Part III Local Government Act 1974; Public Services Ombudsman (Wales) Act 2005; Scottish Public Services Ombudsman Act 2002
2 Local Government Ombudsman *Annual Report* 2003/04

2. What is maladministration
3 House of Commons debates; Parliamentary Commissioner Act 1967
4 UK Parliamentary Ombudsman Report 1993
5 Report by Commissioner Jerry White, Complaint 03/B/12862 29, September 2004

3. Making a complaint
6 *R v Commissioner for Local Administration, ex parte Liverpool CC* [2001] All ER 462 (CA)

Appendix 1

Exempt dwellings

There are 23 classes of exempt dwelling for council tax.

A   An empty unoccupied property undergoing structural alterations or one which requires or is undergoing major repairs to make it habitable and up to six months thereafter. Exemption is available for a maximum period of 12 months overal (whilst the property remains empty and unoccupied. After 12 months between 50 per cent and 100 per cent tax applies according to the local authority concerned.

B   Unoccupied property owned by a charity, for a period of up to six months since last occupied. After six months between 50 per cent and 100 per cent tax applies according to the local authority concerned.

C   Property empty for a period of up to six months since last occupied or the date that the construction of the property was substantially completed (so long as it remains empty and unfurnished). After six months between 50 per cent and 100 per cent tax applies according to the local authority concerned.

D   Property unoccupied because the liable person is in prison (except for fine defaulters and for council tax arrears).

E   Empty property where the person is resident in hospital or a nursing home.

F   Unoccupied property where probate or letters of administration have not yet been granted, and for a period of up to six months after the date of such a grant is made, where no one is liable other than as executor or administrator. After six months from the grant of probate or letters of administration, between 50 per cent and 100 per cent tax applies according to the local authority concerned.

G   Empty property where occupation is prohibited by law (eg, planning or court order).

H   Unoccupied property kept for ministers of religion.

I   Unoccupied because the owner or tenant has moved elsewhere to receive care.

J   Unoccupied because the owner or tenant has moved elsewhere in order to provide care.

K   Unoccupied, where the person subject to the tax is a student and has been since s/he last occupied the property.

L   Property repossessed under a mortgage.

M   Student halls of residence.

N   Premises where all of residents are students.

O   Property owned by the Ministry of Defence and used for serving personnel.

P   Property occupied by members of, or associated with, visiting forces.

Q   Property empty on bankruptcy of the taxpayer.

R   An unused caravan pitch or boat mooring.

S   Property occupied only by persons under 18 (eg, property occupied by a lone mother under 18).

T   An unoccupied separately banded part of a property (eg, annexes) which may not be let separately without being in breach of planning regulations.

U   Property occupied only by people who are severely mentally impaired.

V   Property occupied by foreign diplomats or members of certain international organisations headquartered in the UK.

W   Any separately banded part of a property – eg, an annex, which is occupied by a dependent relative of the family in the other part of the building where the relative is over 65, severely mentally impaired or substantially and permanently disabled.

Appendix 2

··

National Standards for Enforcement Agents (page 9)

Vulnerable situations

- Enforcement agents/agencies and creditors must recognise that they each have a role in ensuring that the vulnerable and socially excluded are protected and that the recovery process includes procedures agreed between the agent/agency and creditor about how such situations should be dealt with. The appropriate use of discretion is essential in every case and no amount of guidance could cover every situation, therefore the agent has a duty to contact the creditor and report the circumstances in situations where there is potential cause for concern. If necessary, the enforcement agent will advise the creditor if further action is appropriate. The exercise of appropriate discretion is needed, not only to protect the debtor, but also the enforcement agent who should avoid taking action which could lead to accusations of inappropriate behaviour.
- Enforcement agents must withdraw from domestic premises if the only person present is, or appears to be, under the age of 18; they can ask when the debtor will be home – if appropriate.
- Enforcement agents must withdraw without making enquiries if the only persons present are children who appear to be under the age of 12.
- Wherever possible, enforcement agents should have arrangements in place for rapidly accessing translation services when these are needed, and provide on request information in large print or in Braille for debtors with impaired sight.
- Those who might be potentially vulnerable include:
  - the elderly;
  - people with a disability;
  - the seriously ill;
  - the recently bereaved;
  - single parent families;
  - pregnant women;
  - unemployed people; *and*

– those who have obvious difficulty in understanding, speaking or reading English.

Issued in April 2002 by The Lord Chancellor's Department (now The Ministry of Justice). For full text of the guidance, see www.dca.gov.uk/enforcement/agentso2.htm

Appendix 3

Adjournment letter

TO: The Magistrates' Chief Executive
The [NAME] Magistrates' Court
[ADDRESS OF MAGISTRATES' COURT]

Dear Sir/Madam

RE: Summons number [INSERT REFERENCE NUMBER]
RE: Liability order application – Hearing date [STATE DATE]
RE: [NAME OF COUNCIL] v [NAME OF TAXPAYER]

I hereby apply to the court sitting at [GIVE NAME OF MAGISTRATES' COURT] for an adjournment of the above proceeding for the recovery of council tax to be heard on [STATE DATE CONTAINED ON SUMMONS].

The basis for seeking the adjournment is:
[GIVE DETAILS OF WHY ADJOURNMENT IS REQUESTED]
[IN A CASE WHERE AN APPEAL IS MADE TO A VALUATION TRIBUNAL ABOUT LIABILITY, EXEMPTION OR AN AMOUNT OF TAX, GIVE DETAILS OF THE APPEAL]

Accordingly, I have made an appeal to the valuation tribunal under section 16 of the Local Government Finance Act 1992 against this decision, and I would ask that the magistrates' court please considers adjourning this case until the tribunal has determined this matter.

Naturally, I hope that it will be possible to settle this matter without unnecessary proceedings and I await hearing from you with your decision.

Thanking you for your attention, I await hearing from you.

Yours faithfully
[NAME]

Note: a copy of the request should also be served on the local authority.

Appendix 4

Abbreviations used in the notes

ACR	Appeal Case Reports	LJ	Lord Justice
ALR	Administration Law Reports	KB	King's Bench Reports
All ER	All England Reports	para(s)	paragraph(s)
Art(s)	Article(s)	PN	Practice Notes
CA	Court of Appeal	QB	Queen's Bench Reports
CO	Crown Office	QBD	Queen's Bench Division
COD	Crown Office Digest	RA	Rating Appeals
EWHC	England and Wales High Court	reg(s)	regulation(s)
GM	Housing Benefit and Council Tax	RVR	Rating & Valuation
	Benefit Guidance Manual		Reports
HLR	Housing Law Reports	KB	King's Bench Reports
JP	Justice of the Peace Reports	Sch(s)	Schedule(s)
		s(s)	section(s)

Acts of Parliament

CSPSSA 2000	The Child Support, Pensions and Social Security Act 2000
LGA 2003	The Local Government Act 2003
LGFA 1988	The Local Government Finance Act 1988
LGFA 1992	The Local Government Finance Act 1992
SSAA 1992	The Social Security Administration Act 1992
SSCBA 1992	The Social Security Contributions and Benefits Act 1992

Regulations

Each set of regulations has a statutory instrument (SI) number and date. You ask for them by giving their date and number.

CCCTNR(E)(MC) Regs	The Community Charges, Council Tax and Non-Domestic Rating (Enforcement) (Magistrates' Courts) England Regulations 2000 No.2026
CT(AE) Regs 1992	The Council Tax (Administration and Enforcement) Regulations 1992 No.613

CT(AE) Regs 2004	The Council Tax (Administration and Enforcement) Regulations 2004 No.927
CT(AE)(S) Regs	The Council Tax (Administration and Enforcement) (Scotland) Regulations 1992 No.1332
CT(AE)(A)(W) Regs	The Council Tax(Administration and Enforcement) (Amendment) (Wales) Regulations 2007 No.582
CT(ALA) Regs	The Council Tax (Alteration of Lists and Appeals) Regulations 1993 No.290
CT(ALA)(E) Regs	The Council Tax (Alteration of Lists and Appeals) (England) Regulations 2009 No.2270
CT(ALA)(S) Regs	The Council Tax (Alteration of Lists and Appeals) (Scotland) Regulations 1993 No.355
CT(APDD) Regs	The Council Tax (Additional Provisions for Discount Disregards) Regulations 1992 No.552
CT(CD)O	The Council Tax (Chargeable Dwellings) Order 1992
CT(CVL) Regs	The Council Tax (Contents of Valuation Lists) Regulations 1992 No.553
CT(D)(S)(A) Regs	The Council Tax (Discounts) (Scotland) Amendment Regulations 1995 No.597
CT(D)(S) Amdt O	The Council Tax (Discounts) (Scotland) (Amendment) Order 1993 No.343
CT(D)(S) Amdt Regs	The Council Tax (Discounts) (Scotland) Amendment Regulations 1993 No.342
CT(D)(S)CAO	The Council Tax (Discounts) (Scotland) Consolidation and Amendment Order 2003 No.176
CT(D)(S)O	The Council Tax (Discounts) (Scotland) Order 1992 No.1408
CT(D)(S) Regs	The Council Tax (Discounts) (Scotland) Regulations 1992 No.1409
CT(DD)O	The Council Tax (Discount Disregards) Order 1992 No.548
CT(DD)(A)(E)O	The Council Tax (Discount Disregards) (Amendment) (England) Order 2006 No.3396
CT(DD)(A)(W)O	The Council Tax (Discount Disregards) (Amendment) (Wales) Order 2006 No.580
CT(DDED)(A)O	The Council Tax (Discount Disregards and Exempt Dwellings) (Amendment) Order 1995 No.619
CT(DIS) Regs	The Council Tax (Deductions from Income Support) Regulations 1993 No.494
CT(DN)(W) Regs	The Council Tax (Demand Notices) (Wales) Regulations 1993 No.255
CT(DUD)(S) Regs	The Council Tax (Discounts for Unoccupied Dwellings)(Scotland) Regulations 2005 No.512

CT(Dw)(S) Regs	The Council Tax (Dwellings) (Scotland) Regulations 1992 No.1334
CT(ED)O	The Council Tax (Exempt Dwellings) Order 1992 No.558
CT(ED)(A)(E)O 2005	The Council Tax (Exempt Dwellings) (Amendment) (England) Order 2005 No.2865
CT(ED)(A)(E)O	The Council Tax (Exempt Dwellings) (Amendment) (England) Order 2006 No.2318
CT(ED)(A)(W)O	The Council Tax (Exempt Dwellings) (Amendment) (Wales) Order 2000 No.1025
CT(EDDD)(A)O	The Council Tax (Exempt Dwellings and Discount Disregards) (Amendment) Order 1998 No.291
CT(ED)(S)O 1992	The Council Tax (Exempt Dwellings) (Scotland) Order 1992 No.1333
CT(ED)(S)O 1997	The Council Tax (Exempt Dwellings) (Scotland) Order 1997 No.728
CT(ED)(S)O 2002	The Council Tax (Exempt Dwellings) (Scotland) Order 2002 No.101
CT(ED)(S)(A)O 1995	The Council Tax (Exempt Dwellings)(Scotland) Amendment Order 1995 No.59
CT(ED)(S)(A)O	The Council Tax (Exempt Dwellings) (Scotland) (Amendment) Order 2006 No.402
CT(LO) Regs	The Council Tax (Liability of Owners) Regulations 1992 No.551
CT(LO)(A)(E) Regs	The Council Tax (Liability for Owners) (Amendment) (England) Regulations 2003 No.3125
CT(LO)(A)(W) Regs	The Council Tax (Liability of Owners) (Amendment) (Wales) Regulations 2004 No. 2920
CT(LO)(S) Regs	The Council Tax (Liability of Owners) (Scotland) Regulations 1992 No.1331
CT(PCD)(E) Regs	The Council Tax (Prescribed Classes of Dwellings) (England) Regulations 2003 No.3011
CT(PCD)(W) Regs	The Council Tax (Prescribed Classes of Dwellings) (Wales) Regulations 1992 No.3023
CT(RD) Regs	The Council Tax (Reductions for Disabilities) Regulations 1992 No.554
CT(RD)(S) Regs	The Council Tax (Reductions for Disabilities) (Scotland) Regulations 1992 No.1335
CT(RDTA)(W)(A) Regs	The Council Tax (Reductions for Disabilities and Transitional Arrangements) (Wales) (Amendment) Regulations 2005 No.702
CT(SVD) Regs	The Council Tax (Situation and Valuation of Dwellings) Regulations 1992 No.550

CT(SVD)(W)(A) Regs	The Council Tax (Situation and Valuation of Dwellings) (Wales)(Amendment) Regulations 2005 No.701
CT(TA)(W) Regs	The Council Tax (Transitional Arrangements) (Wales) Regulations 2004 No.3142
CT(VALA)(E) Regs	The Council Tax (Valuations and Alterations of Lists and Appeals) (England) Regulations 2008 No.315
CT(VD)(S) Regs	The Council Tax (Valuation of Dwellings) (Scotland) Regulations 1992 No.1329
CTB Regs	The Council Tax Benefit (General) Regulations 1992 No.1814
CTB(SPC) Regs	The Council Tax Benefit (Persons who have Attained the Qualifying Age for State Pension Credit) Regulations 2006 No.216
CTNDR(DN)(E) Regs	The Council Tax and Non-Domestic Rating (Demand Notices) (England) Regulations 1993 No.191
DFA Regs	The Discretionary Financial Assistance Regulations 2001 No.1167
HBCTB(DA) Regs	The Housing Benefit and Council Tax Benefit (Decisions and Appeals) Regulations 2001 No.1002
VCCT(Amdt) Regs	The Valuation and Community Charge Tribunals (Amendment) Regulations 1993 No.292
VT(Amdt)(E) Regs	The Valuation Tribunals (Amendment) (England) Regulations 2000 No.409
VTE(CTRA)(P) Regs	The Valuation Tribunal for England (Council Tax and Rating Appeals) (Procedure) Regulations 2009 No.2269

Council tax Practice Notes

England and Wales

PN No.1	Valuation Lists
PN No.2	Liability, Discounts and Exemptions
PN No.3	Council Tax Benefit
PN No.4	Transitional Arrangements
PN No.5	Administration (including Billing and Collection)
PN No.6	Appeals
PN No.7	Tax Setting, Precepting and Levying
PN No.8	Data Protection
PN No.9	Recovery and Enforcement

Wales

PN A	The Council Tax in Wales
PN B	Tax Setting, Precepting and Levying in Wales

Index